Economic Adjustment:
Policies and Problems

Economic Adjustment: Policies and Problems

Edited by Sir Frank Holmes

Papers presented at a seminar held in
Wellington, New Zealand,
February 17–19, 1986

International Monetary Fund • 1987

© International Monetary Fund, 1987

Library of Congress Cataloging-in-Publication Data

Economic adjustment : policies and problems : papers presented at a
  seminar held in Wellington, New Zealand, February 17–19, 1986 /
  edited by Sir Frank Holmes.
      p.   cm.
   Bibliography: p.
   ISBN 0-939934-98-1
      1. Oceania—Economic policy—Congresses.   2. Korea (South)—
Economic policy—1960—Congresses.   3. New Zealand—Economic
policy—Congresses.   I. Holmes, Frank Wakefield, Sir, 1924–
II. International Monetary Fund.
   HC681.E28 1986
   338.99—dc19

87-30382
CIP

Price: $16.00

Foreword

Economic adjustment continues to be a major issue demanding the attention of the authorities of developed and developing countries alike. This volume, which contains the proceedings of a seminar held in 1986 in Wellington, New Zealand, focuses on the adjustment problems faced by countries in the South Pacific, and particular attention is devoted to the situation of the small island economies in the South Pacific. One of the most important aspects of adjustment for these countries, as well as for New Zealand and Australia, is the formulation of liberalized trade and exchange policies in the face of increasing worldwide protectionism, and a number of participants in the seminar addressed themselves to this issue.

As is suggested in several of these papers, many of the problems of adjustment are not unique to the South Pacific region. Accordingly, these papers also consider general adjustment policy issues that are applicable to a wide range of economies. Specific examples are provided by two case studies of the adjustment effort in a developed and a developing economy.

In the past few years, the International Monetary Fund, in collaboration with the World Bank, has become progressively more involved with the adjustment efforts of its member countries, especially the developing countries. This seminar, which was jointly sponsored by the Fund and the Reserve Bank and Treasury of New Zealand, is a part of the Fund's continuing effort to provide a forum for an open discussion and exchange of views about the role of international financial institutions in the adjustment process.

Michel Camdessus
Managing Director
International Monetary Fund

Acknowledgements

One of the most important functions of the International Monetary Fund is to promote informed discussion on issues of fundamental significance for international financial stability and economic development. This volume contains papers from a seminar that the Fund co-sponsored with the Reserve Bank and Treasury of New Zealand in Wellington in February 1986. At this seminar, staff members of the Fund and the World Bank came together with a group of central bankers, officials, financiers, researchers, and journalists from New Zealand, Australia, Korea, and several South Pacific countries. The papers included in this volume stimulated constructive discussion on the policy options available to those countries compelled to undergo economic adjustment and on the problems that adjustment brings.

Appropriately, given the origin of the participants, particular attention was given to developments in the Pacific. Case studies were presented of adjustment in New Zealand and Korea, and a special session was devoted to the design of adjustment programs in small economies. However, the general papers on trade policy, private capital and aid, fiscal and monetary policies, exchange rate policies, and long-term structural adjustment drew on experience from a wide range of economies throughout the world. Thus, they should be interesting and relevant to people concerned with issues of adjustment everywhere.

The technique of appointing leading discussants was helpful in focusing attention on key issues and provoking useful interchanges among the participants. The value of the seminar was also enhanced by good organization by officers of the Fund, the Reserve Bank, and the Treasury, and in particular, through the efforts of Graham Newman, Grant Spencer, Alison Scott, and Jean Kerr. Sara Kane, of the Fund's Editorial Division, assisted in the editing of this volume from draft to publication.

Sir Frank Holmes
Wellington, October 1987

Contents

	Page
Foreword	v
Acknowledgements	vii

Introduction
   Sir Frank Holmes 1
1. Trade Policies and their Impact on Individual Economies
   P.J. Lloyd 8
   Comment
   Cho Soon 30
2. Economic Adjustment in New Zealand: A Developed Country Case Study of Policies and Problems
   Ralph Lattimore 34
   Comment
   Colin James 85
3. A Case of Successful Adjustment in a Developing Country: Korea's Experience During 1980–84
   Bijan Aghevli and *Jorge Márquez-Ruarte* 91
   Comment
   Sang Woo Nam 114
4. The Role of Aid and Private Capital Inflows in Economic Development
   Helen Hughes 120
   Comment
   Christopher Findlay 147
5. Fiscal and Monetary Policies: Their Role in the Adjustment Process
   Grant H. Spencer and *Robin T. Clements* 154
   Comment
   Christopher Higgins 185

Page

6. The Role of Exchange Rate and Other Pricing Policies in the Adjustment Process
    Peter Wickham 192
    Comment
    David Mayes 210
7. Long-Term Structural Adjustment Policies
    Stanley Please 217
    Comment
    Te'o I.J. Fairbairn 232
8. Some Aspects of Economic Adjustment in Small Island Economies
    Bruce J. Smith 237
    Comment
    Peter Nicholl 263
Appendix 273

The following symbols have been used throughout this book:
  ... to indicate that data are not available;
  — to indicate that the figure is zero or less than half the final digit shown, or that the item does not exist;
  - between years or months (e.g., 1983–84 or January–June) to indicate the years or months covered, including the beginning and ending years or months;
  / between years (e.g., 1983/84) to indicate a crop or fiscal (financial) year.
"Billion" means a thousand million.
Details may not add to totals shown because of rounding.

Introduction

Sir Frank Holmes

When I was invited to be moderator for this seminar, I looked in my dictionary to see what the job involved. I was obviously not being asked to be "president of an ecclesiastical body of the Presbyterian Church," though I have no doubt there will be some dogma (economic, if not religious) in our discussions. I am not an "examiner for Oxford Moderations" (though as editor of the proceedings, I am told to take a critical view of the papers). I could be called on as "arbitrator or mediator," but I trust that you will not put my skills in that role too severely to the test. But I do accept gratefully the opportunity to be your "presiding officer." And I trust that I can help, not hinder, constructive discussion and your general enjoyment of our time together.

My most arduous responsibility comes now, when I must take you around the Pacific in 15 minutes, generalizing heroically about recent economic developments. I turned for help to a recent study by ANU's [The Australian National University] Australian-Japan Research Center. Tables 1,2, and 3 indicate that the Pacific region's share of world output and trade has been growing in the past two decades. Japan and other northeast Asian economies have done best, sufficiently so to offset the relatively laggard performance of North America, Australasia, and, until recently, ASEAN (Association of South East Asian Nations) (Table 1). In the process of expansion, most economies have become much more export oriented (Table 2), with the significant exceptions of Australia and New Zealand.

The interdependence among the region's economies has also grown (Table 3). The share of trade going to other Pacific countries ranges from about 50 percent for the United States and 55 percent for Japan to above 70 percent for ASEAN and 75 percent for the People's Republic of China. Reorientation of trade into the Pacific has been strong for China, Australia, and especially New Zealand, which has perforce dramatically

Table 1. Share of World GNP, Exports, and Imports for Selected Pacific Economies, 1962, 1981, 1990
(In percent)

	World GNP Actual 1962	World GNP Actual 1981	World GNP Projected 1990	World Exports Actual 1962	World Exports Actual 1981	World Exports Projected 1990	World Imports Actual 1962	World Imports Actual 1981	World Imports Projected 1990
North America	31.0	28.3	26.7	21.7	17.0	16.5	17.3	15.1	17.6
Japan	4.2	9.9	10.7	3.9	8.8	7.6	4.5	6.1	5.4
China, People's Rep. of	2.2	2.3	3.3	0.6	1.2	1.6	0.5	0.8	1.5
Other Northeast Asia	0.4	1.2	1.8	0.7	3.3	5.5	1.5	3.6	4.5
ASEAN	1.9	1.7	2.0	3.3	4.1	4.6	3.3	3.8	4.0
Australia	1.2	1.5	1.4	1.9	1.2	1.4	1.7	1.3	1.4
New Zealand and other Pacific	0.3	0.3	0.3	0.7	0.4	0.4	0.6	0.4	0.4
Total Pacific	**41.2**	**45.2**	**46.0**	**32.8**	**36.0**	**37.5**	**29.4**	**31.2**	**34.8**
Western Europe	28.3	27.4	27.5	45.8	42.8	41.4	50.7	42.5	42.9

Source: For 1962 and 1981: Anderson, K., et al., "Pacific Growth and its Prospects for Australian Trade," Pacific Economic Papers No. 122 (Canberra: Australia-Japan Research Center, Australian National University, May 1985), p. 44. For 1990: approximate midpoint of Wharton and JRC estimates, given in text.

Table 2. Exports as a Share of GNP and Export Growth for Pacific and Other Economies, 1962-1981
(In percent)

	1962	1981	1962-70	1970-81
Australia	14	13	7.2	3.8
Japan	8	14	16.8	8.7
China, People's Rep. of	3	8	1.1	12.5
Other Northeast Asia	14	45	1.2	14.1
ASEAN	10	37	3.9	12.0
Total East Asia	**8**	**17**	**12.8**	**10.5**
North America	7	9	8.4	4.3
New Zealand and other Pacific	22	22	5.5	1.6
Total Pacific	**7**	**12**	**9.3**	**6.9**
Western Europe	14	24	9.8	5.1
Middle East	7	17	13.0	14.5
Centrally planned	2	4	10.1	7.1
Rest of world	16	34	7.5	1.6
Total world	**9**	**16**	**9.5**	**5.9**

Source: World Bank, *World Tables*, Third Edition (Baltimore: Johns Hopkins University, 1983).

Table 3. Regional Trade as a Share of Total Trade in Pacific Economies, 1962, 1970, and 1981
(In percent)

	Share of Exports Going to Other Pacific Economies			Share of Imports Coming from Other Pacific Economies		
	1962	1970	1981	1962	1970	1981
Australia	49	65	60	41	51	63
Japan	56	62	56	59	58	53
China, People's Rep. of	48	56	74	48	54	77
Other Northeast Asia	60	72	65	71	75	70
ASEAN	68	70	74	64	67	64
North America	39	50	48	48	59	52
New Zealand and other Pacific	29	48	58	44	53	68

Source: Australia-Japan Research Center/ASEAN-Australia Project Trade Data Bank, based on World Bank trade statistics.

reduced its previous heavy dependence on the British market and on pastoral exports.

In general, the developing countries of Asia have adapted much better than their counterparts in Latin America and Africa to the oil crises and economic fluctuations of the 1970s and early 1980s. With the exception of the Philippines, they have kept their debt service ratios within prudent bounds, and below those now prevailing in Australia and New Zealand, both of which have drawn heavily on foreign capital to ease the process of adjustment. Nevertheless, ASEAN and the North Asian developing countries continue to depend greatly on healthy expansion and reasonably liberal trade policies in the bigger industrial economies. Even those that have been most outward looking and adaptable can occasionally go astray with domestic policy. Who, for example, expected two or three years ago that Singapore would be experiencing negative growth, in an expanding world economy, and needing to reappraise its fiscal, construction, incomes, and exchange rate policies?

Overall, however, the record of the past 15 years provides encouraging evidence that most of the developing countries of the region manage their economies well and adapt effectively to change. I have had the pleasure of visiting Korea several times recently for various PECC [Pacific Economic Cooperation Conference] meetings. One cannot fail to be impressed by the Korean achievement in turning a poor, war-torn country into such a dynamic economy in such a short period. It is appropriate that it has been selected for special attention here.

New approaches to economic policy in China, including a more open attitude to overseas trade, are potentially very significant developments for trade and adjustment in the Pacific. It has proved necessary for the Chinese to slow down their early hectic pace of change. It will take time for them to devise satisfactory pricing and trade regimes for the more decentralized and market-oriented system they are trying to create. But we can expect to see growing market opportunities and growing competitive challenges from China in the next decade.

In the meantime, developments in the United States and Japan remain of dominant importance in the region. The sustained expansion, with low inflation, which has been achieved in the recent past in North America has assisted greatly the exports and general economic development of most Pacific countries. However, the durability of the improvement has been in doubt, with the American deficit on current account growing, the U.S. dollar held high through net capital inflow, and growing pressure on the President and the Congress for action to exclude imports and subsidize exporters. The "Baker Initiative," leading to collective action by the "Gang of Five," seems to have achieved a significant, rapid change in exchange relationships in the "right" direction in a few months. But whether this action will endure and/or achieve the desired results depends on its being accompanied by complementary domestic adjustments in the major economies.

We should not underestimate the political obstacles to adjustment. In the United States reduction of the federal budget deficit is a contentious issue of vital importance. In Japan, which has been politically comfortable with its high savings ratio, large surpluses on current account, and high investment overseas, the Government has felt obliged, because of the dangers facing international trade, to make genuine efforts to reduce trade barriers, gradually free up its financial markets, and vigorously counsel Japanese to buy imports. But the habit of buying Japanese is deeply ingrained, and the resistance is strong to adopting policies that will stimulate domestic consumption and investment.

We from the South Pacific are very much aware that the Pacific Region has many small economies with difficult problems of development and adjustment. Some, like Papua New Guinea, are physically large and have considerable resource potential. Others are tiny and resource-poor. Geoff Bertram has dubbed some of those with which New Zealand has close ties "MIRAB" economies.[1] They are very dependent on migration of "surplus" population to cities overseas; on remittances from the emigrants; on aid from other countries; and on a bureaucracy which administers the spending of the aid and other revenue. Members from several different types of small economies are here to help us understand their special adjustment problems. Those of us from Australia and New Zealand have a special interest in what forms of assistance and other relationships with our South Pacific neighbors would best help them deal with those problems.

I trust that those who are not Australians and New Zealanders will be tolerant of any outbreaks of hostility over cricket in the next three days. Please press us to concentrate on what I think is a very timely opportunity to compare notes on how we are approaching our problems of adjustment. We have both enjoyed comparatively strong growth in the past two years. But the world recovery has not been as beneficial as usual to the prices of several of the major commodities which we export. And trends in our balance of payments have been cause for some concern.

We both have Labour Party governments that accept the need for some radical changes of policy, designed to improve the efficiency and flexibility of our economies. Both have removed or reduced many old regulations, floated their dollars, opened their financial systems to the world, embarked on attempts to reform their tax systems, and reduced

---

[1] Geoffrey Bertram, "Sustainable Development in Pacific Micro-Economies," *World Development* (Vol. 14, No. 7), July 1986, pp. 809–22.

the high protection and other supports previously accorded to selected industries. In New Zealand the end of some "sacred cows," such as import licensing, is now in sight.

Understandably, the process of adjustment is not proving easy, nor is getting the balance of policies right. In New Zealand, particularly, we are not yet on top of our propensity to inflate faster than our trading partners. Curbing that propensity must be a top priority for the Government in its package of adjustment policies.

For us, as for others, the adjustment process will be greatly eased if the major economies continue on a path of stable expansion and reverse the tendencies for protection to increase. Our concern about recent increases in trade barriers is not solely with agricultural protection, which has been worsening, not only in the European Communities (EC) but also in countries like Japan and Korea. Nor is it solely with disposal of surpluses arising from protection. We must all be concerned at the consequences of the growth of non-tariff barriers, voluntary export restraints, orderly market agreements, and the like, which are impeding the exports and frustrating the development potential of so many of our Pacific neighbors.

Recent efforts to contain and reverse this protection have been disappointing. But a recent PECC Task Force on Trade Policy recommended that Pacific countries should pursue the possibilities on a number of fronts—multilateral, regional, bilateral, and unilateral.

At least, we now have agreement in principle that there should be another General Agreement on Tariffs and Trade (GATT) round. One cannot be optimistic about early action, however, when one considers the problems of even reaching an agreement to start another round, and the differences among participants on many critical issues. Nevertheless, there is general recognition in the Pacific that the multilateral approach is first-best, and that every effort should be made to get a GATT round started promptly and in a way that faces, not evades, the issues of major concern to Pacific participants.

What of a Pacific approach? Australia and Japan, particularly, have been active in promoting the concept of a Pacific Economic Community, or at least more active Pacific cooperation, most recently via the "Hawke" initiative. I think a Community is a long way off. But cooperation is gathering momentum in a number of forms, for example, in business via the Pacific Basin Economic Council (PBEC); in research with the Pacific Trade and Development (PAFTAD) conferences; and on a tripartite basis, through the Pacific Economic Cooperation Conferences. The PECC Task Force recently recommended Pacific cooperation in laying the groundwork for successful multilateral negotiations. If the multilateral approach failed, the Task Force saw merit in attempting more limited exchanges within the Pacific. The difficulties of achieving Pacific-wide agreement were acknowledged; but less comprehensive arrangements were deemed worth investigating, provided they left room for subsequent access by others and reduced rather than increased barriers overall.

Bilateral deals are rightly suspect. When the United States, for example, succeeds in persuading Japan to free access for U.S. produce, it has sometimes meant less access for others in the Pacific. On a broader scale, free trade areas or customs unions can be damaging, especially if protection against nonmembers is increased in important areas, as the EC has done with some agricultural products. However, we need not apologize for regional arrangements like the CER Agreement (Closer Economic Relations and Trade) (ANZCERT) between Australia and New Zealand. It aims to be outward-looking, and in New Zealand's case, it has been an important stepping stone toward the measures now being taken to get rid of import licensing generally and reduce the higher rates of tariff. Further development of ANZCERT, and possibly its extension to additional participants, could be a useful element in the adjustment policies of Australia and New Zealand in future.

The reaction of the United States to difficulties in reaching multilateral arrangements could well confront us, and others in the Pacific, with the need to consider seriously the possibility of bilateral or "plurilateral agreements." The United States has already negotiated a Free Trade Deal with Israel and is talking seriously about one with Canada. Not too long ago, it was informally sounding out possibilities in New Zealand, Australia, and ASEAN.

It was only a few years ago that the prospect of freeing trade with Australia struck fear into many New Zealand hearts. Now it is not beyond the bounds of possibility that a New Zealand Government would contemplate free trade with North America. The old mercantilist attitudes have been seriously eroded, including the assumption that protection should be reduced only in exchange for concessions made by others. More recently, governments have been more disposed to ask what benefits high protection and other supports to producers are bringing, in relation to the costs imposed on consumers, taxpayers, and the less protected producers. The present New Zealand Government has concluded that the answers suggest less protection and support—and that, if we wish to do better economically, we cannot wait for a successful GATT round, but must start the process of adjustment now.

Accordingly, this seminar on economic adjustment is a timely one for New Zealand. I hope that the attitudes toward reducing protection which have been developing here will also gain ground elsewhere in the Pacific. The path of adjustment is not an easy one, and I am delighted that our hosts have brought such a strong team together to share ideas on the problems ahead.

1
Trade Policies and Their Impact on Individual Economies

P.J. Lloyd

I. Introduction

International trade in manufactured commodities as a group has exhibited several definite long-term trends in the developed market economies.

- Tariff rates have been falling for more than two decades. When the reductions negotiated at the Tokyo Round are fully implemented, according to data supplied by the General Agreement on Tariffs and Trade (GATT), tariffs on manufactured products will average 4.9 percent in the United States, 6.0 percent in the European Communities (EC), and 6.0 percent in Japan (GATT (1979)).
- Nontariff instruments that assist import-competing production of manufactures have been rising in terms of commodity coverage in all developed market countries. According to the United Nations Conference on Trade and Development (UNCTAD) inventory of nontariff measures, which has been used to calculate incidence in terms of the percentage of actual imports affected by nontariff measures, import trade so affected in 1980 was 6.2 percent for the United States, 7.2 percent for Japan, and 10.9 percent for the EC. These percentages rose in 1981, 1982, and 1983 (Balassa and Balassa (1984)).
- It is probable that the average level of effective protection by combined tariff and nontariff instruments has increased since the conclusion of the Tokyo Round in 1965 in most developed market economies, although there are no comprehensive estimates of the average levels of nominal or effective assistance resulting from the measures that were included in the incidence studies. For the United States, Morici and Megna (1983) estimated that quantitative restrictions alone were equivalent to an average nominal tariff of 0.57 percent for all manufacturing. Even fewer data are available for Japan and most other countries, with the exception of Australia (see Section IV).

- The growth of import restrictions in each country has been concentrated in a few areas of production. In the United States, for example, apart from temporary protection and antidumping duties and subsidies introduced after an investigation by the International Trade Commission, nontariff restrictions on manufactured products have been concentrated in only three industries—textiles and apparel, steel, and automobiles. In the Federal Republic of Germany the major manufacturing recipients of nontariff assistance have been steel, shipbuilding, and the electrical industries (Lawrence (1985)).
- Few exports of manufactures are subject to export taxes or other restrictions, and, in fact, manufactures receive export subsidies in most countries. However, the overall structure of trade interventions in most countries seems to restrict the size of the trade sector.

Many domestic industry policies affect trade, and the distinction between border protection and nonborder protection policies is arbitrary. Nevertheless, this paper will be confined to border policies.

The features outlined above are remarkably consistent across countries, as several authors, as well as the International Monetary Fund (IMF), have noted (for example, Page (1981) and IMF (1982)). This consistency has a number of implications. From the point of view of the countries imposing import restrictions, the increases in the number and severity of the restrictions have been concentrated in manufacturing industries that are already receiving above-average levels of assistance. Consequently, the restrictions have increased the dispersion of nominal and effective rates among industries.

There is no measure of dispersion of these rates that has a one-to-one correspondence with the aggregate costs of the distortions; for any structure of rates, these costs also depend on the relationships among industries of substitutability and complementarity in both demand and supply. However, one theorem that has emerged from recent welfare theory is that an increase in extreme distortions worsens the welfare of the residents under general conditions (see Woodland (1982), Chapter 11). While in many economies higher rates of distortion undoubtedly apply to some nonmanufacturing industries (especially agricultural products such as meat, sugar, cereals, and dairy products), these activities are separable from manufacturing activities, in that they generally have very low rates of substitutability or complementarity with the manufacturing products. These two features together imply that the costs of manufacturing protection have almost certainly increased in these countries.

From the point of view of the exporting countries, the concentration of these new restrictions in a few areas, such as textiles and clothing, steel, and electrical goods, means that world trade in these areas is now heavily restricted. Thus, the restrictions discriminate indirectly against those exporting countries that have a greater comparative advantage in these areas. Moreover, many individual nontariff instruments discriminate by country in their application (for example, voluntary export restraints, orderly marketing agreements, discretionary licensing), or by groups of countries such as developing countries (for example, the Multi-Fiber Agreement (MFA) quotas on textiles and clothing). These two characteristics of the restrictions imply that the growth of protectionism has tended to discriminate against developing countries as a group.

The growth of protection of manufacturing production has been viewed with concern by international economists and by international organizations such as the GATT, the IMF, UNCTAD, and the Food and Agricultural Organization (FAO). Yet, this trend should be seen in the perspective of trends in international trade in all goods and services. The value of exports of manufactures accounted for 58 percent of total world merchandise trade in 1983 (GATT (1984)). For the individual developed market economies, the corresponding shares varied among countries and between export and import trade, but they were generally above the world average. For the United States, the shares of manufactures in export and import trade in 1983 were 67 and 61 percent, respectively (GATT (1984)). However, international trade includes trade in services as well as goods. Total world exports of services including investment income in 1980 were estimated to be valued at $610 billion (UNCTAD (1983)), or 35 percent of merchandise trade; trade in manufactures in that year was about 43 percent of world trade in all goods and services.

It would be interesting to compare the restrictions on trade in manufactures with those on other merchandise trade and on trade in services. Statistics of the nominal rates of protection for some agricultural commodities (see, for example, IMF (1982)) show a greater dispersion than the rates for manufacturing industries; however, it should be remembered that the sample of agricultural products is restricted and these data relate to individual commodities, whereas the rates for industries are averages across commodities. Few measures exist of the nominal rates of protection for mineral commodities, but it appears that most of these resource-based imports are unrestricted, presumably because they are more frequently noncompetitive with domestic production.

There are few, if any, estimates of the nominal rates of protection or assistance for tradable services. Trade in some services, such as for tourists, seems to be almost free in many countries, or it has become less restricted, as with foreign investment income, banking, air transport, and reinsurance (UNCTAD (1983)). However, trade in other services such as international goods freight is known to be severely restricted, in some cases by prohibitive barriers. As a broad generalization, it could be said that trade in manufactures and agricultural products is on average more restricted than other tradables, but it is possible that the price distortions within the manufacturing sectors are less than those for other tradables in some countries.

This paper will examine further some aspects of the impact of these trade restrictions. It will be concerned solely with the impact in the restriction-imposing countries. Section II gives some perspectives on these trends. Section III considers some general aspects of the impact of the restrictions, and Section IV examines Australia in greater detail as an illustrative case study. Section V draws some conclusions.

II. Recent Trends in Growth of Protectionism

The growth of protection of manufacturing industries has tended to be concentrated in areas within the manufacturing sector that have experienced declines in absolute levels of employment and, in some cases, in real output. For example, according to data provided by the Organization for Economic Cooperation and Development (OECD), in the clothing and textile industries, value added in constant prices has fallen in the developed market economies as a group since 1973, and employment has fallen more rapidly than real output (OECD (1983)). The share of these industries in total manufacturing production and employment has fallen steadily in all developed market economies (OECD (1983)). For industrial market economies, the share of the manufacturing sector in gross domestic product fell from 30 percent in 1960 to 24 percent in 1982 (World Bank (1984)).

It is customary to examine the relationship between trade flows, on the one hand, and domestic production and consumption, on the other, in terms of changes in import shares. The World Bank has prepared comprehensive tapes of "import penetration" (i.e., the share of imports in total production plus exports) for the industrialized economies. Consider, for example, trade by the Pacific Basin in clothing and textile industry products, a product group that has experienced large increases in protection. For the individual Pacific Basin countries, the import penetration ratios follow a rising trend in a majority of the four-digit International Standard Industrial Classification (ISIC) groups over the period 1970–80 (Lloyd (1985)).

Several studies have attempted to estimate the significance of import penetration of manufacturing markets through changes in domestic output and employment relative to changes in consumption and exports and to changes in labor employed per unit of output (see Baldwin (1984), pp. 595–97, for a survey). These studies have invariably found that the changes in import shares have accounted for only a small share of the change in employment in these import-competing industries and that this component has been swamped by the effect of increases in labor productivity. However, it is now accepted that these decompositions cannot be interpreted as cause and effect, because changes in the labor input coefficients, imports, exports, and consumption are all interdependent (see Martin and Evans (1981)). For example, an increase in actual or threatened imports may induce an increase in labor productivity because of the cessation of the least competitive lines of production or of low-vintage equipment, or because of induced innovation.

Trends in import shares cannot be interpreted as an indicator of market performance for several reasons. The changes in the shares reflect in part increases (and decreases) in the levels of protection of domestic producers. Also, import share data ignore all exports. Increasing intra-industry specialization between, say, two countries results in mutual interpenetration of the markets of both countries. Furthermore, a rise in the import penetration ratios covering low-cost foreign materials may be necessary for the international competitiveness of downstream domestic activities.[1] The use of net imports/exports as a percentage of apparent consumption is preferable to the use of gross imports. In the case of textiles and clothing, these net ratios have also risen, though less dramatically than the increase in import shares (Lloyd (1985)). These import shocks are themselves the result of other factors which must be the ultimate exogenous cause of disturbances to market demands and/or supplies.

Manufacturing trade and production have been subject to abnormal shocks since the early 1970s, as the rates of unemployment of labor and capital stocks have increased in all developed market economies compared to the levels prevailing before this period. Page (1981) identified 1973 as the beginning of the "new protectionism." This was the year in which the IMF in its *Annual Report on Exchange Arrangements and Exchange Restrictions* (1973) first found more increases than decreases in restrictions and the industrialized or OECD countries first pledged to avoid restrictions in the future. The GATT and others have frequently noted the correlation between these events.

A second source of market shocks has been technology change. The possibility of intercountry differences in average rates of change can have a decided impact on long-run trends. The technological lead of U.S. producers in technology-intensive products has been steadily

---

[1] There are a number of other problems. Many imports include a domestic content due chiefly to domestic equity participation in overseas assembly operations and to the use by overseas suppliers of materials produced domestically at an earlier stage. Furthermore, the shares are derived from data in current prices. Where imports from, say, developing countries have improved in quality over the sample period, these shares overstate the quantity growth over time. These problems derive from the aggregation of flows across multiple stages of production or different commodities. Finally, the omission of inventory accumulation and decumulation and year-to-year variability make it difficult to identify trends.

reduced, and the decline in the competitiveness of U.S. manufactures is sometimes partly attributed in part to this falling off. (For an elegant formal model of technology gap trade, see Krugman (1985).) In his survey of U.S. industrial policy, Lawrence (1985, p. 10) observes: "Reflecting these pressures, the U.S. industries seeking assistance have gradually moved up the technological spectrum—first, agriculture, then steel and automobiles, and increasingly, high-technology products such as semiconductors." Similar differentials between the rates of technological improvement of domestic producers and those of the most competitive trading partners may also exist for some Pacific Basin countries. On the other hand, in the case of Japan, this factor has improved competitiveness in a range of manufacturing industries. The increased penetration by the so-called newly industrialized countries (NICs) of the markets for manufactures in the old industrialized countries seems primarily to reflect improved technologies in the NICs.

A third set of shocks, which have systematically affected the manufacturing sectors of some countries, is variable exchange rates. Among the world's principal currencies, exchange rates have now floated for over a decade. Has this increase in flexibility produced greater variability? Recent studies have shown that bilateral nominal exchange rates have become more volatile since the advent of floating exchange rates (see Williamson (1983); IMF (1984); and Argy (1985)). But movements in real exchange rates are more closely related to competitiveness.[2] The studies indicate that real exchange rates, too, have become more variable. Taking March 1973 as the base and using the Morgan Guaranty index of real effective exchange rates,[3] Argy calculates that the maximum deviations from the base were about 52 percent real appreciation for sterling (February 1981), 25 percent appreciation for the U.S. dollar (early 1985), and 23 percent real devaluation for the yen (October 1982). Moreover, deviations from purchasing parity rates have persisted for long periods. If these rates are used as a measure of the "fundamental equilibrium" rates, the U.S. dollar may be currently overvalued by about 25 to 30 percent, and the yen undervalued by about the same magnitude (Argy (1985)). These differentials may be explained in some countries such as the Netherlands by the existence of a "booming sector," and in others by tight monetary policies combined with a much greater level of international mobility of short-term money and by exchange

---

[2] This is unsound for a number of reasons. Changes in technologies which are not reflected in price levels, new product developments, changes in demand, resource discoveries, and other factors may cause movements in real exchange rates and competitiveness to diverge.

[3] This is published in *World Financial Markets*. It uses the wholesale price indices for nonfood manufactures to adjust for rates of inflation.

rate expectation effects. There is also a possibility that macroeconomic policies may have been fashioned to assist the tradables sector—what Corden (1982) calls "exchange rate protection." Whatever the cause, these deviations have no doubt contributed substantially to the decline in competitiveness of some outputs of the manufacturing segment of the tradables sector, in the United States and the United Kingdom in particular, and to the continued growth of Japanese exports of manufactures.

Downward trends in output and employment of many manufacturing industries have prompted concern about "de-industrialization" in the United States, the United Kingdom, and some other countries. More recently, "re-industrialization" has emerged as a policy objective. In the late 1970s, many economists attributed the growth of the new protectionism to the global recession. Lately, it has been recognized that real exchange appreciations may have been important in fostering de-industrialization in some countries over some periods. Yet, it is definitionally impossible for all countries to experience real exchange rate appreciations, and most countries have experienced substantial variations in unemployment rates. The widespread and persistent nature of de-industrialization suggests more fundamental factors, such as differentials in the income elasticities of final demand. The manufacturing sector, as a whole, exhibits the symptoms of secular decline, rather like agriculture in the early post-World War II period. It may be that macroeconomic shocks such as a sharp increase in unemployment or real exchange rate appreciations increase structural adjustments, which, in turn, lead to increased assistance to the least competitive industries.

These shocks and other disturbances have an important implication for trade policy formation. Most increases in protection are today a defensive response to adverse market trends, rather than an offensive strategy to shift resources from other economic activities into the protected activities. The arguments used nowadays in most countries to justify increases in protection relate to structural adjustment difficulties. The arguments usually run along two lines. First, if there are distortions in domestic markets owing to, say, rigid or sticky factor prices or monopolies, markets might fail to take account of the full social costs of adjustment. If an economy is characterized by perfect competition in product and factor markets, adjusting to increased import competition will not involve any social welfare costs. However, if distortions exist, the shift of resources associated with increased import competition will entail production losses that must be offset against the welfare gains to consumers/users (see, for example, Bhagwati (1971)). The second line of popular argument is that firms have less than perfect information, which causes them in some instances to undervalue existing assets and to close plants and lay off workers prematurely and/or to underestimate the rates of return on prospective developments.

A second feature of modern protectionism seems to be closely related to its defensive nature. It is sometimes argued that the degree of risk prevailing in international goods markets has increased (see, for example, IMF (1982) and GATT (1984), pp. 8–9). This increased risk has been variously attributed to an increase in the volatility of commodity prices, the unpredictability of monetary and fiscal policies, and the international debt issue, all of which affect exchange rate movements; "last but not least, there is the increasing unpredictability of trade policies" (GATT (1984), p. 8). These factors have been blamed for the hesitant investment recovery in the developed market economies and the high real interest rates. However, they may also be related to the growth of nontariff instruments of protection. Many of these instruments differ from tariffs, or at least ad valorem tariffs, which are the dominant form, in that the protection they give is not constant in ad valorem terms, but rather increases when the foreign price falls and/or foreign market shares increase. With a quota, for example, the implicit ad valorem rate of tariff, which does not affect the level of domestic output, increases when the foreign supply function shifts downward. Similarly, trigger price mechanisms, antidumping duties, and other duties whose rate is contingent upon the landed price yield higher rates of protection in the same circumstances. For all of these instruments, the nominal rate of protection is state-dependent and this state dependence provides more downside protection than a tariff, which gives the same average rate of protection over time. Lloyd and Falvey (1986) have modeled this feature and argue that there is a producer preference for nontariff instruments over tariffs, although other factors such as the GATT tariff bindings and the visibility of tariff rates have also contributed to the growth of nontariff protection.

III. Effects of Protectionism

This section reviews the impact that protectionist trade policies have on the countries that impose them in the light of the developments discussed in Section II. I shall distinguish between effects on efficiency of resource use, on employment, and on the economic system.

Discussions by economists of the effects of protection normally begin with the efficiency effects, that is, the deadweight consumption and production losses due to policies that distort relative prices from those that would prevail in free trade (abstracting for the moment from any market failure arguments which might justify these deviations from free trade). For the consumption effects, one requires estimates of the nominal rates of protection, that is, the percentage increase in the prices to consumers attributable to trade policies. For the production effects, one requires the effective rates of protection (or assistance), that is, the percentage increase in domestic value added attributable to trade policies. The former should relate to individual consumer commodities, and the latter to individual production activities. These two rates may diverge for an individual activity that produces, say, a single consumer commodity, either because the activity used importable inputs which may be protected, or because the instrument of assistance affects the market prices to producers and consumers differentially. A subsidy based on output will, for example, under certain circumstances, increase the rate of assistance to the producers without increasing the prices to consumers/users of this commodity. (One should note that it will increase the prices of some other taxable commodities or reduce the income of some other factors because the subsidy must be financed in some way.)

One should ideally estimate the structure of nominal and effective rates for the whole economy, because it is the structure of relative price distortions in the economy that affects resource allocation and consumption patterns. Unfortunately, few countries compute reliable measures of the nominal and effective rates even for the activities of the manufacturing sector alone. It is especially difficult to obtain reliable estimates of the effects of nontariff instruments of protection.

In practice, the estimates of the efficiency effects of protection have been confined to selected product groups in most countries. A number of excellent studies have been done of individual industries that have received increased protection since the early 1970s, such as textiles and clothing, footwear, and steel (Baldwin (1984), p. 599, provides a partial list up to 1982). Invariably, the studies show that these industries now enjoy relatively high rates of nominal and effective protection; and in many instances, they already had relatively high rates even before recent increases. In some studies, estimates have been made of the dollar value of losses from the distortions. However, such estimates are unreliable, because the information requirements relating to the demand and supply and input substitution parameters are very demanding; also, because they are partial equilibrium studies, they neglect the direct and indirect effects on other industries.

In recent years, the focus has shifted to the pattern of gains and losses caused by protection measures among income groups and the costs per job saved or created. For example, in their recent study of quotas in the United States, Tarr and Morkre (1984) estimated the annual costs of quotas to consumers, the annual costs to the economy (the costs to consumers minus the increase in producer income and government revenue), and the annual costs per job created. According to the authors, the three main manufacturing areas currently covered by quotas are Hong Kong textiles, the voluntary restraint agreement with Japan on automobile imports, and the voluntary restraint agreement with a number of countries that limits imports of carbon and alloy steel products to no more than 18.5 percent of the U.S. market. The annual costs to consumers per job saved ranged from $241,000 for automobiles to $43,000 for textiles. The costs to the economy were lower, ranging from $216,000 per job for automobiles to $42,000 for textiles. Finally, the authors estimate the ratio of the costs to consumers and the economy to the earnings of workers in the activities concerned.

Although no welfare connotation can be attached to this measure, it dramatizes the conflict between income groups. Tarr and Morkre estimate that losses to consumers ranged between 34 percent times the gains in income to workers in the case of steel products, and 21 percent times the gains in the case of automobiles. Tarr and Morkre's estimates of the ratio of gains to workers to losses in the whole economy are somewhat lower, but these estimates were made on the basis of conservative assumptions and parameters. Further, the losses to the economy may be substantially understated for other reasons. All increases in producer income are treated as a gain in the partial equilibrium model, whereas for the economy as a whole, the increased use of resources by one set of activities because of protection represents a production loss in the sense of a reduction in the national output valued at world prices (unless one argues either that the substitutable activities from which resources were drawn were more heavily assisted, or that the resources would have remained unemployed in the absence of the increase in protection).

It is difficult to estimate jobs saved/created. There can be little doubt that nonprohibitive increases in protection increase the demand for labor in protected activities in the short run. Indeed, many instances of industry protection appear in practice to have been designed as job protection measures. Yet, it is notable that the areas of economic activity within the manufacturing sector that have experienced increased levels of assistance have generally continued to shed labor (see, for example, the OECD study of the textile and clothing industries in the OECD countries; and Lawrence (1985)).

There are several reasons why increases in levels of protection from import competition may not be able to avoid substantial adjustments in the form of displaced labor, especially in the long run. One reason is that, if import shares are rising because of continuing deterioration in the competitiveness of the local producers, maintaining current employment levels would require continued increases in the rate of protection. However, many countries that use nontariff instruments appear ready to increase their restrictiveness. A second reason is that high levels of protection may encourage larger increases in wage rates than in the absence of increased protection. Any gains in employment would thus be reduced. In such cases, employed labor benefits at the expense of the labor that would have been employed or would have remained employed in these protected activities at lower wage rates.

Some long-run effects of increased protection may even reduce the demand for labor in the protected activities themselves. Protection may reduce the degree of competition. It may increase the rate of adoption of labor-saving technologies by increasing the rate of return or increasing the supply of internal company finance from higher profits. Protection can also have a negative effect on total factor productivity by reducing awareness of foreign costs and product developments (see Bhagwati (1971)). These effects are somewhat nebulous, but nonetheless may be substantial. They are likely to be greatest when the protection insulates the domestic market from more vigorous foreign competitors. Thus, the long-run effect of output protection on employment is ambiguous. The cost per job saved estimates are erroneous if, in the longer run, output protection results in job losses rather than job gains.

One should note, too, that protection of jobs in declining activities may be at the expense of jobs in other activities in an economy. The effect of protection by means of tariffs or quotas or other instruments that raise output prices is to reduce the levels of assistance received by all downstream producers that purchase these outputs as inputs into their activities. Other general equilibrium effects could be triggered from the adjustment of prices to clear exchange rate and factor markets. These effects could even reverse the effect on net employment gains for the whole economy (for an example of general equilibrium effects, see Section IV).

From a global point of view, if one country succeeds in increasing employment in protected activities through its trade policies, it also reduces employment in the supplying countries. It is sometimes argued that increased protectionism has adverse effects on the global trading system. For example, the GATT report on *International Trade 1983/84* (1984) asserts that protectionism has reduced the levels of trade-related investment expenditures in the world economy and also distorted the allocation of these expenditures, because different prices for the same commodity in different markets distort the location of these investments. However, these effects lie outside the scope of my paper.

IV. The Case of Australia

This section examines in detail some aspects of Australian trade policies for manufactured products. Australia's experience is a good case study, as the data relating to the structure of assistance are probably better than those for any other country. The Australian estimates of nominal and effective rates cover both tariffs and the major nontariff instruments; the series date back to 1968/69. There are comparable estimates for agricultural products (IAC (1983 b), and the Industries Assistance Commission (IAC) is now undertaking a study of assistance to the mineral sector. The series for manufacturing industries are calculated at the four-digit ISIC level.

In most respects the experience of Australia parallels that of the developed market economies as a group. In 1982/83 the average effective rate of assistance to manufacturing producers in the manufacturing sector was 25 percent. This compares with the average effective rate of 16 percent for agricultural products. However, the commodity coverage of products in the agricultural sector is incomplete. The number of nontariff instruments omitted from the calculation of these averages is greater in the agricultural sector because, proportionately, more of them take the form of tax concessions and subsidies on government-supplied services, such as rail, road, telephone, and electricity supply. The preliminary indication from work in progress at the IAC is that effective rates of assistance are low or negative for many mining activities. There are no estimates for the service sectors. It is a reasonable guess that the manufacturing sector receives more assistance on average than the rest of the economy.

Table 1 reproduces the series for two-digit manufacturing industries since 1968/69. Between 1968/69 and 1973/74 the average fell from 36 percent to 27 percent. These reductions were almost entirely the result of the unilateral and once-for-all, across-the-board reduction of 25 percent in tariffs in July 1973. After mid-1973 there was a revival of the use of quotas, which had almost disappeared in Australia after the abolition of import licensing at the beginning of the 1960s. The main product groups subject to quotas have been textiles and clothing, footwear, automobile assembly, and more recently, steel. This grouping is similar to that in the highly protected manufacturing industries in the United States. These quotas have markedly increased the average rates of effective assistance in these industry groups. However, there have been some tariff reductions, and the average effective rate for the sector as a whole has been stable since mid-1973.

The selective increases in quotas and, to a lesser extent, tariffs and other nontariff instruments have increased the dispersion of effective and nominal rates of assistance in Australian manufacturing. The IAC has calculated "an index of disparity" for both nominal and effective rates, which is defined as the standard deviation normalized by one plus the average rate (IAC (1983a)). These measures have increased steadily since 1973. However, as noted above (see p. 9), there is no single statistic that measures the economic effects of the distribution of nominal and effective rates. A more meaningful characterization of the changes is provided by the group of industries, protected by quotas, whose effective rates of assistance have increased sharply since 1973. This group is textiles (ISIC-23), clothing and footwear (ISIC-24), and transport equipment (largely motor vehicle assembly) (ISIC-32).

Table 1. Average Effective Rates of Assistance to Selected Manufacturing Sub-Divisions, 1968/69 to 1982/83[1]
(In percent)

	1968/1969	1969/1970	1970/1971	1971/1972	1972/1973	1973/1974	1974/1975	1975/1976	1976/1977	1977/1978	1978/1979	1979/1980	1980/1981	1981/1982	1982/1983
21. Food, beverages, and tobacco	16	17	18	19	19	18	21	20	16	10	14	13	10	9	9
23. Textiles	43	42	42	45	45	35	39	50	51	47	47	51	55	54	54
24. Clothing and footwear	97	94	91	86	88	64	87	99	141	141	143	135	140	204	220
25. Wood, wood products, and furniture	26	27	26	23	23	16	18	19	18	18	17	15	15	14	13
26. Paper and paper products, printing and publishing	52	50	50	52	51	38	31	30	30	24	26	25	25	25	24
27. Chemical, petroleum, and coal products	31	31	31	32	32	25	23	23	21	19	19	17	15	14	14
28. Nonmetallic mineral products	15	15	15	14	14	11	11	10	7	5	5	5	4	4	4
29. Basic metal products	31	30	28	29	29	22	16	16	14	10	10	9	10	11	11
31. Fabricated metal products	61	60	60	58	56	44	39	38	34	30	31	30	31	31	27
32. Transport equipment	50	50	51	50	51	39	45	59	54	48	53	59	63	71	72
33. Other machinery and equipment	43	43	43	44	39	29	24	25	22	20	20	21	20	21	18
34. Miscellaneous manufacturing	34	35	32	32	31	24	27	26	25	30	30	29	28	27	25
Total	36	36	36	35	35	27	27	28	27	23	24	23	25	25	25

Source: IAC (1985).

[1] The estimates from 1968/69 to 1982/83 are in three series: 1968/69 to 1974/75; 1975/76 to 1977/78; and 1978/79 to 1982/83. The first series is based on 1968/69 production weights; the second series uses 1974/75 production weights; and the third series employs 1977/78 production weights and also incorporates forms of assistance not included in previous series estimates.

These are the troubled or problem quota-protected industries. In 1968/69 the average rate of effective assistance for this group was already roughly double that for the rest of the sector. By 1981/82 the average rate for this group had doubled, whereas the average rate for the rest of the sector had fallen sharply. Consequently, the average rate for this group was roughly four times the average rate for the rest of the sector. To a much greater extent than previously, a specific group can now be clearly identified as receiving higher levels of assistance than other manufacturers and all other producers in the economy, with the exception of rural producers of tobacco, marketing milk, eggs, and deciduous canning fruit. As there is little substitutability in production between these manufactured and rural products, the recent increases in the already extreme distortions have worsened the efficiency of resource use in the economy.

The IAC has not—wisely, in my view—attempted to construct a money measure of the aggregate costs of protection policies. However, it has computed other measures, such as the consumer tax equivalent and the net subsidy equivalent of nontariff interventions. In 1981–82 the consumer tax equivalent of the quota-protected industries was estimated to be A$3.9 billion, that is, around A$600 to A$800 per Australian household (IAC (1983a)).

There are no estimates of the costs of jobs saved in Australia. The IAC and others have, however, calculated job subsidies implicit in the protection. One simple method of doing this is to divide the net subsidy equivalent of tariffs and quotas by the number of persons employed in the industry. For the quota-protected industries, this calculation shows that the job subsidies as a percentage of the annual wage in the industries rose from 49 percent before the introduction of quotas to 79 percent of the average annual wage in 1981/82 (Gregory (1984), pp. 14–15). However, this calculation overstates the job subsidy by assuming that protection benefits only the labor factor, while ignoring its effect on the number employed.

To evaluate these government actions we must first consider the objectives of the government's policies. Australian governments have declared their intention of preventing large losses in employment in the protected industries while at the same time maintaining their efficiency. For example, in announcing the current seven-year plan for the textile and clothing industries, the Australian Government saw the plan as ". . . safeguarding employment . . . [encouraging] further improvements in the efficiency of the industry, reductions in costs and responsiveness to changing consumer needs" (Joint Statement (1980)).

There is a stark contrast between the large increases in average rates of assistance to the troubled, quota-protected industries on the one hand, and the continued decline in employment in the same industries,

Chart 1. Employment Indexes: Manufacturing, Troubled Industries
(1968/69 = 100)

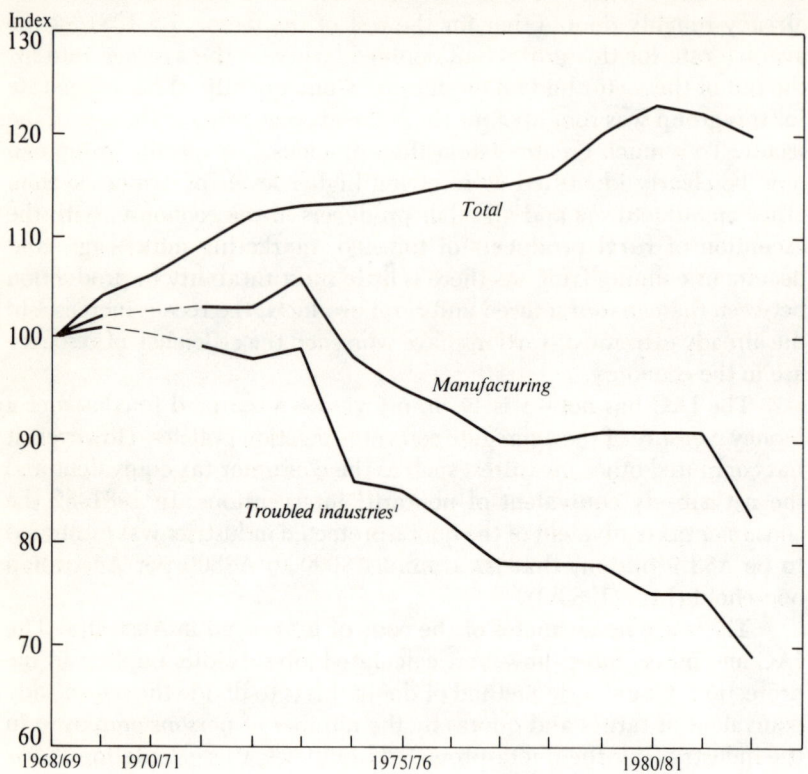

Source: Gregory (1984)
[1]ISIC subdivisions: Textiles (23), Clothing and Footwear (24), Transport Equipment (32).

on the other (see Chart 1). In reviewing these trends, the IAC (1983a) observed (p. 11):

> The above analysis has shown that the group of most highly assisted industries has the worst employment record. Employment in these industries declined much more rapidly than the manufacturing average, not only during the current recession, but also over the past decade. Over the longer term, quota protection allowed these industries to maintain the value of their production more or less unchanged and to limit increases in imports as a share of their domestic markets. Quota protection may have slowed down the rate of decline of employment.

Moreover, the industry plans for textiles, clothing and footwear, and automobile assembly have been constructed with the express intention of maintaining employment in these industries. There is a strong *prima facie* case, therefore, that these instruments of policy have been ineffective in achieving their employment objectives. (This argument is pursued in greater detail in a study of the textile and clothing industry group by Lloyd (1985).)

By themselves, the effects of these protection policies are pervasive enough to disturb the equilibrium of the entire economy. It is therefore necessary to conduct a general equilibrium analysis to determine their employment effects. Conveniently, Soo Sun Chai and Dixon (1985) have conducted such an analysis in their study of the changes in manufacturing protection between 1968/69 and 1977/78—the period in which most of the quota increases occurred. As noted above, the average effective rate of assistance declined, but the spread of rates increased. Soo Sun Chai and Dixon use the general equilibrium model ORANI, which takes account of effects on real wages via consumer price index (CPI) adjustments, aggregate demand effects, and other inter-industry relations. Their calculations show that these increases in assistance to selected industries led to increased employment in the manufacturing sector by some 0.53 percent and, in the economy as a whole, by some 0.77 percent. Resources were drawn into the manufacturing sector primarily from the exporting rural and mining sectors, in which employment fell.

In their calculations, Soo Sun Chai and Dixon also show that the effects of protection differ among manufacturing industries. Increased protection in some industries will destroy more jobs outside the protected industry than it creates within the industry, but for others the reverse is true. The quota-protected industries, especially automobile assembly and footwear, fall into the category of net employment-creating industries. Thus, although increased protection for these industries creates jobs, the magnitude of the additional jobs is small relative to the loss in employment over the same period due to other factors that have caused employment in manufacturing to fall by more than 20 percent since 1968/69.

It is important to know what the other factors are that cause the continued decline in manufacturing employment. Unfortunately, there has been little systematic work on this question in Australia. The main evidence comes from some empirical studies of the effect of the 25 percent tariff cut in 1973 compared with the effect of other measures. Gregory and Martin (1976) estimate that the appreciation of the exchange rate in 1972 (by 7 percent) and 1973 (by 5 percent) had approximately four times the effect on the subsequent increase in imports than the tariff cut. According to the IAC (1977, p. 35), the increase in the manufacturing wage bill between October 1973 and 1975 was equivalent in its effects on the competitiveness of Australian industry to either a 19.7 percent tariff cut or a 5.5 percent revaluation. The increase in the wage bill was due to an explosion in wage rates in 1972–75, particularly female wage rates.

Chart 2. Index of Australian Real Effective Exchange Rate

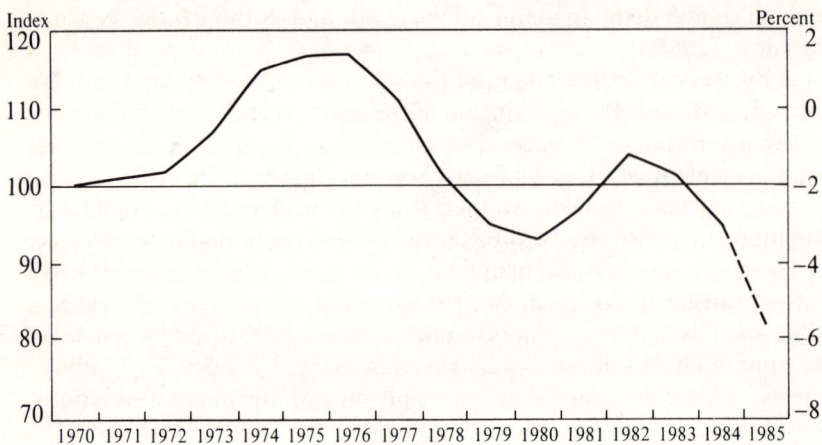

The separate effects of costs and of the change in the effective exchange rate can be combined in the index of the real (effective) exchange rate. Chart 2 plots a series calculated by the Institute of Applied Economic and Social Research.[4] This series shows that the real exchange rate appreciated from 1973 to 1975, the same period in which the quotas were introduced. However, the real exchange rate has followed a downward trend since then and is subject to pronounced cycles, which disturb the competitiveness of the trade-exposed manufacturing sector. The 1973–75 appreciation cannot explain the long-term downward trend of manufacturing employment. The continuation and strength of this trend since the late 1960s suggest that it must be driven by underlying structural factors, rather than important, but short-term factors such as resource booms, exchange rate appreciations, variations in aggregate unemployment, and changes in relative wage rates. However, the 1973–75 appreciation, perhaps combined with the 1973 tariff cut, seems to have triggered demands for protection for the least competitive segments of the manufacturing sector.

Concerning the government's stated objective of using protection policies to promote efficient industries, one must conclude that the increases in protection to selective industries have not induced them to become more competitive internationally, enabling them to survive in the future with lower levels of assistance.

---

[4] The IAC and Treasury have computed alternative indices of the real exchange rate or "competitiveness." These are rather sensitive to the choice of price series and the method of weighting (see, for example, IAC (1980a), but the swings are evident in all of the series.

Studies have also been conducted on the Australian experience with the effects of protection on incomes distributed by region, income groups, and source of factor income. Protection affects the real incomes of each of the units in these distributions differentially. Regionally, the gains have been concentrated in three of the six States—Victoria, principally, and New South Wales and South Australia. The consumption tax component of all tariffs and quotas in Australia falls most heavily on low-income households and especially on the lowest income group (IAC (1980b)). Since the structure of industry assistance does not generally favor the suppliers of unskilled labor vis-à-vis other factor owners, it is a fair guess that the total effect of the structure of industry assistance is regressive, in that it shifts income from the lower-income groups to some higher-income groups in the economy.

V. Conclusions

Democratic governments must be free to choose the objectives they want to achieve through their economic policies. The central questions in an evaluation of these policies are whether the government has made the best choice of policy instruments and, whether these instruments have been successful in moving the economy toward attainment of the stated objectives. The costs that trade policies impose on income earners in the nonprotected industries have long been debated. There is growing awareness in many countries of the failure of trade policies to promote increased efficiency and to maintain employment in the protected industries themselves. This has been the theme of several recent papers on trade policy (for example, those presented by Lawrence and Lloyd at the 1985 PAFTAD Conference). Given the long-term decline in the manufacturing sector of many industrialized countries, protective policies, which are intended to protect jobs, seem to be a Canute strategy.

Other government policy instruments may be more effective in the Mundellian sense of being more closely geared to the objectives and imposing smaller incidental costs on other agents in the economy. About ten years ago, many economists advocated the introduction of adjustment assistance policies as the appropriate policy response to problems of adjustment to disturbances in the markets for tradables. Recently, these policies have been viewed with a growing skepticism. This skepticism is reflected in arguments by OECD, the GATT, and others, that the price system is capable of sending the correct signals about future prices to both producers and consumers and should be permitted to do so. Recent models of structurally adjusting economies suggest that the case for introducing structural adjustment assistance policies to counter market disturbances is severely weakened if prices are flexible and expectations are rational (see, in particular, the papers by Neary and Mussa, in Bhagwati (1982)).

Several recent papers have indicated that the U.S. economy is more flexible than Western European economies (Sachs (1983); Emerson (1984); and Balassa (1984)). Various indicators of flexibility have been used, e.g., firm deaths and births, worker mobility between jobs and industries, relative and absolute flexibility of real wages, and entreprenurial activity. These intercountry differences have been used to explain differences in unemployment rates and employment trends between the United States and European economies. This explanation leads to the suggestion that the appropriate policy response to structural adjustment problems is to increase market flexibility by removing obstacles to the exit and entry of firms and workers, and increasing real wage flexibility. Of course, these measures will be opposed by some interest groups because they threaten the real incomes of factors in their present occupations, especially specific factors.[5]

The ultimate objection to distortionary trade policies is not that they impose costs on consumers and other income groups. Virtually any economic policy will adversely affect some group(s) in an economy. The objection is that they harm these groups unnecessarily because there are other policy options, including, importantly, the option of the government's doing nothing, which come closer to achieving the objectives and reduce the costs.

References

Anjaria, Shailendra J., Zubair Iqbal, Naheed Kirmani, et al., *Developments in International Trade Policy*, Occasional Paper No. 16 (Washington: International Monetary Fund, 1982).

Argy, V., "Flexible Exchange Rates—Twelve Years After—Are There Alternatives?" *The Australian Economic Review* (Melbourne), 2nd Quarter, No. 70 (July 1985), pp. 27–36.

Australia, Ministry of Industry and Commerce and Ministry for Business and Consumer Affairs, Joint Statement on Government Policy Toward the Textiles, Clothing, and Footwear Industries (Canberra, August 15, 1980).

---

[5] A dramatic example is provided by the clothing industry in Australia. There are two groups of workers, one unionized and covered by wage awards, and the other, nonunionized—the so-called "outworkers" working under contracts. Union officials contend that these outworkers make up clothing articles at 1/4 to 1/5 of the labor cost per unit of the unionized labor. In a free and integrated market the wage rate would settle somewhere between the fixed award rate and the outworker rate. The effect of movement to a market-clearing wage rate may be at least as great as the output subsidy equivalent of the present protection, especially for the employment of the labor factor.

Balassa, Bela, "The Economic Consequences of Social Policies in the Industrial Countries," Bernhard Harms Lecture, *Weltwirtschaftliches Archiv*, Vol. 120, No. 2 (1984), pp. 213-27.

——, and Carol Balassa, "Industrial Protection in the Developed Countries," *The World Economy* (London), Vol. 7, (June 1984), pp. 179-96.

——, and Constantine Micholopoulos, "The Extent and the Cost of Protection on Developed-Developing Country Trade," (mimeographed, (Washington: World Bank, 1985).

Baldwin, R. E., "Trade Policies in Developed Countries," Chap. 12 in *Handbook of International Economics*, Vol. 1, ed. by Ronald Winthrop Jones and Peter B. Kenen (Amsterdam: North-Holland, 1984).

Bhagwati, Jagdish N. "The Generalized Theory of Distortions and Welfare," in *Trade, Balance of Payments and Growth*, ed. by Jagdish N. Bhagwati, et al. (Amsterdam: North-Holland, 1971), pp. 69-90.

——, ed., *Import Competition and Response*, National Bureau of Economic Research Conference on Import Competition and Adjustment: Theory and Practice (Chicago: University of Chicago Press, 1982).

Corden, W. Max, "Exchange Rate Protection," in *The International Monetary System under Flexible Exchange Rates: Global, Regional, and National*, ed. by Richard N. Cooper, et al. (New York: Ballinger Publishing House, 1982), pp. 17-34.

Emerson, Michael "The European Stagflation Disease in International Perspective and Some Possible Therapy," in *Europe's Stagflation*, ed. by Michael Emerson (Oxford: Clarendon Press, 1984), pp. 195-228.

General Agreement on Tariffs and Trade, *The Tokyo Round of Multilateral Trade Negotiations*, Supplementary Report by the Director-General of GATT (Geneva: GATT, 1979).

——, *International Trade 1983/84* (Geneva: GATT, 1984).

Gregory, R. G., "Industry Protection and Adjustment: The Australian Experience," Center for Economic Policy Research Discussion Paper No. 111 (Canberra: Center for Economic Policy Research, Australian National University, November 1984).

——, and L. D. Martin, "An Analysis of Relationships Between Import Flows to Australia and Recent Rate and Tariff Changes," *Economic Record* (Victoria, Australia), Vol. 52 (March 1976), pp. 1-25.

Industries Assistance Commission, *Structural Change in Australia* (Canberra: Australian Government Publishing Service, 1977).

——, (1980a), *Annual Report 1979-80* (Canberra: Australian Government Publishing Service).

——, (1980b), *Tariffs as Taxes*, Approaches to General Reductions in Protection, Information Paper No. 2 (Canberra: Australian Government Publishing Service).

——, (1983a), *Annual Report 1982-83* (Canberra: Australian Government Publishing Service).

———, (1983b), *Assistance to Australian Agriculture* (Canberra: Australian Government Publishing Service).

———, *Assistance to Manufacturing Industries: 1977-78 to 1982-83* (Canberra: Australian Government Publishing Service, 1985).

International Monetary Fund, *Annual Report on Exchange Arrangements and Exchange Restrictions, 1973* (Washington: International Monetary Fund, 1973).

———, *Developments in International Trade Policy* (Washington: International Monetary Fund, 1982).

———, *Exchange Rate Volatility and World Trade*, Occasional Paper No. 28 (Washington: International Monetary Fund, 1984).

Krugman, Paul, "A 'Technology Gap' Model of International Trade," *Structural Adjustment in Developed Open Economies*, ed. by Karl Jungenfelt and Sir Douglas Hague, proceedings of conference sponsored by the International Economic Association (New York: St. Martin's Press, 1985), pp. 35-61.

Lawrence, Robert Z., "Industrial Policy in the United States and Europe: Economic Principles and Political Practices," Brookings Discussion Papers in International Economics, No. 41 (Washington: Brookings Institution, 1985).

Lloyd, P. J., "The Australian Textile and Clothing Industry Group: Untowards Effects of Government Intervention," in *Structural Adjustment in Developed Open Economies*, ed. by Karl Jungenfelt and Sir Douglas Hague, proceedings of conference sponsored by the International Economic Association (New York: St. Martin's Press, 1985), pp. 485-522.

———, and R. E. Falvey, "The Choice of Instrument of Industry Protection," in *Issues in World Trade Policy*, ed. by R. H. Snape (London: Macmillan, 1986).

Martin, John P., and John M. Evans, "Notes on Measuring the Employment Displacement Effects of Trade by the Accounting Procedure," *Oxford Economic Papers*, Vol. 33 (March 1981), pp. 154-64.

Morici, Peter, and Laura L. Megna, *U.S. Economic Policies Affecting Industrial Trade: A Quantitative Assessment* (Washington: National Planning Association, 1983).

Organization for Economic Cooperation and Development, *Textile and Clothing Industries: Structural Problems and Policies in OECD Countries* (Paris: OECD, 1983).

Page, S. A. B., "Protectionism and Its Consequences for Europe," *Journal of Common Market Studies* (Oxford), Vol. 20, (September 1981), pp. 17-40.

Sachs, Jeffrey D. "Real Wages and Unemployment in the OECD Countries," *Brookings Papers on Economic Activity: 1* (1980), The Brookings Institution (Washington), pp. 255-303.

Soo, Sun Chai, and Peter B. Dixon, "Protection in Australia: A Description," IAESR Working Paper No. 8, Institute of Applied and Social Research (Melbourne: University of Melbourne, 1985).

Tarr, David G., and Morris E. Morkre, "Aggregate Costs to the United States of Tariffs and Quotas on Imports," report presented to the Federal Trade Commission by the staff of the Economics Bureau (Washington: Federal Trade Commission, 1984).

United Nations Conference on Trade and Development, "Protectionism and Structural Adjustment: Production and Trade in Services, Policies, and Their Underlying Factors Bearing upon International Services Transactions," report prepared for Secretariat of UNCTAD (New York: UNCTAD, April 18, 1983).

Williamson, John, "The Exchange Rate System," Policy Analyses in International Economics, No. 5 (Washington: Institute for International Economics, 1983).

Woodland, A. D., *International Trade and Resource Allocation*, (Amsterdam: North-Holland, 1982).

World Bank, *World Development Report* (New York: Published for the World Bank by Oxford University Press, 1984).

Comment

Cho Soon

Professor Lloyd, in his lucid and instructive paper, cogently analyzes the economic effects of rising protectionism in industrial countries in general and in Australia in particular. The focus of his discussion is mainly on the effects of protection on the countries taking protective measures. I agree with him on most of the points he makes. I shall discuss the nature and causes of protectionism, particularly in the context of structural change in the Pacific economies.

Protectionism has been rising since the early 1970s. Traditionally, protectionism primarily meant tariffs and nontariff measures such as quotas. But for the last decade or so, these traditional means of protectionism have ceased to be the primary instruments for protecting domestic industries. Instead, the industrial countries have discovered a "new protectionism," consisting of such measures as "voluntary export restraints" (VERs), and "orderly marketing agreements" (OMAs). The United States, in particular, is in the process of deliberating in Congress a number of legislative proposals aimed at restricting imports, while the administrative branch is pressing its trade partners in the Western Pacific region to liberalize international trade further. We are living in an age of "fair" trade (rather than of "free" trade) and of "new protectionism."

Broadly, there seem to be two kinds of protectionism—"defensive" and "infant industry." The former is aimed at protecting mature, or in many cases, declining industries; the latter, at infant industries. The distinction is often not very clear, but generally, protectionism in advanced countries is defensive, and protectionism in developing countries is aimed at the infant industries. Traditionally, only the latter type of protectionism has been held justifiable, with a proviso that the infant industry must eventually grow up. The traditional theory did not posit the need for the second type of protectionism. However, there is a certain symmetry between the two types. The infant-industry argument aims at mobilizing resources to the protected industry, while the defensive protectionism aims at withdrawing resources from the protected industries. The success of protection depends, in either case, upon whether or not resources are moved, i.e., whether or not the structures can be adjusted. Protectionism, whether for infant, mature, or declining industry, is justified only in the short run as a temporary relief or a breathing spell for these industries during which they may prepare themselves for more fundamental adjustment. Protectionism is only a short-run substitute for structural adjustment.

Has the United States, through new protectionism, succeeded in attaining short-run as well as long-run objectives? In some cases, protectionism did give the protected industries short-run relief, but in general, this was not the case. As Professor Lloyd points out, the new protectionism has been applied mainly to such industries as textiles, apparel, footwear, steel, and automobiles. The records of trade in the first half of the 1980s show that, in spite of these import restriction measures, imports of these items to the United States continued to increase rapidly.

How can the import of these goods continue unabated? The fact of the matter is that the new protectionism has not been a systematic, long-run policy, but rather an ad hoc policy, so that the exporting countries—mostly Asian newly industrialized countries (NICs)—have been able to take advantage of the many loopholes in such ad hoc measures. The new protectionism is, unlike traditional protectionism, sector-specific and country-specific, intended to discriminate against developing countries in the northeast area. So far, the policy has not been able to attain even the short-run objective, to say nothing of the long-run objective. This does not mean that the variants of new protectionism in the future will be as ineffective as in the past. As the U.S. authorities acquire more experience and become more intent on attaining policy objectives, protection may become much more effective.

The root cause of protectionism is structural imbalance, which develops in an ever more interdependent world. The increase in interdependence involves possibilities of structural imbalance among trade partners with respect to particular industries. As structural imbalance develops, so protectionism develops, no matter how adverse it may be to the trading economies. This explains the irony that the VERs were introduced by the United States, the leader of the postwar free trade movement. Such industries as textiles, apparel, steel, and automobiles attribute the surrender of a large portion of the domestic market not to the natural market force of competition, but to present and past U.S. government policies and to the "unfair" trade practices employed by foreign competitors. They urge the U.S. Government to enforce more strictly the U.S. trade laws against dumping and subsidies. Whatever the justifications for the demand of these industries for more protective measures, the U.S. Government has no choice but to comply with it. Trade is inherently political.

Most economists maintain that protectionism is bad, always and everywhere. However, protectionism persists no matter what economists say about it. It persists because it is always ready at hand and easy to adopt, while other alternatives are either unavailable or too slow to take effect. When the disparity in rates of growth of productivity among the trade partners diverges steadily, and measures for structural adjustment are too slow to yield desired results, protectionist measures would be the only short-run remedies for it.

Structural adjustment is a very slow process, which can be brought about by flexibility in movement of resources and, above all, by improvement in productivity of the industries concerned. The improvement in productivity seems to originate as much from "noneconomic" factors. Recently, there has been talk about a nebulous concept called "industrial policy." If it means intervention by the government in the private sector of the economy, industrial policy is against the basic tenets of a free enterprise economy.

Since 1981, the U.S. Government has been exerting great pressure on Japan and Korea to liberalize their import policies and to "open up" various service industries. The United States may be hoping to offset the balance of payments deficit in the manufacturing sector with a surplus in the service sector. It remains to be seen whether this expectation will be borne out in reality, but it seems to me that liberalization of service industries in Korea and Japan, desirable as it might be on some grounds, would not be a good substitute for structural adjustment in the U.S. economy. In recent years, the service industries in the United States have been absorbing an ever larger proportion of the labor force. This is one of the causes of the slow growth of productivity in the manufacturing sector. One would conjecture that the more successful the United States became in international competition with respect to service industries, the greater would be the employment of resources by service industries, with the result that the manufacturing industries would be still less competitive.

Professor Lloyd cites an Australian study on the effect of protection on income distribution in Australia. He thinks that "it is a fair guess that the total effect of the structure of industry assistance is regressive, in that it shifts income from lower-income groups to some higher-income groups in the economy." I find this statement somewhat puzzling, though I do agree that the incidence of protection on consumers would be regressive. I would consider, however, that if labor-intensive industries are protected, the income of the workers in protected industries will be supported, and it would be difficult to maintain that protection will shift income from the low-income groups to some high-income groups.

Professor Lloyd seems to be in favor of taking a laissez-faire approach in international trade. He maintains that protection should be considered in the light of policy alternatives, including one of doing nothing. One can easily see that doing nothing will be the best course of policy if everything goes well; i.e., if the trade partners perform roughly equally in technological improvement and efficiency in industrial management, if they do not experience balance of payments difficulties, and if the structural changes are slow enough to be corrected by measures other than protection. But there seem to be many circumstances which render protectionism unavoidable, if not positively desirable. I doubt that in our interdependent world the country that has beleaguered industries can afford to do nothing. It will be forced to devise and adopt some measures to effect structural adjustment, without being fully confident that that device will, in fact, be an appropriate one.

2

Economic Adjustment in New Zealand: A Developed Country Case Study of Policies and Problems

Ralph Lattimore

I. Introduction

New Zealand serves as a good case study of the processes of economic adjustment for a number of reasons. Its economic structure has strong similarities with both the developed and less-developed country groupings; it is a small, relatively open economy with a large export-agricultural sector like many less-developed countries, but with a relatively high income level. New Zealand has followed a more intense import substitution and generally interventionist economic strategy than most other high-income countries. Furthermore, New Zealand is an island state with high transport costs to and from overseas markets.

Perhaps, in part because of the country's size, isolation, cultural heritage, and historical ties, New Zealanders have stimulated and supported a particular form of economic and political organization over a long period of time. New Zealand was, for example, at the forefront of developments leading to the "welfare state" during the 1930s and universal accident compensation in the 1970s. The New Zealand public education system and women's suffrage were at the leading edge of parallel global initiatives. Nationalization and state control of industry have been important throughout most of the period of European settlement. On the development side, successive New Zealand governments (at least until recently) have tended to rely heavily on economic regulations, trade policy instruments, and subsidies and grants to affect the growth and shape of industry at all levels.

In short, government planning and intervention have played a major role in New Zealand's development. Many New Zealanders have viewed our country as a rather unique ensemble of resource endowments and, at the same time, have supported the use of policy instruments to conduct numerous and far-reaching social and economic experiments. Some of these experiments have been lauded for their success, others have failed, and the jury is still out on many others.[1]

The analysis presented in this paper is static in nature and abstracts from important dynamic considerations. Recent government liberalization attempts have raised questions as to the timing of policy and regulatory changes (Stewart (1984)). Should not policy liberalization be applied to fix-price sectors before it is applied to the flex-price sectors to ensure a smooth resource response to policy change? Proponents of this view argue that in New Zealand the liberalization attempts are being made back to front. In addition, the whole question of exchange rate overshooting with financial deregulation is an open one at this stage. In the interests of space, these dynamic issues are left to another paper.

The paper is designed to trace one strand of these economic experiments—that of policy toward the tradable sectors of the economy over the last thirty years, with particular focus on the policy adjustment of the last few years. This period is chosen because it encompasses a number of major turning points in the development strategy and, hence, may provide greater insights into the processes of policy adjustment in New Zealand.

The paper documents the changing economic performance in relation to some aspects of changes in government intervention in trade policy, tax expenditures, production subsidies, and regulations. This work consists of a synthesis of past empirical studies with new estimates of direct export assistance, tax expenditures, and a recent assessment of import protection. The second aspect of the paper is to assess the impact of the development strategy on growth and employment.

There are major gaps in our understanding, both of the trade policy path of the last 50 years and, in particular, of how recent policy changes are affecting the neutrality of trade policy. There is no long-term consistent series of nominal or effective protection rates, for example. Further, the degree of precision in measuring export assistance is greater than for import protection. In part, this is because export assistance is based on tax expenditures and direct assistance. The reader needs to bear these inadequacies in mind throughout.

II. Economic Setting

Until the 1960s New Zealand's per capita income level ranked in the top ten on a world scale (Gould (1982)), when it is measured in terms

---

[1] The interested reader is directed to the following three references for a succinct economic history of New Zealand from the time of European settlement to 1982: Condliffe (1930), Hawke (1985), and Gould (1982). Each has an excellent set of further references.

of gross domestic product (GDP) at the market exchange rate. Subsequently, New Zealand's position has fallen. The structure of the economy, however, does not match that of other countries currently experiencing a high level of performance. This is shown in Table 1. The primary sector of the economy is two to three times the size of its counterparts in Western European and North American countries. Within the primary sector, farming is the dominant industry.

The manufacturing sector is highly oriented toward the manufacture and processing of farm inputs and agricultural products. It has been estimated (Guthrie and Lattimore (1984)) that in 1976/77, 20 percent of GDP was generated by the broadly defined agricultural production, processing, and distribution sector. Furthermore, this broad sector (agriculture) employed 18 percent of the work force, as indicated in Table 1.

The manufacturing subsector involved in industrial activities (i.e., not related to food and natural fiber products) appears to be relatively small in New Zealand. The service sector is similar in size to that of other developed economies. Table 1 also shows that while New Zealand agriculture tends to be more capital-intensive than manufacturing and services, the differences overall are not great. This reflects the composition of farm output and the labor-intensive nature of processing livestock products.

The high degree of agricultural orientation is magnified in the balance of payments. Table 2 presents the results of a two-way breakdown of New Zealand's visible exports. Products have been roughly classified into either crude or manufactured product forms and according to whether the export product is derived from one of five sets of raw ingredients—livestock commodities (animals, milk, raw wool, etc.), crops (barley, peas, seeds, etc.), timber, metals (iron ore, etc.), or other. The final residual category includes imported raw materials, like aluminum and human capital (e.g., skill-based products such as computer software). Some of the highlights of Table 2 are drawn out in the summary statistics at the bottom. In 1985, 75 percent of New Zealand export earnings were crude materials, a small drop from 80 percent in 1977. Over this nine-year period, about 90 percent of export receipts were from the sale of products based on local materials, and that figure has been quite stable. Manufactured exports, comprising 25 percent of the total, have tended to switch to a local material base over this period.

The composition of imports is not given here, but it tends to complement exports. Imports consist mainly of industrial raw materials (chemicals, oil and resins, etc.), equipment, and semi-durable and durable consumer products, or their components.

International trade has represented a high (23 percent in 1980), but slightly decreasing, proportion of GDP in the post-World War II period.

Table 1. New Zealand: Gross Domestic Product and Employment by Sector, 1950/51–1976/77

Year	Proportion of Total GDP Attributable to Each Sector				Proportion of Employment In Each Sector			
	Rural	Mining	Manufacturing	Services	Rural	Mining	Manufacturing	Services
1950/51								
1954/55	20.4	0.9	23.8	54.5				
1955/56					19	1.0	25	55
1960/61	19.0	0.9	23.0	57.0	16	0.9	24	59
1965/66	15.0	0.7	25.0	59.0	14	0.8	25	63
1970/71	12.0	0.5	26.0	61.0	13	0.6	27	63
1971/72	13.0	0.5	23.0	64.0	11	0.5	25	62
1972/73	15.0	0.4	22.0	63.0	12	0.4	24	62
1973/74	13.0	0.4	22.0	64.0	12	0.4	25	62
1974/75	9.0	0.5	23.0	67.0	12	0.4	25	62
1975/76	11.0	0.3	22.0	67.0	12	0.4	24	62
1976/77	12.0[1]	0.5	22.0[1]	66.0[1]	11[2]	0.4	25[2]	62[2]

Source: Lloyd, et al. (1980), adapted.
[1] Includes agricultural production, processing, and distribution component, which combined totals 20 percent.
[2] Includes agricultural production, processing, and distribution component, which combined totals 18 percent.

Table 2. New Zealand: Composition of Visible Exports

Exports Based On:	1977 Crude	1977 Mnfd.[1]	1977 Total	1978 Crude	1978 Mnfd.[1]	1978 Total	1982 Crude	1982 Mnfd.[1]	1982 Total	1983 Crude	1983 Mnfd.[1]	1983 Total	1985 Crude	1985 Mnfd.[1]	1985 Total
	(In millions of NZ dollars, f.o.b.)														
a. Livestock	2,123	53	2,176	2,080	96	2,176	4,112	194	4,306	4,748	266	5,014	5,781	864	6,645
b. Crops	144	43	187	144	97	241	519	82	601	626	1,345	760	1,120	223	1,343
c. Forestry	150	71	221	145	116	260	363	232	595	289	248	537	337	391	728
d. Metals	140	3	143	165	11	176	291	2	293	366	116	483	849	22	871
e. Mainly imported or other materials	—	457	457	—	282	282	—	799	799	—	896	896	—	1,201	1,201
Total exports	2,557	627	3,184	2,534	602	3,135	5,285	1,309	6,594	6,029	1,660	7,690	8,087	2,701	10,788
	(In percent)														
Summary															
Total exports	80	20	100	81	19	100	80	20	100	78	22	100	75	25	100
Percentage based on local materials (a) to (d), above		86			91			88			88			89	
Manufactures based on:															
Local materials		27			53			39			46			55	
Imported materials		73			47			61			54			45	

Source: Derived from Department of Statistics, *External Trade* (various years).
[1] Manufactured or highly processed products.

Whereas New Zealand's trade dependence was among the highest in the world up to the 1950s, it has been surpassed to a considerable extent by countries like Belgium, Canada, the Netherlands, and the Scandinavian countries. This is one of the results of the trade policy balance and the rapid growth in world trade in manufactures in the 1950s and 1960s.

New Zealand's external terms of trade are highly volatile (Table 3). This volatility reflects the composition of exports and imports, and, over the last decade, the degree of dependency on imported oil.

While resource endowments and demand conditions can be used to explain the economic structure and performance of the New Zealand economy, the degree of government intervention has played a major role as well. For example, does the relative size of the agriculture and industrial sectors in New Zealand solely reflect resource endowments, or has the development strategy of import substitution led to the stagnation of some elements of the manufacturing sector and the maintenance of a relatively large agricultural sector? A second set of questions revolves around the stability question. World agricultural product prices tend to be less stable than those of manufactures. One might well ask to what extent the volatile external terms of trade conditions New Zealand has experienced are the result of, rather than the stimulus for, government intervention in industrial development.

III. Exchange Rate Policy

On December 7, 1938 foreign exchange controls were introduced in New Zealand. These controls eventually involved monopoly control of foreign exchange dealing by the Reserve (Central) Bank for a period of 40 years, with some adjustments. Up until the breakdown of the Bretton Woods Agreement, the New Zealand dollar was pegged to the pound sterling. This was subsequently changed to the U.S. dollar for a short period in 1973 (Economic Monitoring Group (1984)). For the next ten years the New Zealand dollar adjustment mechanism included a crawling peg and a fixed basket approach, interspersed with nine autonomous realignments (three revaluations and six devaluations). There was a large 20 percent devaluation in July 1984. This last adjustment was followed by the adoption of a floating exchange rate in March 1985.

Coupled with this exchange rate policy was a long history of interest rate controls in a variety of forms. These regulations set ceilings on interest on deposits and lending and quantitative restrictions on the source and use of funds. This repressive financial market system remained in force until 1984, with a break from 1976–81 when a "relatively flexible interest rate policy" was in place (Deane, et al. (1983)).

From 1950 to 1967, New Zealand's inflation rate averaged 3 percent. After that date, and particularly over the period from 1975 to

Table 3. New Zealand: Exchange Rate Balance and Overseas Debt

	Market Exchange Rate Index (NZ$/unit foreign exchange) (1)	Real Exchange Rate Index (NZ$/unit foreign exchange) (2)	External Terms of Trade (1957 = 100) (3)	Degree Overvaluation (percent) (4)	Official Foreign Debt (percent of GDP) (5)
1958	1.200	1.077	85	+11	9.4
1959	1.207	1.139	100	0	12.3
1960	1.213	1.139	96	+4	11.1
1961	1.212	1.128	90	+11	9.5
1962	1.215	1.123	94	+6	10.1
1963	1.221	1.121	99	0	10.6
1964	1.220	1.127	111	−11	9.9
1965	1.220	1.137	108	−7	9.3
1966	1.227	1.128	107	−8	8.7
1967	1.230	1.141	101	−1	9.8
1968	1.071	1.008	89	0	12.1
1969	1.069	1.012	88	0	11.7

1970	1.070	1.009	87	+1	10.2
1971	1.069	1.048	83	+10	10.0
1972	1.044	1.039	93	−1	9.5
1973	1.143	1.132	113	−11	7.1
1974	1.259	1.214	112	−5	5.1
1975	1.181	1.109	78	+23	10.8
1976	1.004	0.970	72	+19	17.3
1977	0.996	0.997	79	+9	18.6
1978	0.996	1.074	78	+19	21.4
1979	0.996	1.098	86	+11	21.0
1980	0.910	1.032	82	+10	20.6
1981	0.853	1.025	76	+18	20.1
1982	0.799	1.029	77	+18	22.8
1983	0.742	1.026	74	+23	28.4
1984	0.742	1.013	74	+22	26.7
1985	0.593	0.863	73	+4	35.1

Sources: Columns (1), (2), and (3), Bascand and Carey (1985); column (4), the percentage difference between the real exchange rate and the terms of trade normalized to be zero in 1968, the year following a devaluation; column (5), Reserve Bank of New Zealand, *Bulletin* (various issues).

1982, New Zealand's inflation rate exceeded the Organization for Economic Cooperation and Development (OECD) average. The rate of inflation contributed to negative real interest rates for long periods of time in many areas of the financial market, with associated nonprice rationing and low savings rates. This continued until 1984, when the deregulation of the financial and foreign exchange markets led to an immediate reversal in the sign of the real exchange rate. Over the last 18 months, real interest rates have been positive, ranging between 5 and 10 percent.

These financial factors have combined over the years to cause major differences between real income and expenditure in New Zealand, with differences being taken up by changes in foreign exchange reserves and changes in foreign borrowing. Bascand and Carey (1985) have analyzed these effects and some of their data are reproduced in Table 3. They have computed the real exchange rate by correcting the administered market exchange rate index for New Zealand's major trading partners with relative cost differences between those countries and New Zealand. Changes in the real exchange rate influence real expenditure by affecting the relative price of tradables to nontradables. Changes in the external terms of trade, on the other hand, influence the future real income prospects.

The real exchange rate index is given in column 2 of Table 3. If the terms of trade were stable, differences in the rate of change of the market rate (administered) and the real rate would roughly indicate the degree to which the New Zealand dollar was over- or undervalued by the exchange rate policy (given no change in trade, subsidy, or other structural policy). Alternatively, such differences would indicate the degree to which foreign borrowing or foreign reserves must change to equilibrate the foreign exchange market. Given the volatile nature of the external terms of trade, it is preferable to use a measure which includes an adjustment for world prices.

Starting from a stable, balanced position, the extent to which the real exchange rate does not adjust in line with the terms of trade is a crude indication of the degree of over- or undervaluation of the exchange rate. It is crude because of the difficulty of establishing a starting point. Furthermore, this approach abstracts from other important components of the foreign exchange market, including invisibles and the capital account.

The degree of exchange rate overvaluation[2] presented in Table 3 is computed by assuming that in 1969, the year immediately following a

---

[2] This concept of disequilibrium in financial terms needs to be distinguished from the degree of *structural* overvaluation of the exchange rate which is introduced in the next section. Structural overvaluation refers to trade policy imbalances or the non-neutral treatment of the import substitute and export sectors.

devaluation, the exchange market was in equilibrium relative to the terms of trade.

The index given in column 4 indicates that over the period 1958–74, the degree of overvaluation (or undervaluation, if negative) fluctuated plus or minus 11 percent around its equilibrium value. This appears to be reasonably consistent with changes in foreign borrowing during the periods 1958–59, 1963–66, and 1972–75. It does not appear to be consistent for the periods 1960–61 and 1967–69. However, after 1974 the index of overvaluation clearly reflects the need for overseas borrowing. It suggests that the New Zealand dollar was seriously overvalued from 1975 to 1984, by amounts varying from 10 percent to 23 percent. While this measure suffers from a number of deficiencies, the fact that the 1985 value is close to zero and that the March 1985 float did not initially result in a major appreciation or depreciation is evidence of robustness. It is also worth noting that, following the float, the concept of "overvaluation" is not relevant in the absence of exchange market intervention. However, that begs the question as to whether the exchange rate has been "overshooting" since the float.

One of the major effects of the currency misalignment was that it modified the effectiveness of the trade policies which were in place at the time. Currency overvaluation tends to lower import prices and thereby reduces the effectiveness of import protection for the importable sector. The *true* rate of import protection ought to reflect this overvaluation effect.

On the exportable side, an overvalued currency would tend to reduce perceived export prices and lower the value of export subsidies to those industries. This index of overvaluation is important in the following section, which examines true protection rates over the period.

IV. Historical Outline of Import Substitution Policy

The second part of the story begins with a diversion of sorts: a policy change which occurred in 1932 and which lay dormant for over fifty years.

In 1932, in the depths of the Great Depression, New Zealand concluded a tariff agreement with the United Kingdom and the British Commonwealth which established British Preferential Tariffs (BP) at low levels (around 5 percent) for Commonwealth trade, and distinguished these from Most Favored Nation (MFN) tariffs, which were at least 20 percent higher. This Ottawa Agreement resulted in new customs tariff legislation being passed in 1934. Given the high proportion of New Zealand imports sourced in the United Kingdom at the time, this action probably had little immediate impact on New Zealand's cost structure.

In 1938 New Zealand embarked upon a major swing in the thrust of its development policy with the introduction of quantitative restrictions on imports and foreign exchange controls (Hawke (1985)). This import licensing arrangement, added to higher tariff rates that had been established following the British Commonwealth Trade Conference, raised the level of import protection considerably and ushered in a major import substitution phase in New Zealand's economic history.

This last statement benefits from hindsight, of course. At the time, Hawke (1985) argues, the controls were adopted as a crisis measure. Viewed in this fashion, increased import protection and exchange controls could be viewed as New Zealand's reaction to the global trading difficulties that accompanied the Great Depression. Such reactions were common around the world, though these "beggar thy neighbor" policies were introduced by most other countries in the early part of the 1930s.

The first major attempt to remove quantitative restrictions on imports occurred in the early 1950s, and by 1955 they had been almost entirely eliminated. This liberalization phase was reviewed in 1957 when the new government reacted to a serious decline in New Zealand's terms of trade by reimposing import licensing.

During this period, the relative importance of the tariff as an import protection instrument was increasing. Given the high proportion of imports originating in the United Kingdom in 1934, tariff protection was low. However, during the period 1950-70, the significance of the United Kingdom as an import supplier fell considerably in favor of MFNs, particularly Japan. Given the higher (essentially default) MFN rates introduced in 1934, the relative importance of the tariff gradually changed.

The period 1955-58 is the first for which a detailed analysis of the degree of import protection is available (Table 4). This is unfortunate because by that time, a full cycle of what Giles and Hampton (1984) term "forced industrialization" had been completed. Prior to 1934, import protection had been on the order of 15 percent to 20 percent based on tariffs alone (Lattimore (1984)). In 1938 virtually all imports were subject to quotas (licensing), and after that date, it is reasonable to assume that the rate of protection rose to an average figure in excess of 35 percent, perhaps by a large margin because the rate of import protection averaged 34 percent during the period of liberalization. By the mid-1960s, nominal import protection had risen to 54 percent.

In the late 1960s there was increased concern about the level of import protection following the Agricultural Production Conference and the National Development Conference. According to Hawke (1985), the Government again came close to removing import licensing in 1969, but drew back from the proposal. Apparently, a consensus could not be reached on introducing a more neutral trade policy stance.

Table 4. New Zealand: Nominal Rate of Trade Policy Intervention, 1955–84
(In percent)

Year	Nominal Rate Import Protection	Nominal Rate Export Subsidy
1955-58	34.2	0.1
1964-67	53.6	0.5
1972/73	31.5	1.7
1978/79	(20.3)[1]	2.3
1983/84	30.9	11.1

Source: Appendix B.
[1] This estimate is thought to be seriously underestimated and is reproduced only because it appeared in the source report. For a fuller explanation, see text, pp. 45-46.

This period may turn out to have been another turning point in New Zealand's development history because, around this time a 15-year period of "tariff compensation" to the export sector began. Tax expenditures to farmers increased and direct production and export subsidies were introduced, reaching a peak in the period 1982–83 with large subsidies for selected export products. The farm subsidies are documented here, but others in the forestry, tourist, and international transport industries have had to be omitted for lack of data.

The export subsidy component of the farm measures is given in detail in Appendix B and an average for the tradable sector is reproduced in Table 4. During the 1950s, exports were indirectly subsidized to a small extent through grants to agricultural research and subsidies for transport and for the control of noxious weeds. Explicit export subsidies for manufactured exports were also introduced in the first half of the 1960s.

The pace of tariff compensation began to quicken in 1970 in the form of both higher agricultural production subsidies, tax concessions for farmers, and export subsidies to manufacturers.

During the 1960s the import licensing system was increasingly liberalized for raw materials and capital equipment. The proportion of goods exempt from license rose from around 15 percent in 1963 to 60 percent in 1970. After 1970 the exemption list plateaued at about the 60–70 percent level until 1979. Although some sources suggest that this movement led to a reduction in the rate of import protection to 20 percent by 1978/79 (as presented in Table 4), this is known to be an incorrect conclusion as the weighted average tariff alone at that time was higher than 20 percent. For this reason it might be better to assume that the nominal protection rate remained in the 30–50 percent range throughout the period 1960 to 1984.

Two years after the first major oil shock, the New Zealand authorities accelerated the growth in export assistance again, using both forms of intervention, export and production subsidies. As shown in Table 4, the rate of export assistance overall increased almost sevenfold to 11 percent from 1972/73 to 1983/84. However, this average rate masked a wide variation across export sectors. The beef and dairy sectors (and a number of smaller industries excluded from this study) received the lowest rate of export assistance, as presented in Tables 15–22. The sheepmeat industry was granted the highest rate of export assistance, with the nominal rate of export subsidy to the sector rising to 34 percent in 1983/84 (Table 15)—on a par with the average rate of nominal import protection.

Before we examine the degree of neutrality in trade policy, an explanation is required of the import protection rates for 1983/84. The import protection rate for 1983/84 was estimated by adding the ad valorem tariff rates to the average successful bid price of the import licenses tendered. By contrast, the earlier studies are more indirect, having had to use price list comparisons to assess the protective effect of the import licensing arrangements. The direct procedure ought to be more accurate.

The import license tender scheme was introduced in 1980, and since that time, data on successful premiums paid are available for 26 rounds of tendering. Pickford (1984) has analyzed the data for the first 12 rounds which took place over the period 1981–84. A summary of his results are shown in Chart 1. This Chart shows that around half the nominal protection rate for the limited number of items offered was in the form of the customs tariff. The remainder consisted of import quota rent. The distribution appears to be bimodal, with a high incidence of protection rates between 50 and 60 percent and another peak between 80 and 90 percent.

The number of licenses was expanded in subsequent rounds both in terms of the value offered per item and the number of items. When the data for these later rounds (13–26) were analyzed, the distribution of protection rates changed considerably, as shown in Chart 2. The distribution becomes unimodal around nominal protection rates between 40 and 50 percent, and license premiums are very small in relation to the tariff. The later tender data are used as the basis for estimating nominal protection rates for 1983/84 because they encompass a broader range of products.

Nevertheless, the 1983/84 import protection estimate in Table 4 is not as inclusive as the earlier ones, since it is limited to product lines open to tender or exempt from licensing. Hence, it excludes some impor-

**Chart 1. Import License Tenders
Distribution of Import Protection Rates, 1981-84**
(Tender Rounds 1-12)

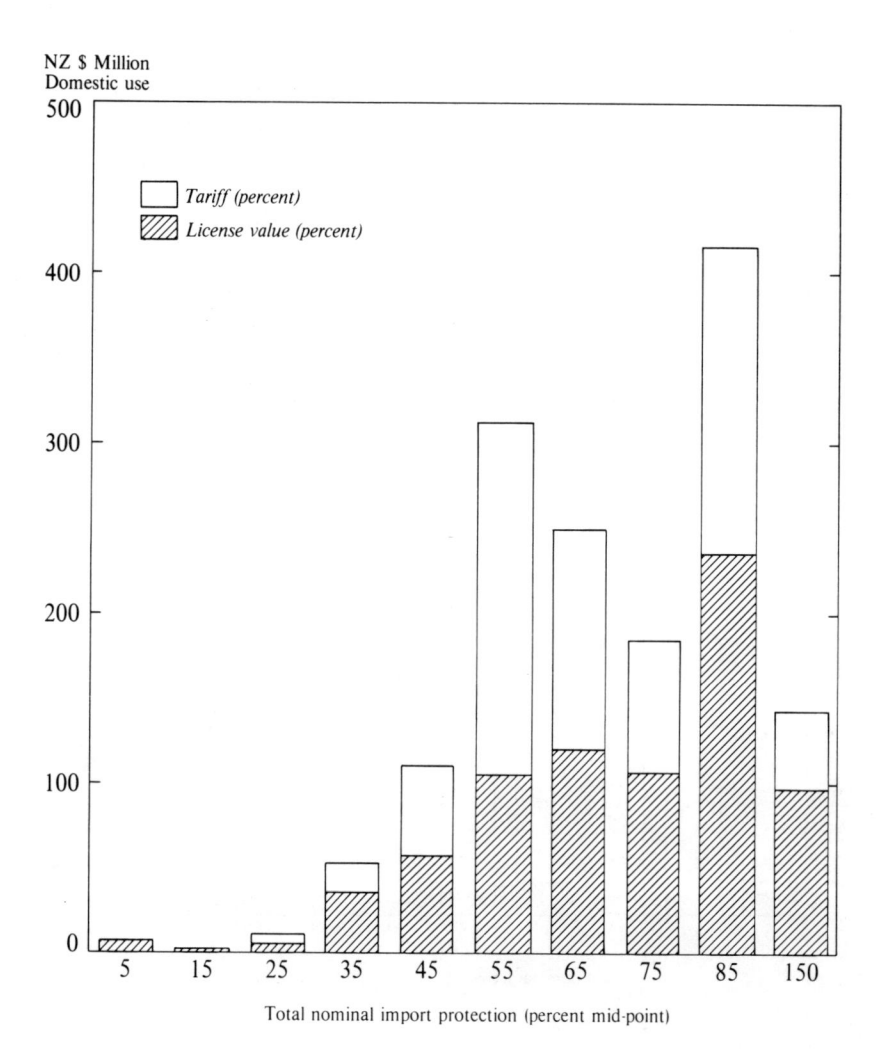

Total nominal import protection (percent mid-point)

tant sectors subject to "industry plans" and other industries, notably crude oil and petroleum products, which have special and perhaps more restrictive protection rates. This factor suggests that the 1983/84 protection estimate is biased downwards, and further analysis will be necessary to clarify the issue.

The items covered by industry plans and other special arrangements are important because the performance of the sectors involved is

**Chart 2. Import License Tenders
Distribution of Import Protection Rates, 1984-85**
(Tender Rounds 13-26)

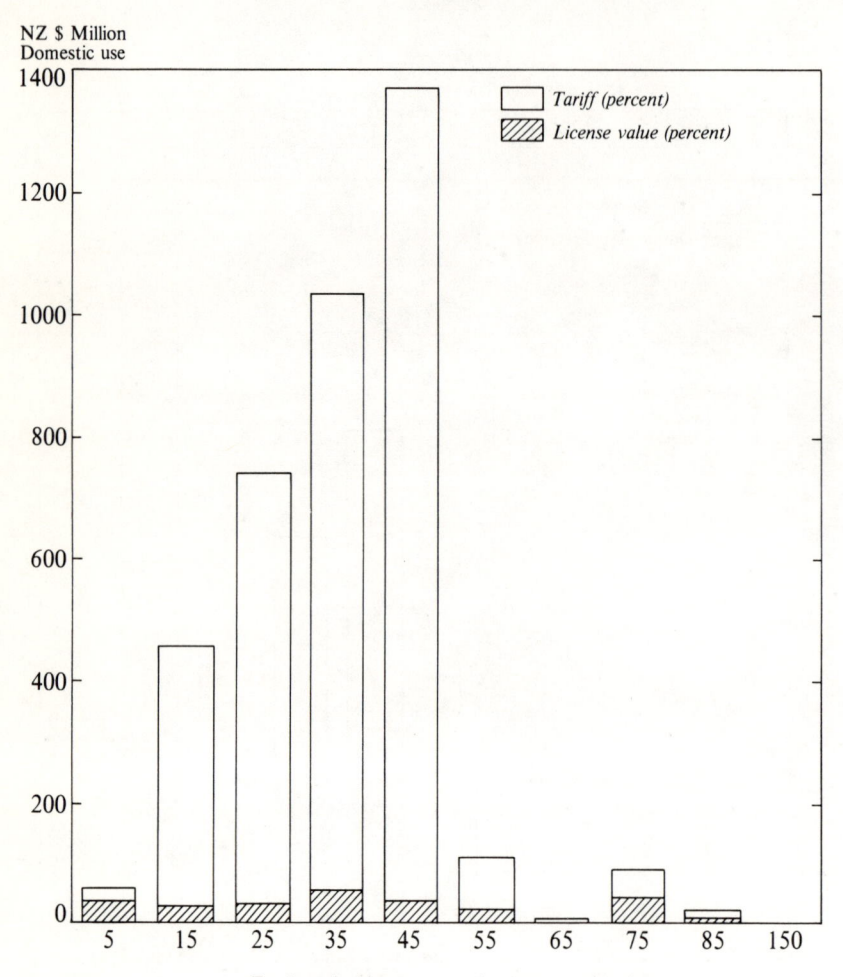

less transparent than other sectors at present, and some brief outline of the industries involved may be warranted. Three types of arrangements are involved. The industries listed in Table 5 have been the subject of public hearings by the Industries Development Commission (IDC) since 1979. For each of these industries (except town milk for which no decision has yet been taken) the Government has decided on a gradual phasing out of import protection following an IDC recommendation and dis-

ADJUSTMENT IN NEW ZEALAND 49

Table 5. **New Zealand: Industries Under Special Arrangements or Industry Plans**
(Industries Development Commission Industry Study Program)

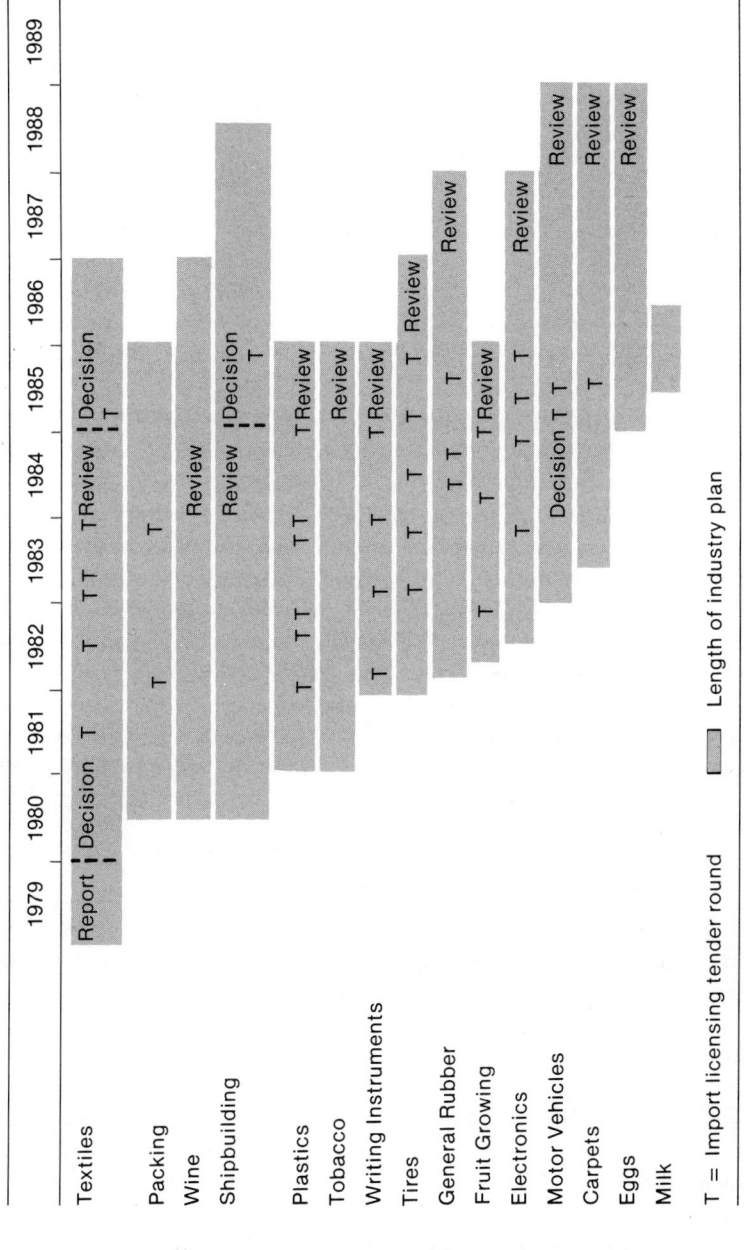

Industry	1979	1980	1981	1982	1983	1984	1985	1986	1987	1988	1989
Textiles	Report	Decision	T	T	T T	T Review	Decision T				
Packing				T							
Wine					T						
Shipbuilding						Review	Decision T				
Plastics				T	T T		T Review				
Tobacco				T			Review				
Writing Instruments				T	T	T	T Review				
Tires				T	T	T	T	Review			
General Rubber					T T	T T	T				
Fruit Growing					T	T	T Review				
Electronics					T	T T T	T T T	Review			
Motor Vehicles						Decision T T		Review			
Carpets							T		Review		
Eggs									Review		
Milk											

T = Import licensing tender round   ▓ Length of industry plan

Source: Industries Development Commission, Study Program (Wellington: IDC, various years).

cussions with the industry. While some product lines have been opened for public tender, there is no clear picture of the protection that remains. A second group of industries, listed in Table 6, have followed a similar process except that the background study was carried out by government departments rather than the IDC. In addition, a few industries producing strategic material, like petroleum, have been granted monopoly import rights. Elements of protection are involved in these cases, but the full effect of the intervention is not known.

In spite of the tentative nature of the results shown in Table 4, a major conclusion may be drawn. The rate of nominal import protection has always exceeded the rate of export subsidy by a wide margin. Even when the level of export subsidization peaked in 1984, the rate of subsidy was probably only one third of the level of import protection. Furthermore, as demonstrated in Table 14 in Appendix B, there is a wide distribution of protection rates on the export and import substitute sides of the trade ledger.

If we examine effective rates of assistance, the variation in industry protection is much wider. This is true for both exportable and importable products. Effective rates of import protection are given in Table 21, and effective rates of export assistance in Table 22.

Effective import protection ranged from 140 percent to −48 percent in 1978/79. In earlier periods, rates tended to be much higher and, accordingly, more variable—the same pattern as that observed in nominal rates.

In the early periods (1955–73), effective rates of assistance for exports tended to be zero or small positive amounts (by New Zealand standards). However, during the late 1970s, export assistance rose to high levels in many cases, sometimes rivaling the rates for importables.

V. True Protection Rates and Optimal Trade Policy

It is clear from the range of policies discussed so far that intervention has been extensive. Accordingly, it is likely that the policies have had important effects on the cost structure of the New Zealand economy as a whole over the last 30 years or so.

In this environment, the nominal (or effective) rates of protection computed at the sectoral level may be a poor guide to the degree of "resource-pull" operating in the economy, and, hence, to the real effects of intervention on the efficiency of resource allocation. These latter effects depend upon the so-called true (or net) protection rates. One way to examine these effects is given in Appendix A, based on the work of Sjaastad and Clements (1982).

The approach taken is to examine the effect of protection on the price of nontraded goods. Import and export protection of a general

Table 6. New Zealand: Industries Under Special Arrangements or Industry Plans
(Interdepartmental Studies)

	1983	1984	1985	1986	1987	1988	1989
Footwear	T T T		T Review				
Glassware		CER[1] 10 percent	T 10 percent		Review T 15 percent–20 percent		25 percent
Starch		T 10 percent	T 10 percent	T 10 percent	T 20 percent		Review
Ceramics		5–30 percent[2]	5–30 percent[2]	5–30 percent[2]	Review		
Electric Motors[3]							

T = Import licensing tender round
▓ Length of industry plan

Source: Industries Development Commission, Study Program (Wellington: IDC, various years).
Note: Percentage increases refer to the value of import license tenders to be made available.
[1] Closer Economic Relations Agreement (ANZCERT) between Australia and New Zealand, which came into force on January 1, 1983 and which provided for the allocation of import licenses for specified products from Australia.
[2] Licenses of varying values within this range were allocated to various groups within the ceramics industry.
[3] Exempt effective September 30, 1986.

nature will affect the economy by raising the price of nontraded goods. To the extent that it does so, the true protection rate is simultaneously reduced. This is the so-called incidence-of-protection factor.

Recent empirical work in Australia (as detailed in Appendix A) demonstrates that import protection tends to push up nontraded goods prices four times as much as export subsidies do. Sjaastad and Clements (1982) use a preferred value of 0.8 for the incidence of import protection. Russel (1985) has made a tentative estimate of 0.5 for the import incidence parameter. This figure is subject to change as his work proceeds. In the meantime, if we assume that the incidence parameter for New Zealand is of the order of 0.7, the true protection rates can be computed from the nominal estimates in Table 4 using the method given in Appendix A. These true nominal protection rates are given in the first two columns of Table 7.

The first thing to notice is that the true rates of import protection are considerably lower than their uncorrected values. This is simply because when the incidence of import protection is 0.7, each 100 percentage points of import protection lead to an increase of 70 percentage points in nontraded goods prices, particularly through factor costs. The true rate of protection for the import substitute sector is accordingly eroded significantly. At the same time, the rise in nontraded goods prices constitutes an implicit export tax.

In the New Zealand case where there have been explicit export taxes as well as import duties, the two sets of policies work against each other. The net effect is given in Table 7. While the import substitute sector has received low to modest true rates of assistance in recent years, the export sector has been taxed by the mix of policies used.

Table 7. New Zealand: Average True Rates of Assistance
(In percent)

Year	True Rate of Protection (nominal terms) Import Substitutes	Export	Average Degree of Exchange Rate Overvaluation (+)
1955–58	+ 14.7	− 14	− 5
1964–67	+ 22.9	− 20	− 7
1972/73	+ 16.4	− 10	− 1
1978/79	+ 10.4	− 6	+ 13
1983/84	+ 13.8	− 3	+ 20

Source: Table 4 and Appendix A.

There appears to have been a downward trend in the degree of the export tax since the period 1964–67, which has coincided with an increase in manufactured exports. However, as late as last year (1985), there remained a significant gap between the relative incentives to produce for the export market versus production for the domestic market. In short, policies in 1984/85 continued to have an anti-export bias as a result of continuing distortions in the economy-wide cost structure.

The degree of exchange rate overvaluation (given in column 3 of Table 7) has compounded the structural policy problem. The exchange overvaluation that persisted throughout the mid-1970s to the mid-1980s is a monetary phenomenon that can offset or magnify the real protection incidence. Take 1978/79 as an example. In that year the balance of import and export protection policies appears to have resulted in a true export tax of 6 percent or so. At the same time, the exchange rate was overvalued by around 13 percent and being financed by foreign borrowing. The degree of overvaluation constituted a further tax of 13 percent on the export sector. At the same time, the overvalued exchange rate lowered import prices and reduced import protection by 13 percent, so that net true import protection was itself negative. The negative protection of the whole tradable sector would indicate that the nontradable sector was exerting a resource pull.

It is important to examine also the true assistance rates at the sectoral level. These results are given in Tables 8 and 9. As with the uncorrected rates, the true effective protection for importables has been high, declining, and variable. The rates for exportables are illuminating. In the 1950s and 1960s, the true export assistance levels were negative and most restrictive for manufactured products. In this environment, it is hardly surprising that manufacturing exports remained very small. These rates may also help to explain why overall trade declined in relative importance to the New Zealand economy over the period. Indeed, had the degree of agricultural comparative advantage and technical advance been less, the farm sector would not have achieved the growth it exhibited. Prior to 1972/73 when the exchange rate was occasionally undervalued $(-)$, the rate of import (export) protection, was raised above the true rates given in Table 7.

How do these estimates of general cost effects compare with other studies? Gibson (1984), in his analysis of agricultural protection, included an offsetting item which he called the "cost excess" to agriculture of import protection. He used an assumed value of 20 percent. If the nominal rate of import protection in 1984/85 was around 34 percent, (with $\omega = 0.7$), then his assumption is broadly in agreement with the estimates made here.

Philpott (1985) has also estimated the effect of import protection on the cost structure of the export sector including agriculture. He estimates that the removal of all current (presumably 1984/85) protection would

Table 8. New Zealand: True Effective Rates of Assistance for Importables
(In percent)

Sector	1955–58	1964–67	1972/73	1978/79	1982/83
Beverages, etc.	−41	−28	42	11	
Other textiles	21	137	48	33	179
Footwear	34	59	50	39	
Clothing	91	864	138	120	
Furniture	64	140	25	−35	51
Printed products	−1	3	−28	−19	26
Leather goods	17	134	88	69	
Rubber goods	4	53	87	54	
Chemical fertilizer	−35	−44	−13	0	
Petroleum products	22	−51	−70	−52	
Other chemicals	25	41	81	62	
Nonmetallic minerals	−27	−9	9	7	
Basic metal products	−20	110	−3	−6	
Metal products	56	474	77	60	
Machinery	102	59	39	66	
Electrical products	85	305	312	66	
Vehicle assembly	2,060	62	very negative	29	
Other transport	19	6	33	29	
Miscellaneous manufacturing	44	129	71	62	

Source: Table 21 rates adjusted by the procedure described in Appendix A, equation (16).

reduce current (capital) costs in agriculture by 3.5 percent (8 percent). This is significantly lower than the estimates given here or assumed by Gibson. If the Philpott figure were correct, it would imply that the import protection incidence parameter was less than 0.1. Such a low value has not been observed in the ten studies cited by Sjaastad and Clements (1982) for a range of countries not dissimilar to New Zealand in economic structure. It is possible that the Philpott analysis has constrained the outcome in some fashion, so that it is unable to measure the full extent of the cost shifts involved in import protection.

What is the optimal trade policy stance for New Zealand? If, for policy purposes, New Zealand is a price taker in the world market for tradable goods, and if the "infant industry" argument is not valid for New Zealand at our present stage of development, then the trade policy stance ought to be neutral as between exportables and importable prod-

Table 9. New Zealand: True Effective Rates of Assistance for Exportables
(In percent)

Sector	1955-58	1964-67	1971-73	1978/79	1983/84
Agriculture					
Sheepmeats	-13	-14	-3	21	large
Wool	-13	-14	1	8	70
Beef	-12	-14	-4	4	18
Dairy	-13	-12	0	46	24
Beverages, etc.	-15	-15	-15		
Other textiles	-15	-15	-15		
Footwear	-15	-15	-15	32	25
Clothing	-15	-15	-15	28	21
Furniture	-15	-15	-15	6	1
Printed products	-15	-15	-15	24	17
Leather goods	-15	-15	-15	74	65
Rubber goods	-15	-15	-15		
Chemical fertilizer	-15	-15	-15		
Petroleum products	-15	-15	-15		
Other chemicals	-15	-15	-15		
Nonmetallic minerals	-15	-15	-15	21	15
Basic metal products	-15	-15	-15	-7	-12
Metal products	-15	-15	-15	27	20
Machinery	-15	-15	-15		
Electrical products	-15	-15	-15		
Vehicle assembly	-15	-15	-15		
Other transport	-15	-15	-15		
Miscellaneous manufacturing	-15	-15	-15		

Source: Table 22 rates adjusted by the procedure described in Appendix A, equation (18).

ucts. This would involve eliminating the implicit export tax which has existed for decades in New Zealand.

The price-taker condition is concerned with the degree of responsiveness of world demand and supply to changes in New Zealand's export supply and import demand. But the condition is also dependent upon the source of the international responsiveness and the ability of New Zealand to manage the intervention mechanism should it be appropriate. That is to say, it is necessary but not sufficient to show that export demand elasticities facing New Zealand are not infinite before considering an optimal export tax. The sufficient condition requires also that the

New Zealand Government can institute and manage an instrument that will capture the additional trade gains available. Given the serious concerns that have been raised over the efficiency of government regulation and intervention here and abroad over the past twenty years, the management question may be more important than the elasticity one.

Let us examine the consensus of the profession on the trade elasticities facing New Zealand. This is not a simple question, because there are serious difficulties associated with trying to estimate trade elasticities directly. The results tend to be biased downwards, exaggerating the potential intervention gains. Analysts apppear to be in agreement that the importable supply to New Zealand is perfectly elastic, and that would coincide with a micro approach to the world market, given New Zealand's extremely small world market share (Cronin (1979)). There is less consensus on the export side. It is common (see, for example, Bascand and Carey (1985)), for analysts to assume on the basis of the evidence that New Zealand is a price taker in world markets for policy purposes (O'Brien (1981)). Furthermore, the micro foundations of the excess demand elasticities outlined by Cronin would support this contention if the level of product aggregation under consideration is limited to the one- or two-digit level, e.g., meat, wool, metal products, consulting services, or grain. This again is a function of the New Zealand market share and the responsiveness of its export competitors or close substitutes in world markets.

It may be worth noting that the above framework is completely different from that of marketing managers of firms. At a lower level of aggregation, marketing experts often argue that New Zealand has significant levels of influence over conditions of sale including price. This argument, however, is beside the point when discussing trade policy intervention in the form of government export taxes or their second best alternatives, import tariffs and quotas.

The infant industry condition is another issue about which a range of opinion exists. While it has yet to be proven, there is growing evidence in New Zealand that the import substitution bias that has existed in New Zealand since the 1930s has hindered industrial development, stimulated foreign ownership, reduced employment growth, and reduced real income. These results would be expected if New Zealand's trading environment were that of a small country and the domestic market alone offered few (if any) opportunities to exploit economies of size.

The empirical evidence also points in this direction. New Zealand's per capita GDP fell from third place in the world to nineteenth by 1975, a period which encompasses a high level of implicit export tax. It appears that the manufacturing sector completely missed the opportunity to participate in the worldwide trade growth in manufactures of the 1950s and 1960s, in part because of the high disincentive to produce for export. In more recent years, the manufacturing sector has increasingly shared in export growth. Perhaps in part this is due to the reduction in the true export tax as a result of the changing trade policy balance. Furthermore, New Zealand's rate of growth of real GDP has been above average over the last five years, as compared to the OECD group (Philpott (1985)).

VI. Recent Policy Changes Affecting Trade

In July 1984 a new government came into power. Since that time a number of major policy changes have been made. Some of these policies have reinforced or accelerated policy thrusts which were underway. Others were new policy directions (though such distinctions are often undefined in policymaking circles!).

Two days after the election, the exchange rate was devalued 20 percent, and this was followed by major changes in intervention in capital markets. In March 1985 the exchange rate was floated. The effect of these changes was to remove the high level of overvaluation of the New Zealand dollar which had persisted for some years, as shown in Table 3. Nominal interest rates rose in the face of rising inflationary expectations and the large government borrowing requirement, both of which caused an appreciation of the exchange rate following the float. For a period in late 1985, the rate was close to its predevaluation level (in terms of foreign exchange).

On the real side of the economy, the Government quickly modified the trade policy stance by announcing the phasing out of export incentives and export production grants and subsidies over a two-year period. In the import substitute sector, the Government referred a number of additional industries to the IDC for review and continued the practice of introducing industry plans to phase out high levels of import protection (wheat and flour, eggs, and town milk). The import licence tendering system (introduced in 1980) was continued, and in September 1985 it was announced that tariff rates were to be slowly reduced by 5 percent of their existing levels (which averaged 30 percent), except for high tariffs (above 50 percent), which would have 5 percentage points removed in July 1986. In July 1987 it was anticipated that all tariffs would be reduced by 10 percent, with another review in 1988. While this was to have been a final tariff agreement, it was further announced in early December 1985 that all tariffs on items not produced in New Zealand would be reduced to zero on January 1, 1986 and that some other tariffs on key export sector inputs would also be reduced.

Each of those policy changes is potentially important for the balance of trade policy. Although very recent data of this type are difficult to obtain, we will attempt the following forecasting exercise. It must be borne in mind that much of the data are preliminary or even speculative in nature.

Table 10 shows the degree to which nontraded goods prices have been raised by the balance of trade policy interventions in the past. This is the amount by which the incidence of protection parameter (or degree of structural overvaluation of the exchange rate referred to earlier) has raised general prices and costs relative to traded goods prices. It includes the effects of import protection and export assistance.

The forecast of the nontraded goods price effect has been made assuming that the announced 5 percent tariff reductions in 1986 proceed, that export incentives and all import licensing arrangements are phased out, and that the scheduled eliminations and reductions in grants and subsidies to agriculture are carried out. This would imply that import protection would remain in the form of tariffs alone. The average nominal tariff in 1986/87 would be 28.5 percent, but in many cases effective protection rates in the importable sector would be considerably higher than that figure. It is important to note that this forecast is conditional on policy changes up to September 1985. It takes no account of the December tariff decision, nor does it attempt to speculate on what additional policy changes might be made in the future. The forecast is based on this snapshot of policy as it existed in late 1985.

In the exportable sector, under the same assumptions, there would be a large reversal in true effective export assistance rates. As shown in Table 11, effective rates of export assistance are planned to fall to between zero and 17 percent by 1986. The maintenance of relatively high tariffs means that the true rates (Table 12) would become negative for industries exporting wool, dairy products, and industrial products

Table 10. New Zealand: Increase in Nontraded Goods Prices Resulting from Trade Policies
(for $\omega = 0.70$)[1]

	Nontraded Goods Prices (percent increase)
1955–58	17
1964–67	25
1972/73	13
1978/79	(9)
1983/84	15
1986/87 (forecast)	12

Source: Appendix A.
[1] Incidence of protection parameter. See Appendix A for details.

Table 11. New Zealand: Forecasts of Effective Rates of Assistance—Major Exportables
(In percent)

Sector	1983/84	1986/87
Sheepmeat	large	17
Wool	95	9
Beef	36	12
Dairy	43	11
Industrial (simple average)	38	0

Source: Values for 1983/84 from Tables 15–18. Forecast values are based on market performance in 1983/84 (1982/83 for sheepmeat) and the policy changes described in the text. The details are given in Tables 15–18.

Table 12. New Zealand: Forecasts of True Effective Rates of Assistance—Major Exportables
(In percent)

Sector	1983/84	1986/87
Sheepmeat	large	4
Wool	70	−3
Beef	18	0
Dairy	24	−1
Industrial (simple average)	20	−11

and close to zero for beef and sheepmeat. Taken together, these elements would continue the import substitution stance of the past.

VII. Summary and Conclusions

Over the last 50 years, successive New Zealand governments have experimented widely with economic policies. It is almost as if they have attempted simultaneously to test the infant industry argument, the Prebisch/Singer hypothesis, the command economy model, and tariff compensation. It is increasingly clear that the experiment has failed.

The present government has clearly stated its intention to reform government policy as a whole. Much has already been accomplished.

However, the long-term goals for the trade policy stance are not entirely clear. As export assistance has been removed since 1984, the trade strategy has tended to become oriented more toward import substitutes and accordingly biased against exports. If this trend were to persist, real income and employment growth and industry development would be affected accordingly.

Appendix A
The Incidence of Trade Policy Intervention

A trade policy incidence model has been developed by Sjaastad and Clements (1982), which is based upon the impact of intervention on the home (or nontraded) goods market in a real economy setting. This approach abstracts from the monetary sector and parallels other models such as those of Balassa (1971) and Corden (1971), which attempt to characterize the general equilibrium impact of major trade policy settings. This effect has various names, including the degree of structural overvaluation of the exchange rate due to trade policy intervention (Lattimore (1984)). This outline summarizes in a more pedestrian fashion the Sjaastad and Clements model and provides the formula required to compute the true protection rates afforded various export and import substitute industries in New Zealand since the period 1955–58.

Sjaastad and Clements derive the incidence of import protection (ω) in a three-sector model of the real economy involving exportables, importables, and home goods. The supply (q_s) and demand (q_d) for home goods may be written as follows:

$$q_s = f(P_e, P_m, P_h; \ldots\ldots\ldots) \tag{1}$$

$$q_d = f(P_e, P_m, P_h; \ldots\ldots\ldots), \tag{2}$$

assuming that real income and factor endowments are fixed and where the P's represent the prices of exportables, importables, and home goods, respectively. Totally differentiating and dividing both sides by q we have:

$$\frac{dq_s}{q_s} = \frac{\delta q_s}{\delta P_e}\frac{dP_e}{q_s} + \frac{q_s}{\delta P_m}\frac{dP_m}{q_s} + \frac{\delta q_s}{\delta P_h}\frac{dP_h}{q_s} \tag{3}$$

$$\frac{dq_d}{q_d} = \frac{\delta q_d}{\delta P_e}\frac{dP_e}{q_d} + \frac{\delta q_d}{\delta P_m}\frac{dP_m}{q_d} + \frac{\delta q_d}{\delta P_h}\frac{dP_h}{q_d}. \tag{4}$$

If the rate of change *(dx/x)* is denoted by a hat (^), equations (3) and (4) may be rewritten as:

$$\hat{q}_s = \eta_e^s \hat{P}_e + \eta_m^s \hat{P}_m + \eta_h^s \hat{P}_h \tag{5}$$

$$\hat{q}_d = \eta_e^d \hat{P}_e + \eta_m^d \hat{P}_m + \eta_h^d \hat{P}_h, \tag{6}$$

where the η_j^i are compensating supply and demand price elasticities (both own and cross price).

The homogeneity condition and market equilibrium requires that:

$$\Sigma_i \, \eta_i^s = \Sigma \eta_i^d = 0 \tag{7}$$

$$q_s = q_d, \tag{8}$$

so that combining equations (5) through (8) gives:

$$\hat{P}_h = \omega \hat{P}_m + (1 - \omega) \hat{P}_e, \tag{9}$$

where

$$\omega = \frac{\eta_m^d - \eta_m^s}{\eta_h^s - \eta_h^d}.$$

Under reasonable assumptions, ω will be positive and is referred to as the protection incidence parameter. It is the proportion of import protection that is an implicit tax on the exportable sector. Conversely, $(1 - \omega)$ is the proportion that explicit export subsidization is an implicit tax on the importable sector.

If the tradable sectors are affected solely by a uniform ad valorem import tariff *(t)*, the true tariff (true net protective effect), τ is given by:

$$\tau = \Delta(P_m/P_h), \tag{10}$$

where prices will move from their free trade position (superscript *f*) by:

$$P_m = P_m^f(1 + t) \text{ and } P_h = P_h^f(1 + \omega t).$$

If the free trade price ratio is normalized, then:

$$\tau_t = \Delta\left(\frac{P_m}{P_h}\right) = (1 + t)/(1 + \omega t) - 1. \tag{11}$$

Furthermore, the true export subsidy (σ) in this situation would be given by:

$$\sigma_t = \Delta(P_e/P_h) = 1/(1-t) - 1, \tag{12}$$

where $\sigma < 0$ for all σ, and $t > 0$.

Alternatively, if a uniform export subsidy (s) was the sole intervention instrument in the tradable sector, the true tariff protection would be given by:

$$\tau_s = 1/[1 + (1-\omega)s] - 1, \tag{13}$$

where $\tau_s < 0$ for $0 < \omega < 1$, and $s > 0$.

In this case, the value of the true export subsidy (σ_s) would be:

$$\sigma_s = \Delta\left(\frac{P_e}{P_h}\right) = (1+s)/[1 + (1-\omega)s] - 1. \tag{14}$$

In the presence of many importables and exportables, the true nominal and effective tariff and export subsidy is then given by:

true nominal tariff

$$\tau_i = \Delta(P_m^i/P_h) = (1+t_i)/(1 = \omega\bar{t})[1 + (1-\omega)\bar{s}] - 1 \tag{15}$$

true effective tariff

$$\tau_i^e = (1 + t_i^e)/(1 + \omega\bar{t})[1 + (1-\omega)\bar{s}] - 1 \tag{16}$$

true nominal export subsidy

$$\sigma_i = \Delta(P_e^i/P_h) = (1+s_i)/(1 + \omega\bar{t})[1 + (1-\omega)\bar{s}] - 1 \tag{17}$$

true effective export subsidy

$$\sigma_i^e = (1 + s_i^e)/(1 + \omega\bar{t})[1 + (1-\omega)\bar{s}] - 1, \tag{18}$$

where $\bar{t}$ and $\bar{s}$ are trade weighted averages of all rates.

The incidence factor (ω) has been estimated for a number of countries by Sjaastad and Clements (1982), and preliminary work has been started on the New Zealand case by Russel (1985). These results are given in Table 13.

Since the New Zealand estimates are very tentative, a value of 0.70 is used in this paper as it lies between the more reliable Australian estimate using ORANI and the estimate by Russel (1985).

Appendix B
Nominal and Effective Rates of Protection

Introduction

Given the time frame and wide industry coverage involved in this study, an effort has been made to draw upon previous studies whenever possible. The main sources of previous estimates of protection at the sector level are a recompilation of four effective protection studies for New Zealand manufacturing industries for the periods 1955–58 and 1978/79 summarized by the Economic Monitoring Group (EMG (1984)); a study of protection using early import licensing tender information by Pickford (1984), a detailed study of agricultural assistance (Gibson (1984)); the first report of the Syntec consultants to the Treasury (1984); and studies on tax expenditures and long-term agricultural assistance carried out by the Agricultural Economics Research Unit (Lattimore (1984)) and (Lattimore and Wood-Belton (1986)).

Table 13. Long-Run Estimates of Protection Incidence (ω)

Country	Period	(ω)
Chile	1959–71	0.53–0.59
Uruguay	1966–79	0.51–0.57
Argentina	1935–79	0.38–0.48
El Salvador	1966–76	0.70
Australia (1)	1950–80	0.59–0.67
(2)	Computable G.E. Model	0.65–0.88
(3)	ORANI	0.83
New Zealand	1959–84	0.42–0.57

Note: Since the New Zealand estimates are very tentative, a value of $\omega = 0.70$ is used in this paper, as it lies between the more reliable Australian estimate using ORANI and the estimate by Russel (1985).

Sectoral Classification

The economy is disaggregated into 23 tradable sectors, 4 based on primary agricultural commodities (wool, beef, sheepmeat, and manufacturing milk) and 19 industrial sectors. The so-called agricultural sectors comprise the input supply and farm and processing subsectors, which can be closely identified with the production and processing of the raw farm commodities into tradable products at the wholesale level. They correspond to the sectors identified by Gibson (1984). The industrially based manufacturing sectors are taken from EMG (1984). The Standard International Trade Classification (SITC) and Customs Cooperation Council Nomenclature (CCCN) concordances for these sectors are given in Tables 19 and 20.

An additional concordance is required to compute the import licensing premiums and tariffs between domestic manufactured output and the tariff codes (CCCN basis). This classification for 1981/82 is taken from the Department of Trade and Industry (DTI) (1985), based on worksheets prepared by DTI. In this data set, manufacturing output from the 1981/82 Census of Manufacturing was classified by tariff code for nonindustry plan items. It was inflated to approximate 1983/84 values using the producer price index deflator of 8.8 percent. Exports by CCCN category were deducted to estimate domestic use of locally manufactured products.

Periods of Study

Five periods are chosen to measure the balance of export subsidization and import protection: 1955–58, 1964–67, 1972/73, 1978/79, and 1983/84.

Export Assistance

Subsidies to New Zealand exports have arisen from two broad types of instruments. Since 1964, a range of explicit export subsidy programs have been in place for exports of manufactured products. These programs are outlined in Treasury (1984) and have excluded most, but not all, products of agricultural origin.

It has been estimated by Morgan (cited in Tweedie and Spencer (1981)) that the nominal rates of export subsidy for export of industrial products in 1955–58, 1964–67, and 1972/73 were 0, 9, and 14 percent, respectively. These values are shown in Table 14. Industrial export subsidy rates for the latter two periods are taken from Syntec (1984) for selected sectors.

The recent type of export subsidy consists of a range of grants and production subsidies to the major export industries. Only the agricultural sectors are included here. This is an important restriction, because a number of subsidy and grants programs and regulations are thought to provide assistance to the international transport, tourist, forestry, and other service industries. In the absence of estimates for these sectors (implicitly assumed to be zero), the following estimates of export assistance overall are biased downwards. This will tend to exaggerate the true protection and assistance rates estimated in the report.

The rate of assistance to the four major agricultural industries is estimated in detail and the results given in Tables 15–18. The data for the years 1979/80 to 1983/84 and the methodology are mostly taken from Gibson. However, it is important to note that the sectoral definitions used here differ significantly from Gibson. No assumptions regarding the incidence of agricultural subsidies within the sector are made in this study.

Agricultural industry output and value added have been derived from the Agricultural Statistics and various input-output tables. The latter are available for five yearly intervals from 1954/55 to 1981/82.

The estimates of value of assistance from 1979/80 to 1982/83 are taken from Gibson, with the exception of tax expenditures. The value of tax expenditures (concessions) is based on more recent analysis, including the value of explicit export subsidies to agriculture, from Lattimore and Wood-Belton (1986). All assistance data for years prior to 1979/80 have been taken from Lattimore (1984) and computed using the Gibson methodology.

The rate of assistance is taken as the export subsidy equivalent, since 70 percent to 90 percent of output in each of these sectors is exported.

Import Protection

The nominal rates of import protection for each sector for the periods 1955–58 to 1978/79 are taken from EMG (1984). The rates for 1983/84 are estimated from import license premium information for rounds from the DTI (1985). These data were classified according to a concordance of tariff codes and industrial output less exports given in DTI. The average premium value was used for the latest tender round for each item open to tender. In many cases, this was zero in the latest rounds. All tenders of partial categories (termed "Ex" in the item codes) were excluded to prevent bias, and the DTI domestic use weights were used to aggregate from the seven- to the two-digit level used here.

It is important to recognize that the procedure used tends to bias the level of import protection downwards. First, some protection, notably for oil and petroleum products, is derived from special importing and domestic profit and pricing arrangements. In the absence of detailed research in this area, a rate of 25 percent has been assumed for

Table 14. New Zealand: Nominal Export Subsidies and Import Protection Trade Weighted, Selected Years 1955 to 1984

	1955–58				1964–67			
	Exports ($NZ million)	Nominal Export Subsidy 1954/55 (In percent)	Imports ($NZ million)	Nominal Import Protection (In percent)	Exports ($NZ million)	Nominal Export Subsidy 1965/66 (In percent)	Imports ($NZ million)	Nominal Import Protection (In percent)
Agriculture[1]								
Sheepmeat	84.002	0.1	—	0.0	141.004	0.4	—	0.0
Wool	211.918	0.0	—	0.0	209.350	0.0	—	0.0
Beef	41.610	0.1	—	0.0	60.080	0.3	—	0.0
Manufactured milk	127.328	0.2	—	0.0	180.902	0.2	—	0.0
Beverages and tobacco	0.386	0.0	11.934	120.0	0.914	9.0	8.764	134.0
Other textiles	0.236	0.0	72.614	29.0	0.914	9.0	73.722	62.0
Footwear	0.004	0.0	2.250	36.0	0.096	9.0	1.240	59.0
Clothing	0.018	0.0	6.511	48.0	0.316	9.0	3.532	103.0
Furniture	0.010	0.0	0.875	44.0	0.078	9.0	0.159	68.0
Printed products	0.183	0.0	7.623	21.0	0.446	9.0	13.896	30.0

ADJUSTMENT IN NEW ZEALAND

Leather goods	0.152	0.0	2.132	21.0	0.320	9.0	1.318	53.0
Rubber goods	0.103	0.0	3.330	22.0	0.358	9.0	4.867	56.0
Chemical fertilizers	0.006	0.0	3.528	0.0	0.032	9.0	6.783	0.0
Petroleum products	1.340	0.0	43.648	17.0	4.588	9.0	64.344	3.0
Other chemicals	5.124	0.0	34.381	28.0	18.672	9.0	61.613	45.0
Nonmetallic minerals	0.081	0.0	10.131	4.0	0.528	9.0	11.070	23.0
Basic metal products	0.208	0.0	60.643	5.0	0.920	9.0	80.236	61.0
Metal products	0.656	0.0	26.540	39.0	1.848	9.0	22.680	81.0
Machinery	0.996	0.0	74.644	46.0	2.438	9.0	88.601	59.0
Electrical products	0.272	0.0	30.938	42.0	1.200	9.0	58.491	92.0
Vehicle assembly	0.143	0.0	48.544	61.0	0.335	9.0	77.039	48.0
Other transport goods	0.319	0.0	6.765	35.0	0.750	9.0	17.347	35.0
Miscellaneous manufactured goods	0.231	0.0	12.176	34.0	1.666	9.0	9.696	74.0
Subtotal	*475.326*	*0.1*	*459.207*	*34.2*	*627.756*	*0.5*	*605.398*	*53.6*
Other goods and services	141.2	0.0	193.4	0.0	239.9	0.0	312.6	0.0
Total visible and invisible trade (June years)	**616.5**	**0.1**	**652.6**	**24.1**	**867.7**	**0.4**	**918.0**	**35.3**

Table 14 (continued). Nominal Export Subsidies and Import Protection Trade Weighted, Selected Years 1955 to 1984

	1972/73				1978/79			
	Exports ($NZ million)	Nominal Export Subsidy 1971/72 (In percent)	Imports ($NZ million)	Nominal Import Protection (In percent)	Exports ($NZ million)	Nominal Export Subsidy 1979/80 (In percent)	Imports ($NZ million)	Nominal Import Protection (In percent)
Agriculture[1]								
Sheepmeat	452.556	0.3	—	0.0	589.778	2.2	—	0.0
Wool	397.223	0.0	—	0.0	678.392	0.0	—	0.0
Beef	230.852	0.1	—	0.0	505.183	0.7	—	0.0
Manufactured milk	306.225	0.2	—	0.0	483.025	2.1	—	0.0
Beverages and tobacco	3.553	14.0	16.502	64.0	9.826	34.3	35.068	13.0
Other textiles	17.097	14.0	119.515	29.0	18.220	12.1	279.723	21.0
Footwear	0.434	14.0	2.405	43.0	3.997	15.0	7.785	36.0
Clothing	2.878	14.0	4.232	63.0	28.110	12.1	9.339	54.0
Furniture	1.430	14.0	0.663	28.0	15.871	11.7	3.227	21.0
Printed products	2.902	14.0	31.055	0.0	11.070	17.9	71.306	0.0
Leather goods	7.015	14.0	1.842	36.0	55.221	7.2	5.099	29.0

Rubber goods	1.628	14.0	11.703	44.0	3.948	(7.2)[2]	28.102	37.0
Chemical fertilizers	0.064	14.0	18.331	0.0	1.074	4.6	36.423	9.0
Petroleum products	13.683	14.0	96.593	−10.0	68.762	(0.0)	542.395	0.0
Other chemicals	35.244	14.0	157.159	33.0	127.430	(4.6)[2]	433.018	26.0
Nonmetallic minerals	3.734	14.0	17.951	19.0	17.117	13.1	50.191	13.0
Basic metal products	34.985	14.0	121.247	12.0	200.203	3.6	316.880	6.0
Metal products	9.036	14.0	40.910	39.0	45.155	13.9	100.052	32.0
Machinery	16.460	14.0	198.900	33.0	77.959	(13.9)[2]	587.068	36.0
Electrical products	14.964	14.0	78.010	63.0	50.961	(13.9)[2]	126.458	
Vehicle assembly	5.939	14.0	172.691	52.0	24.531	(13.9)[2]	346.445	23.0
Other transport goods	6.432	14.0	29.160	45.0	42.917	(13.9)[2]	160.176	
Miscellaneous manufactured goods	11.402	14.0	26.479	45.0	53.018	(13.9)[2]	61.873	37.0
Subtotal	*1,575.736*	*1.7*	*1,145.348*	*31.5*	*3,111.768*	*2.3*	*3,200.628*	*20.3*
Other goods and services	525.9	0.0	795.8	0.0	1,864.2	0.0	2,247.4	0.0
Total visible and invisible trade (June years)	**2,101.6**	**1.3**	**1,941.1**	**18.6**	**4,976.0**	**2.0**	**5,448.0**	**11.9**

Table 14 (concluded). Nominal Export Subsidies and Import Protection Trade Weighted, Selected Years 1955 to 1984

		1983/84		
	Exports ($NZ million)	Nominal Export Subsidy 1983/84 (In percent)	Imports ($NZ million)	Nominal Import Protection (In percent)
Agriculture[1]				
Sheepmeat	1,022.021	34.0	—	—
Wool	1,119.595	7.0	—	—
Beef	815.755	1.0	—	—
Manufactured milk	1,287.517	0.0	—	—
Beverages and tobacco	17.775	7.7	66.319	18.0
Other textiles	36.459	19.1	432.452	(21.0)[2]
Footwear	7.767	19.0	14.951	(36.0)[2]
Clothing	58.568	(19.1)[2]	33.669	(54.0)[2]
Furniture	23.248	19.3	9.813	73.0
Printed products	33.445	18.4	135.049	58.0
Leather goods	96.350	19.1	12.851	45.0
Rubber goods	19.190	(19.1)[2]	61.139	(37.0)[2]

Chemical fertilizers	1.405	11.4	(9.0)²
Petroleum products	3.119	(0.0)²	(25.0)²,³
Other chemicals	314.307	(11.4)²	29.0
Nonmetallic minerals	41.560	19.9	9.0
Basic metal products	352.042	3.3	26.0
Metal products	103.751	17.4	36.0
Machinery	162.727	(17.4)²	36.0
Electrical products	78.784	(17.4)²	35.0
Vehicle assembly	26.742	(17.4)²	29.0
Other transport goods	185.501	(17.4)²	41.0
Miscellaneous manufactured goods	113.964	(17.4)²	45.0
Subtotal	*5,921.591*	*11.1*	*30.9*
Other goods and services	3,742.4	0.0	0.0
Total visible and invisible trade (June years)	**9,664.0**	**6.8**	**17.5**

Sources: Department of Statistics (various years), and Economic Monitoring Group (1984).

¹The agricultural sectors are defined here as the farm and processing industries based on pastoral farming producing beef, sheepmeat, wool, and dairy products.

²Values in parentheses are assumed to be the same rate of protection as for similar products.

³Taken from Stewart (1984).

Table 15. New Zealand: Assistance to Sheepmeat Sector, 1954/55–1986/87
(In millions of New Zealand dollars, current)

	1954/55	1959/60	1965/66	1971/72	1976/77	1979/80	1980/81	1981/82	1982/83	1983/84	1986/87 (Forecast)[1,2]
Value of output (gross revenue)	131.2	206.0	296.8	335.7	666.5	923.8	1,042.8	992.0	1,100.8	1,177.0	1,100.8
Value added	74.4	109.5	156.9	181.3	351.2	281.7	320.5	280.9	337.6	219.9	337.6
SMP exports effect	—	—	—	—	—	—	—	45.000	156.000	223.000	0
SMP domestic effect	—	—	—	—	—	—	—	8.403	26.809	41.544	0
SMP total effect	—	—	—	—	—	—	—	*53.403*	*182.809*	*264.544*	*0*
Meat inspection	0.128	0.188	1.187	0.859	8.343	19.152	20.772	29.631	33.567	33.241	15.0
Meat industry hygiene grants	—	—	—	—	—	0.800	1.390	1.025	1.254	1.158	
Total assistance on output	**0.128**	**0.188**	**1.187**	**0.859**	**8.343**	**19.952**	**22.162**	**84.059**	**217.630**	**298.943**	**15.0**
Assistance on input											
Fertilizer	0.278	0.186	0.466	8.160	26.555	15.150	14.154	12.468	11.422	11.083	0
Livestock incentive scheme	—	—	—	—	—	0.627	1.839	3.501	3.451	4.847	0
Agricultural pest control	0.237	0.246	0.415	0.416	0.817	0.976	1.137	0.990	0.979	1.239	0

Miscellaneous payouts	0.090	0.295	0.076	0.929	0.041	1.537	1.389	1.348	1.401	1.587
Total assistance on inputs	**0.605**	**0.727**	**0.957**	**9.505**	**27.413**	**18.290**	**18.519**	**18.307**	**17.253**	**18.756**	**19.0**
Assistance to value-added factors										
Advisory services	0.132	0.179	0.192	0.363	0.674	1.123	1.554	1.733	1.920	2.243
Labor	...	...	...	...	...	2.972	2.282	3.135	3.437	3.566
Agricultural research	0.126	0.238	3.953	1.231	2.802	5.216	7.517	8.333	9.007	10.685
Agricultural quarantine	...	...	...	...	...	0.464	0.637	0.668	0.723	0.964
Animal health	0.166	0.267	0.115	0.958	2.011	1.201	1.744	1.699	2.072	1.514
Interest concessions	0.135	0.269	0.545	0.565	1.029	5.92	10.46	13.00	19.6	46.033	0
Taxation concessions	0.1	0.4	3.7	3.5	13.7	23.7	18.1	22.0	14.5	27.6	0
Special payment to sheep and cattle	—	—	—	—	—	0.025	0.004	—	—	—
Payment to agricultural allied organizations	0.018	0.015	0.072	0.802	0.595	0.279	0.393	0.468	0.386	0.50
Total assistance to value-added factors	**0.5**	**1.5**	**8.6**	**7.4**	**20.8**	**39.6**	**42.0**	**49.7**	**50.5**	**92.2**	**16.5**
Nominal rate of assistance *(In percent)*	0.1	0.1	0.4	0.3	1.3	2.2	2.2	9.3	24.6	34.0	1.0
Effective rate of assistance *(In percent)*	2.0	2.0	7.0	10.0	18.0	32.0	30.0	85.0	278.0	large	17.0

Sources: Based on Gibson (1984), Lattimore (1984), and Lattimore and Wood-Belton (1986).

[1] Forecast on the basis of estimates by Stonyer (1985) for Tables 15–19.
[2] 1982/83 weights.

Table 16. New Zealand: Assistance to Wool Sector, 1954/55–1986/87
(In millions of New Zealand dollars, current)

	1954/55	1959/60	1965/66	1971/72	1976/77	1979/80	1980/81	1981/82	1982/83	1983/84	1986/87 (Forecast)[1]
Value of output (gross revenue)	190.2	235.9	291.9	218.6	674.3	1,013.9	1,010.3	1,213.5	1,163.2	1,198.4	1,198.4
Value added	107.6	132.3	141.2	113.8	303.7	309.2	310.4	384.3	231.7	303.7	303.7
Assistance on output											
SMP exports effect	—	—	—	—	—	—	—	0	0	0	
SMP domestic effect	—	—	—	—	—	—	—	0	0	0	
SMP total effect	—	—	—	—	—	—	—	148.000	197.000	80.000	
Total assistance on output								148.000	197.000	80.000	
Assistance on inputs											
Fertilizer	0.404	0.213	0.458	5.310	26.865	26.140	20.498	19.761	16.514	14.863	0
Livestock incentive scheme	—	—	—	—	—	1.083	2.663	5.549	4.989	6.499	0
Agricultural pest control	0.345	0.282	0.409	0.271	0.827	1.684	1.646	1.570	1.416	1.662	

Miscellaneous payouts	0.037	0.059	0.073	0.604	0.039	2.646	1.999	2.075	1.985	2.119	
Total assistance on inputs	**0.786**	**0.554**	**0.940**	**6.185**	**27.731**	**31.553**	**26.806**	**28.955**	**24.904**	**25.143**	**3.7**
Assistance to value-added factors											
Advisory services	0.192	0.205	0.189	0.236	0.682	1.937	2.250	2.748	2.776	3.008	
Labor	...	...	...	...	...	2.972	2.282	3.135	3.437	3.566	
Agricultural research	0.202	0.249	4.063	1.061	2.993	7.486	9.067	10.622	11.207	12.279	
Agricultural quarantine	...	...	...	...	...	0.800	0.922	1.058	1.045	1.294	
Animal health	0.242	0.306	0.113	0.624	2.035	2.073	2.525	2.692	2.995	2.030	
Interest concessions	0.195	0.309	0.538	0.368	1.528	7.112	13.103	21.433	27.943	32.869	0
Taxation concessions	0.2	0.5	3.7	2.1	13.8	24.4	18.3	23.0	14.6	28.0	0
Special payment to sheep and cattle	—	—	—	—	—	0.025	0.004	—	—	—	
Payment to agricultural allied organizations	0.026	0.018	0.071	4.334	2.602	0.481	0.540	0.646	0.558	0.671	
Total assistance to value-added factors	**1.1**	**1.6**	**8.7**	**8.7**	**23.6**	**47.3**	**49.0**	**65.3**	**64.6**	**83.7**	**22.8**
Nominal rate of assistance (In percent)	0.0	0.0	0.0	0.0	0.0	0.0	0.0	13.9	20.4	7.0	0.0
Effective rate of assistance (In percent)	2.0	2.0	7.0	14.0	19.0	29.0	27.0	117.0	2,924.0	95.0	9.0

Sources: Based on Gibson (1984), Lattimore (1984), and Lattimore and Wood-Belton (1986).
[1]1982/83 weights.

Table 17. New Zealand: Assistance to the Beef Sector, 1954/55–1986/87
(In millions of New Zealand dollars, current)

	1954/55	1959/60	1965/66	1971/72	1976/77	1979/80	1980/81	1981/82	1982/83	1983/84	1986/87 (Forecast)[1]
Value of output (gross revenue)	78.8	127.9	178.3	342.1	741.8	1,286.8	1,173.4	1,159.61	1,490.2	1,412.8	1,412.8
Value added	49.2	68.5	94.7	181.3	391.6	393.2	360.7	357.8	475.6	358.6	358.6
Assistance on output											
SMP exports effect	—	—	—	—	—	—	0.500	30.000	42.000	—	
SMP domestic effect	—	—	—	—	—	—	0.200	13.063	16.287	—	
SMP total effect							*0.700*	*43.063*	*58.289*		
Meat inspection	0.056	0.083	0.522	0.378	3.670	8.424	9.137	13.034	14.765	14.622	6.0
Meat industry hygiene grants	—	—	—	—	—	0.602	0.923	0.727	0.799	0.607	0.6
Total assistance on output	**0.056**	**0.083**	**0.522**	**0.378**	**3.670**	**9.026**	**10.760**	**56.824**	**73.859**	**15.299**	**6.6**
Assistance on inputs											
Fertilizer subsidies	0.088	0.052	0.120	1.744	6.918	5.381	4.444	3.571	3.568	3.313	0
Livestock incentive scheme	—	—	—	—	—	0.829	1.791	3.466	3.988	4.780	0
Agricultural pest control	0.143	0.153	0.250	0.423	0.909	1.289	1.107	0.980	1.132	1.222	
Miscellaneous payouts	0.040	0.183	0.517	0.945	0.046	2.029	1.353	1.335	1.620	1.566	

	0.271	0.388	0.887	3.112	7.873	9.528	8.695	9.352	10.308	10.881	11
Total assistance on inputs	0.271	0.388	0.887	3.112	7.873	9.528	8.695	9.352	10.308	10.881	11
Assistance to value-added factors											
Advisory services	0.080	0.111	0.116	0.370	0.750	1.483	1.513	1.716	2.219	2.212	
Labor	...	...	...	...	...	0.932	0.766	1.015	1.154	1.235	
Agricultural research	0.070	0.141	2.386	1.271	3.117	6.889	7.322	8.250	10.409	10.539	
Agricultural quarantine	...	...	...	...	...	0.612	0.620	0.661	0.836	0.951	
Animal health	0.100	0.166	0.069	0.974	2.237	5.730	7.633	8.606	9.713	9.489	
Diary beef scheme	—	—	—	—	0.708	0.676	—	—	—	—	
Interest concessions	0.082	0.169	0.330	0.576	2.476	6.002	8.874	14.565	22.109	24.101	0
Taxation concessions	0.9	1.3	2.7	6.7	19.5	48.9	16.9	17.3	9.7	44.5	0
Special payment to sheep and cattle	—	—	—	—	—	0.019	0.003	—	—	—	
Payment to agricultural allied organizations	0.011	0.010	0.043	0.815	0.662	0.368	0.363	0.404	0.446	0.493	
Total assistance to value-added factors	1.2	1.9	5.6	10.7	29.5	71.6	44.0	52.5	56.6	93.5	24.9
Nominal rate of assistance (In percent)	0.1	0.1	0.3	0.1	0.5	0.7	0.9	5.2	5.2	1.1	0.5
Effective rate of assistance (In percent)	3.0	3.0	8.0	8.0	11.0	24.0	19.0	41.0	36.0	36.0	12.0

Sources: Based on Gibson (1984), Lattimore (1984), and Lattimore and Wood-Belton (1986).
¹1983/84 weights.

Table 18. New Zealand: Assistance to Export Dairy Sector, 1954/55–1986/87
(In millions of New Zealand dollars, current)

	1954/55	1959/60	1965/66	1971/72	1976/77	1979/80	1980/81	1981/82	1982/83	1983/84	1986/87 *(Forecast)*[1]
Value of output (gross revenue)	243.0	283.9	358.2	461.2	809.2	1,054.7	1,456.5	1,842.0	2,030.3	1,982.7	1,982.7
Value added	137.6	152.9	180.4	228.2	363.2	300.3	451.7	592.0	656.6	513.7	513.7
Assistance on output											
SMP exports effect	—	—	—	—	—	17.400	—	—	—	—	
SMP domestic effect	—	—	—	—	—	—	—	—	—	—	
SMP total effect	—	—	—	—	—	*17.400*	—	—	—	—	
Inspection and grading	0.397	0.553	0.549	0.816	0.260	4.787	6.432	7.248	8.637	8.457	4
Total assistance on output	**0.397**	**0.553**	**0.549**	**0.816**	**0.260**	**22.187**	**6.432**	**7.248**	**8.637**	**8.457**	**4**
Assistance on inputs											
Fertilizer subsidies	0.196	0.120	0.323	4.516	16.831	13.942	11.739	11.287	11.373	10.581	0
Livestock incentive scheme	—	—	—	—	—	0.411	0.456	1.031	0.964	1.253	
Agricultural pest control	0.440	0.338	0.501	0.571	0.991	1.334	0.593	1.560	1.641	1.876	
Miscellaneous payouts	0.165	0.406	1.040	1.273	0.052	2.776	1.997	2.125	2.348	2.403	

Total assistance on inputs	0.801	0.864	1.864	6.360	17.874	18.463	14.785	16.003	16.326	16.113	16
Assistance to value-added factors											
Advisory services	0.302	0.325	0.310	0.616	0.855	2.218	3.096	3.767	4.509	4.549	
Labor	...	...	...	...	...	3.146	2.594	3.451	3.936	4.221	
Agricultural research	0.265	0.333	4.950	1.955	3.682	6.487	8.919	10.675	12.344	13.330	
Agricultural quarantine	...	...	...	...	...	0.634	0.892	1.052	1.212	1.460	
Animal health	0.309	0.367	0.139	1.313	2.439	6.910	9.272	12.627	10.911	10.326	0
Interest concessions	0.303	0.494	4.311	5.110	23.175	48.228	64.505	54.352	67.320	100.230	0
Taxation concessions	0.5	0.9	5.4	11.2	27.8	45.1	46.2	72.8	78.5	50.5	
Special payment to sheep and cattle	—	—	—	—	—	0.019	0.004	—	—	—	
Payment to agricultural allied organizations	0.033	0.021	0.086	1.099	0.722	0.381	0.523	0.642	0.647	0.758	
Total assistance to value-added factors	1.7	2.4	15.2	21.3	58.7	113.1	136.0	159.4	179.3	185.4	34.1
Nominal rate of assistance (In percent)	0.2	0.2	0.2	0.2	2.1	0.4	0.4	0.4	0.4	0.2	
Effective rate of assistance (In percent)	3.0	10.0	13.0	22.0	59.0	37.0	32.0	32.0	43.0	11.0	

Sources: Based on Gibson (1984), Lattimore (1984), and Lattimore and Wood-Belton (1986).
[1]1983/84 weights.

Table 19. New Zealand: Concordance Agricultural Sectors

Sector	SITC	CCCN
Sheepmeat	011.21.01-011.22.91	02.01.000.01-02.01.000.36
	011.60.01-011.60.39	02.01.000.71-02.01.000.86
Wool	268.10.01-268.20.21	53.01.000.01-53.01.000.51
	268.61.00-268.70.00	53.03.000.00-53.05.000.09
	613.00.01, 613.00.11	43.02.000.01, 43.02.000.11
	613.00.21, 613.00.31	53.05.000.01-53.07.000.11
	651.26.01-651.28.09	53.10.000.01-53.07.000.19
	659.21.01-659.49	58.01.000.01-58.02.000.69

Table 20. New Zealand: Concordance Industrial Sectors

Sector	SITC	CCCN
Beverages, tobacco	11, 12	22, 24
Other textiles	65[1]	50-52; 54-60; 62,63
Footwear	85	64
Clothing	84	61
Furniture	82	94
Printed products	892	49
Leather goods	61	41,42
Rubber goods	62	40
Chemical fertilizers	56	31
Petroleum products	33	27
Other chemicals	51-55, 57-59	28-30, 32-38
Nonmetallic minerals	66	25
Products, basic metal	67, 68	73-76, 78-81[2]
Metal products	69	73.21-73.40, 82, 83[2]
Machinery	71-76[4]	84[3]
Electrical products	71 or 77	85[3]
Vehicle assembly	73 or 78	87
Other transport goods	79	86, 88, 89
Miscellaneous manufactures	81,83,87,88 and 89 (except 892)	39, 66, 67, 70, 71 90-93, 95-99

[1]Except SITC 651.21.000 to 651.23.09, and 659.21.01 to 659.49.39.
[2]Some overlap exists between products, basic metals, and metal products.
[3]Some overlap exists between machinery and electrical products.
[4]For the years 1978/79 and 1982/83, "Machinery" includes SITC Divisions 71-76; for all other years valuation fell under the SITC Division 71, "Machinery, other than electric."

Table 21. New Zealand: Effective Rates of Assistance for Importables, 1955–83
(In percent)

Sector	1955–58	1964–67	1972/73	1978/79	1982/83
Beverages, tobacco	−31	−10	61	21	
Other textiles	41	196	67	45	221
Footwear	57	99	69	51	
Clothing	124	1,105	169	140	
Furniture	92	200	41	−29	74
Printed products	16	29	−19	−12	45
Leather goods	37	193	−112	84	
Rubber goods	22	91	111	68	
Chemical fertilizers	−24	−30	−2	9	
Petroleum products	43	−39	−66	−48	
Other chemicals	46	76	105	77	
Nonmetallic minerals	−15	14	23	17	
Basic metal products	−6	162	10	3	
Metal products	83	617	100	74	
Machinery	136	99	57	81	
Electrical products	117	406	365	81	
Vehicle assembly	2,428	102	−165	41	
Other transport goods	39	33	50	41	
Miscellaneous manufactures	69	186	93	77	

Sources: Economic Monitoring Group (1984), and Syntec (1984), p. 142.

petroleum products for the period 1983/84 based on the ratio of retail bulk prices for diesel oil in New Zealand and the United States in 1984.

A second source of bias arises from special import regimes that have been negotiated in industry plans. In some cases competing imports are not subject to import quota tender procedures and hence are excluded from the estimates in Table 14.

Effective rates of assistance are taken from EMG (1984), Syntec (1984), and Tables 15–18. These data are reproduced in Tables 21 and 22.

Weighting Procedures

The trade-weighted protection rates (current account basis) are given at the bottom of Table 14 for the purposes of estimating the incidence of protection described in Appendix A.

Trade-weighted rates on a trade account basis are used in the texts to measure intersectoral neutrality. For this purpose, domestic use (importables) or output (exportables) would be preferable to trade weights, but time did not allow for this additional computation to be made.

Table 22. New Zealand: Effective Rates of Assistance for Exportables, 1955-84
(In percent)

Sector	1955-58	1964-67	1971-73	1978-80	1983/84
Agriculture[1]					
Sheepmeat	2.0	7.0	10.0	32.0	large
Wool	2.0	7.0	14.0	29.0	95.0
Beef	3.0	8.0	8.0	24.0	36.0
Dairy	0.0	0.0	0.0	0.0	0.0
Beverages, etc.	0.0	0.0	0.0	0.0	0.0
Other textiles	0.0	0.0	0.0	0.0	0.0
Footwear	0.0	0.0	0.0	44.0	0.0
Clothing	0.0	0.0	0.0	39.0	0.0
Furniture	0.0	0.0	0.0	16.0	0.0
Printed products	0.0	0.0	0.0	35.0	0.0
Leather goods	0.0	0.0	0.0	90.0	0.0
Rubber goods	0.0	0.0	0.0	0.0	0.0
Chemical fertilizers	0.0	0.0	0.0	0.0	0.0
Petroleum products	0.0	0.0	0.0	0.0	0.0
Other chemicals	0.0	0.0	0.0	0.0	0.0
Nonmetallic minerals	0.0	0.0	0.0	32.0	0.0
Basic metal products	0.0	0.0	0.0	1.0	0.0
Metal products	0.0	0.0	0.0	38.0	0.0
Machinery	0.0	0.0	0.0	0.0	0.0
Electrical products	0.0	0.0	0.0	0.0	0.0
Vehicle assembly	0.0	0.0	0.0	0.0	0.0
Other transport goods	0.0	0.0	0.0	0.0	0.0
Miscellaneous manufactures	0.0	0.0	0.0	0.0	0.0

[1] The agricultural sector rates are taken from Tables 15-18. Other rates are from Syntec (1984), p. 113.

References

Balassa, Bela, *The Structure of Protection in Developing Countries*, (Baltimore: Published for the World Bank and the Inter-American Development Bank by Johns Hopkins Press, 1971).

Bascand, A., and D. Carey, "Exchange Controls and Real Exchange Rate Adjustment," paper presented at AAES Conference, AERU Discussion Paper No. 97 (Canterbury, New Zealand: Lincoln College, 1985).

Condliffe, J.B., *New Zealand in the Making: A Survey of Social and Economic Development* (London: George Allen and Unwin, 1930).

Corden, W.M., *The Theory of Protection* (Oxford: Clarendon Press, 1971).

Cronin, M.R., "Export Demand Elasticities with Less than Perfect Markets," *Australian Journal of Agricultural Economics* (Sydney), Vol. 23 (April 1979), pp. 69-72.

Deane, R.S., P.W.E. Nicholl, and R.G. Smith, eds., *Monetary Policy and the New Zealand Financial System* (Wellington: Reserve Bank of New Zealand, 1983).

Department of Statistics, *External Trade* (Wellington, New Zealand, various years).

Department of Trade and Industry, "Import Licensing Data Worksheets," (mimeographed, Wellington, New Zealand, 1985).

Economic Monitoring Group, "Strategy for Growth," Report No. 3 (Wellington: New Zealand Planning Council, September 1984).

Gibson, B.C., "Measurement of Assistance to Pastoral Agriculture, 1979/80–1983/84," Draft Discussion Paper 8/84 (Wellington, New Zealand: Ministry of Agriculture and Fisheries, 1984).

Giles, David E.A., and Peter Hampton, "Regional Production Relationships During the Industrialization of New Zealand, 1935–48," *Journal of Regional Science* (Amherst), Vol. 24, (November 1984), pp. 519–33.

Gould, John, *The Rake's Progress? The New Zealand Economy Since 1945* (Auckland, New Zealand: Hodder and Stoughton, 1982).

Guthrie, F., and R.G. Lattimore, "The Agricultural Sector in New Zealand: A Joint Farm Industrial Perspective," AERU Discussion Paper No. 88 (Canterbury, New Zealand: Lincoln College, 1984).

Hawke, G.R., *The Making of New Zealand* (Cambridge: Cambridge University Press, 1985).

Imperial Economic Conference, *Imperial Economic Conference at Ottawa, 1932: Summary of Proceedings and Copies of Trade Agreements* (London: H.M. Stationery Office, 1932).

Lattimore, R.G., "New Zealand Economic Development: A Brief Overview of Unbalanced Industry Growth," AERU Discussion Paper No. 94 (Canterbury, New Zealand: Lincoln College, 1984).

_____ and M.D. Wood-Belton, "Tax Expenditures in New Zealand," AERU Research Paper (Canterbury, New Zealand: Lincoln College, 1986).

Lloyd, P.J., et al., "New Zealand's Long-Term Foreign Trade Problems and Structural Adjustment Policies" (Wellington: New Zealand Planning Council, 1980).

O'Brien, M.B., "The External Sector and the Economy: A Review of the Econometric Evidence," Discussion Paper G81/3 (Wellington: Reserve Bank of New Zealand, May 1981).

Philpott, Bryan, "Economic Research and Economic Policy," Discussion Paper No. 29 (Wellington: New Zealand Institute of Economic Research, 1985).

Pickford, M., "A New Test for Manufacturing Industry Efficiency: An Analysis of the Results of Import Licensing Tendering in New Zealand," Working Paper (Palmerston North, New Zealand: Massey University, 1984).

Reserve Bank of New Zealand, *Bulletin*, various issues (Wellington: Reserve Bank of New Zealand).

Russel, Patrick, "The Incidence of Protection in New Zealand" (unpublished, Wellington, New Zealand: Department of Trade and Industry, 1985).

Sjaastad, Larry A., and Kenneth W. Clements, "The Incidence of Protection: Theory and Measurement," Discussion Paper (Nedlands, Western Australia: University of Western Australia, 1982).

Stewart, J.D., et al., "Economic Management and Land Use Issues," commentary by Independent Study Group to Federated Farmers (Wellington, New Zealand: Treasury Department, 1984).

Stonyer, E.J., "The Impact of Recent Policy Changes in the New Zealand Sheepmeat Industry," paper presented to the Australian Outlook Conference (Canberra: Australian Outlook Conference, 1985).

Syntec Economic Services, and New Zealand Treasury Department, *The Structure of Industry Assistance in New Zealand: An Exploratory Analysis* (Wellington, New Zealand: Treasury Department, February 1984).

Tweedie, A.J., and G.H. Spencer, "Supply Behavior in New Zealand Export Industries," Reserve Bank of New Zealand Discussion Paper G/81/1 (Wellington: Reserve Bank of New Zealand, February 1981).

Comment

Colin James

My first reaction to the invitation to act as discussant to Dr. Lattimore's paper was disbelief. My folkloric impression of the International Monetary Fund is of a body concerned with the technique of economic administration, much involved at present in unscrambling Latin American debt. Not only am I not a technician in economics, I am not an economist (as one or two of this gathering would be happy to testify). I was assured, however, that I had been chosen exactly because I was not an economist (perhaps to give some light relief). It is on that basis that I am here. I pretend to no more than a generalist's interest in, and need to be interested in, economics—what might loosely be called political economy, though without the Marxist connotation that term seems to have acquired in some quarters, most notably, Sydney University.

Accordingly, I will not so much take up the economic arguments of Dr. Lattimore's paper as deal with the political and social background to the change that is central to his paper. This much I do know about economics: that an economy does not exist and operate independently of that political and social background, much as many economists seem to wish it would. An economy is for and of humans, not despite them.

In that context, I note an instructive comment in Professor John Gould's useful little book, *The Muldoon Years*, published a few years ago. Dealing with criticism of New Zealand's external debt, Gould noted that it is only a fraction of its level in relation to gross domestic product (GDP) of 1880, after the heavy borrowing of the Vogel development years.[1] "When therefore we are sternly admonished that in the light of [International Monetary Fund] guidelines the burden of debt today 'must be regarded as being on the high side,' the only retort can be that it is fortunate for New Zealand . . . that there was no IMF around

---

[1] Sir Julius Vogel, Colonial Treasurer from 1869 to 1873 and Premier from 1873 to 1896, initiated a program of heavy borrowing for public works to stimulate the faltering post-gold-rush economy. The levels of indebtedness he incurred attracted widespread criticism both within New Zealand, then still in the early stages of European settlement, and in England.

in the later nineteenth century, for if there had been, countries such as ours would never have got off the ground at all."[2] Sir Robert Muldoon, who repeatedly, and correctly, warned of the destructive social and political potential of too severe IMF and other foreign strictures on debt-ridden developing countries, would have approved.

The human beings have, in fact, been getting on with structural change in New Zealand for some time. That change has been accompanied by a shift in the locus of intellectual debate emphasizing some economic mechanisms and downplaying others that were formerly applauded. It is also accompanied by a generational and psychological shift. These subsidiary considerations create problems for, and opportunities within, the structural change. The elements of the change are:

- Diversification (1) from reliance on a few commodities to a wide mix of land-based and manufactured products, and (2) from reliance on a narrow range of countries to a broad range, with particular emphasis on the Pacific rim countries.
- Departure from a "bonanza" mentality, which looked for a single solution to slow growth such as frozen meat (the 1880s), aerial topdressing (1950s), or big energy-based projects ("think big" in the early 1980s), and movement toward a more fragmented solution—doing a lot of smaller things geared to niches or gaps in foreign markets. (The bonanza still probably lurks in the back of the nation's mind, but hope of one turning up is fading.)
- Emergence of the manufacturing industries from "infant" status, requiring automatic protection, to a capability (uneven and in many cases still unproven, but evident as a trend) to export and sell on the domestic market competitively—that is, to stand on their own feet; coupled with this are a growing recognition that "the market" is not just national but multinational, and the emergence of New Zealand's first indigenously based true multinational companies.
- The freeing up of the commercial infrastructure, most notably internal land and air transport and the financial markets, though not yet to any extent, the labor market.

The impetus for the change has stemmed from a number of factors. Among the most important:

- Government assistance to secondary industry, notably in blanket protection from 1958, in partial integration with Australian industry through the 1965 and 1982 trade agreements, and in export tax incentives.
- Favorable treatment by the government of alternative primary industries, particularly horticulture and fishing.

---

[2] John Gould, *The Muldoon Years* (Auckland: Hodder and Stoughton, 1985), p. 46.

- The relative economic decline of traditional markets, particularly Britain, and the rise of the East Asian newly industrialized countries (NICs).
- A change in the economic environment, notably a severe and prolonged decline in the terms of trade, including two oil shocks, continued and in some cases intensified protectionism against traditional pastoral exports, and new competition for those products.
- A consequent relative decline in economic performance compared with other countries, high unemployment, subsidies for the main exports, and sharply rising foreign debt, which have led to a growing feeling that "something had to be done."
- The ascendancy of a "more market" ideology within both main political parties and, from 1979 onwards, a gradual, then rapid, injection of that ideology into government decision making.
- Growing internal demand for diversity of choice and lower pricing of consumer goods comparable with alternative places to live, particularly Australia, with which New Zealand has a common labor market; this has reduced and maybe eliminated the option of national insulation chosen in 1938 and 1958 and enhanced a sense of international interdependence.
- A generational shift, coupled with and contributing to a psychological shift that values security less and risk more; the new generation has driven the new and innovative companies in the financial markets and increasingly drives the corporations; it is now in power politically and in key parts of the public service.
- A shaky but growing national (and individual) confidence, seen in crafts and the arts from the late 1970s onwards and in business from the early 1980s (last year the Australian press was full of "the Kiwis are coming" stories, bemused and apprehensive in tone); it is also an element in the non-nuclear defense stance.

These factors have all been interactive. Without early government assistance, it is unlikely secondary industry would have grown to its current confident state. An outbreak of "more market" ideology, mainly among younger members in the National Party in early 1979, helped prompt the government into putting this confidence to the test by beginning the relaxation of border protection dating from the 1979 budget (a much undervalued document), and the negotiation of CER.[3] The same influence was instrumental in forcing through a series of internal deregulatory measures, most notably on land and air transport, retailing, the meat processing industry, and union membership. That ideology was

---

[3] Australia-New Zealand Closer Economic Relations and Trade Agreement (ANZCERT).

also instrumental in pulling support away from the National Party from 1982 onwards when Sir Robert Muldoon regulated wages, prices, rents, and interest rates.

Growing confidence in export markets (partly because of the tax incentives) encouraged manufacturers to be accommodating to the closer economic relations agreement with Australia (inconceivable half a decade earlier), and later, to the phasing out of import licensing globally and of tariffs. This in turn diminished an important restructuring constraint at the political level.

The apparent failure of regulation, protection, subsidies, and heavy overseas borrowing to stem or disguise economic malaise undermined belief in the effectiveness of traditional social democratic ideology and mechanisms. The need for massive income maintenance for traditional pastoral farmers undermined city belief in their indispensability at the very time that concrete evidence emerged of greater profitability in other livestock and horticulture and in new exports in manufactures, fishing, tourism, and services. The old guard resistance to change by Sir Robert Muldoon and the dominance, and in the end paralysis, of his government both enhanced the attractiveness of *any* alternative and widened the freedom of action of the subsequent government. The divisiveness of his party in opposition has so weakened it as a political force that the labor government has felt no need to be particularly sensitive to sector group complaints; this may in the final analysis be Sir Robert's principal contribution as a minister of finance—the holding back of change to the point where there was overwhelming demand for it and willingness to accept it relatively uncritically.

The Labor government's freedom of action is due to two more factors: the fact, now clearly apparent, that the economy is on a long-term upswing (and, in 1983–85, strongly growing); and an apparent (subliminal) recognition by the general public that this is so—the Heylen Research Center confidence index of popular economic expectations, while still fluctuating a great deal, has also been on a long-term upswing since 1979. A similar indication is to be found in some business confidence measurements. This perhaps demonstrates the old adage that revolutions occur not at the nadir of human experience, but when things begin to get better.

For a variety of reasons, therefore, the government has been able to take the public with it through a sharp break in political/ administrative policies. That break could not have been achieved even five years ago without serious public resistance that would have wrecked or quickly undone the attempt. The environment was not appropriate; the underlying structural change and rise in self-confidence that were occurring regardless of government policies were not far enough advanced; Sir Robert Muldoon's hands-on style had not yet been discredited, provoking a political demand for change; the underlying economic upswing was only just beginning; the new generation was only beginning to emerge into political and economic power.

It could be argued that the restructuring would have proceeded whatever the government did—had, for instance, a Labor government with traditional social democratic policies taken over in 1984. It is interesting to speculate what would have been done at government level had the 1980 abortive coup against Sir Robert Muldoon within the National cabinet succeeded, and the "more market" men had had their way. Certainly, Sir Robert's later excesses would have been avoided; there would have been faster deregulation and deprotection; but they may not have gone as far as the present government has, and may indeed have given way to an anti-deregulatory and anti-deprotection Labor government in 1981 or 1984.

As it has turned out, the political authorities, after lagging behind the pace of economic restructuring up to 1984, have forced it since. This has probably (but not yet certainly) irreversibly altered the administrative climate, at least for this generation and at least in the sense that the insulated, cross-subsidized economy is not, and is not seen as, a realistic alternative. If nothing else, it has probably (but not yet certainly) cast in cement a sense of the inescapability of international economic interdependence that will encourage readier future adjustment to world economic conditions (for instance, in the next oil shock), drive New Zealand further toward a true developed economy, and encourage reallocation of resources toward more efficient uses and discourage the allocation of resources to inefficient uses.

Forcing the pace has probably also been critical in drawing out the full force of the new psychology of risk, adventure, and self-reliance evident among opinion leaders and the drivers of the emergent elements of the new economy. This encourages hope that, after many false starts, New Zealand may be about to give its economy a new dynamism, more deeply and widely based than the "rich peasant" economy of lambs for cars that sufficed to make it among the richest in the 1950s. The particular ideology of the government's moves is much less important in underpinning this new psychology than the liberating and exhilarating impetus of its taking dramatic, even breathtaking, initiatives. The rise of California, Japan, or Singapore is not a matter of ideology, but the attitudes of its people. Without the right attitudes, no restructuring or more general economic adjustment will succeed convincingly.

There are also problems associated with the government's pace, its insensitivity to sectoral pain, and its particular economic stance. The macroeconomic stance, particularly in deficit management and monetary and exchange rate policy, has worried a number of commentators, including some here today. If that fails, or produces too unstable conditions, popular support for the government, and therefore for its measures taken in their widest scope, might be undermined and cause a retreat. Similarly, if the liberalization, tax changes, and the exchange and monetary policies damage the real economy, support for the measures as a whole might be undermined among the active players in the economy, with a trickle down into unease among the population at large. There are also strains within the Labor Party which suggest the government cannot hold course much into its second term, which may cause uncertainty in business and undermine the development process. Politicians seldom lead. They usually follow. Once this brief period of forcing the pace is over, conditions will need to be in place that will encourage the active players to take over again the initiative for change and development. It is by no means certain yet that that will be the case.

There is another longer-term issue, which is normally lost sight of in economic discussion: the emergence of biracialism, containing within it a cultural challenge to the individualistic basis for much of current economic activity. It remains very much to be seen whether New Zealand's economic development can accommodate, and use to its overall benefit, the collectivist elements of the Maori culture.

The biggest restructuring—economic adjustment—yet in New Zealand's human history was between 1830 and 1920, when an economy based on small, peripatetic agriculture, food gathering, and hunting was converted into a grassland economy exporting livestock products. Since then, in one view of the history of New Zealand's economy it can be seen as a linear development toward a fully industrialized system, with temporary halts, because, unlike the East Asian NICs, it grew rich on the intermediate stage of commodity trading. The real knack of economic adjustment in the successful developed country, which New Zealand is not but now has the chance to be, is to avoid long periods on plateaus and to develop response mechanisms that adjust continually, both at the political/administrative level and in the marketplace. New Zealand has yet to learn that.

3

A Case Of Successful Adjustment in a Developing Country: Korea's Experience During 1980–84

Bijan Aghevli and Jorge Márquez-Ruarte

I. Introduction

Korea's experience following the second wave of oil price increases is an excellent example of how orthodox stabilization policies, effectively implemented, can help a country adjust to domestic and external shocks. There has been wide recognition of the Korean "economic miracle" of the 1960s and 1970s, when an export-led growth strategy resulted in a phenomenal increase of 30 percent a year in export volume and a tripling of real per capita incomes. However, there is markedly less awareness of the severity of the economic problems that Korea faced at the beginning of the 1980s and of the magnitude of the economic adjustment that took place during the subsequent years.

Toward the end of the 1970s, the Korean economy began to experience widening structural imbalances that were associated with a prolonged period of rapid growth and relatively high inflation. The underlying strains and pressures were exacerbated in 1980 by a disastrous harvest, the rise in international oil prices and interest rates, and domestic political disturbances. Consequently, Korea's economic performance worsened sharply. Output declined in 1980 for the first time in Korea's modern history. Inflation soared, and the current account deficit rose to a record level. The authorities responded to the crisis by implementing a comprehensive adjustment program which was supported by two one-year stand-by arrangements with the International Monetary Fund (March 1980–February 1982). Substantial recovery took place during 1981–82. Economic growth resumed at an annual rate of 6 percent. The inflation rate, which had peaked at 35 percent in 1980, fell to 5 percent in 1982. The current account deficit narrowed by more than half to 4 percent of gross national product (GNP).

In spite of the improvement in economic conditions in 1982, the high level of Korea's external debt and its relatively short maturity caused increasing concern, particularly at a time when exports were weakening and the international debt crisis was unfolding. To remedy the situation, the Government intensified its adjustment effort through a far-reaching stabilization program which was supported by another stand-by arrangement with the Fund (July 1983–March 1985). The program proved to be highly successful. Output rose by an average of over 8 percent during 1983–84, while inflation was contained at 2 percent, and the current account deficit fell below 2 percent of GNP. At the same time, the growth of external debt decelerated sharply, and the maturity structure of the debt was lengthened significantly. Korea's outstanding performance during this period ensured that, in contrast to several other large borrowers, its reception in the international capital markets remained favorable.

This paper describes the salient features of Korea's recent adjustment effort. The following three sections deal with the crisis years of 1979–80 (Section II), the recovery years of 1981–82 (Section III), and the adjustment years of 1983–84 (Section IV). A summary of the previous sections and a brief assessment of the medium-term prospects of the economy are provided in Section V.

II. The Years of Crisis (1979–80)

At the turn of the decade, the Korean economy underwent a major crisis, which had its roots in external and domestic shocks that exacerbated the impact of structural imbalances already present in the economy. The main external shocks were the worldwide increase in oil prices and the run-up in international interest rates, which together added the equivalent of 6 percent of GNP to Korea's external payments during 1979–80. Moreover, the slowdown of economic activity in industrial countries magnified the effect of Korea's weak external competitiveness. As a result, export growth dropped markedly. On the domestic side, the economy was buffeted by a drought, which sharply reduced agricultural production, and by severe political disturbances. The shortfall in agricultural output accounted for a decline of more than 4 percent in real GNP.

The authorities' adjustment policies, which were initiated in mid-1978 and strengthened in the subsequent two years, alleviated some of the pressure on the external position. Nevertheless, the magnitude of the external and domestic shocks inevitably led to a pronounced deterioration in economic conditions. Real GNP, which had been rising at an average yearly rate of about 10 percent during the previous two decades, fell by 5 percent in 1980, while inflation surged to 35 percent, and the external current account deficit widened to almost 9 percent of GNP (Table 1).

Table 1. Korea: Selected Economic Indicators, 1979–84

	1979	1980	1981	1982	1983	1984
	(Annual percentage changes)					
National income and prices						
GNP at constant prices	6.5	−5.2	6.2	5.6	9.5	7.6
GNP deflator	21.1	25.6	15.9	7.1	3.0	4.0
Consumer prices (year end)	21.2	34.6	11.7	4.8	2.0	2.4
External sector[1]	15.7	17.1	20.2	1.0	11.1	13.5
Exports, f.o.b.[2]						
Imports, f.o.b.[2]	31.8	13.1	12.5	−3.4	6.4	9.6
Export volume[3]	−1.0	11.5	17.5	6.5	17.3	14.7
Import volume[3]	11.8	−9.1	11.1	0.3	14.5	14.3
Terms of trade	−2.1	−13.3	−2.1	4.4	1.1	1.9
Money and credit						
Domestic credit	35.7	40.6	31.1	25.1	16.0	13.1
Of which: Private sector	39.1	39.6	26.3	25.1	17.6	14.3
Broad money	24.6	26.9	25.0	27.0	15.2	10.6[4]
Interest rate (end of period level, one-year time deposit)	18.6	19.5	16.2	8.0	8.0	10.0
	(In percent of GNP)					
Consolidated public sector						
Revenue	18.5	19.6	20.2	19.4	19.9	20.0
Expenditure	19.9	22.8	24.8	23.7	21.5	21.4
Deficit	−1.4	−3.2	−4.6	−4.3	−1.6	−1.4
Gross domestic investment	35.6	31.3	29.1	27.0	27.8	30.0
Gross national savings[5]	29.2	22.6	22.2	23.3	25.6	28.3
External current account	−6.4	−8.7	−6.9	−3.7	−2.1	−1.7
External debt[6]	32.7	44.6	48.4	52.4	53.6	52.5
Debt service ratio[7,8]	16.9	19.7	20.1	20.6	18.8	20.1
	(In billions of U.S. dollars)					
External current account	−4.2	−5.3	−4.6	−2.6	−1.6	−1.4
Gross international reserves	5.9	6.8	7.2	7.7	7.5	8.2
(In months of imports of goods and services)	2.9	2.9	2.7	2.9	2.8	2.8

Sources: Korean Minister of Finance; and Fund staff estimates.

[1] Based on U.S. dollar values.
[2] Balance of payments basis.
[3] Customs basis.
[4] Includes certificates of deposit issued by commercial bank.
[5] Defined as the sum of gross domestic investment and the external current account surplus.
[6] Includes public, publicly guaranteed, and private sector bank and nonbank debt of all maturities.
[7] As percent of exports of goods and services.
[8] Includes interest on short-term debt, and excludes rollover on interoffice bank accounts.

Policies

The increase in international oil prices complicated economic management considerably. In 1979 the authorities allowed domestic oil prices to rise in line with world prices and, in order to contain inflationary pressures, tightened their financial policies by postponing public investment projects and slowing credit expansion. Nevertheless, domestic inflation continued to increase and, with the fixed exchange rate, led to a deterioration in Korea's external competitiveness. The loss of competitiveness, compounded by slower market growth and greater protectionism abroad, caused export volumes to shrink.

In early 1980, the authorities further strengthened their adjustment effort by formulating a wide-ranging adjustment program which was supported by a one-year stand-by arrangement from the Fund (March 1980–February 1981). The main elements of the program were tight financial policies, a substantial depreciation of the currency, and a comprehensive energy policy designed to reduce Korea's dependence on imported oil. The authorities eased financial policies somewhat in mid-1980, when they were confronted with a pronounced fall in output and rising unemployment.

Fiscal Policy

The principal objectives of fiscal policy in 1979 were to reduce the public sector deficit and minimize its monetary impact. The public sector deficit fell in relation to GNP from 2.5 percent in 1978 to 1.4 percent in 1979. A large share of the adjustment fell on the public enterprise funds whose investment outlays and operating deficits had accounted for a large share of the public sector deficit.

The overall public sector deficit rose to 3.2 percent in 1980, largely reflecting the impact of the economic downturn. The Government adhered to a tight spending policy in the first half of 1980. The devaluation and the oil price increases resulted in some additional outlays, but they were offset by cutbacks in other expenditures. In the second half of 1980, however, the Government accelerated its spending to counteract the downturn in economic activity. In line with a policy of selectively stimulating domestic demand, the Government introduced a supplementary budget that provided for increased assistance to low-income households, implementation of a number of investment projects that had been postponed, and higher public sector wages.

Monetary Policy

The authorities tightened credit policy in 1979 in order to offset the impact of the oil price shock (which was passed through to domestic oil prices) on other domestic prices and the balance of payments. The

Government reduced its debt with the banking system and restrained the expansion of bank credit to the private sector by lowering credit ceilings for each bank. As a result, the rate of growth of bank credit declined from 45 percent in 1978 to 36 percent in 1979. The rate of growth of broad money decelerated even faster than credit—from 35 percent to 25 percent—reflecting a substantial decline in net foreign assets. Broad money in real terms rose by only 3 percent, and velocity increased. The rise in velocity was partly attributable to a decline in real interest rates that took place because domestic inflation rose, while nominal rates remained fixed at the level of June 1978.

The authorities maintained tight credit policy through mid-1980. However, in the face of a severe economic recession, they relaxed credit policy in the latter half of 1980. Net bank credit to the Government increased substantially to finance fiscal expenditures, and the expansion of bank credit to the private sector accelerated. The rate of growth of domestic credit rose from 37 percent (seasonally adjusted annual rate) in the first half of the year to 44 percent in the second half. Nevertheless, given the surge in inflation induced by the rise in energy prices and the devaluation of the won, credit conditions remained tight and contributed to the slowdown of domestic demand and the decline in output.

The growth of broad money accelerated to 27 percent in 1980, but the real stock of money declined by almost 6 percent. The contraction in real money balances during 1980 can be attributed largely to the behavior of real income (which fell sharply during this period) and to the sizable decline in the real yield of bank deposits. Net foreign assets of the banking system fell further, by the equivalent of 8 percent of broad money as the commercial banks increased sharply their short-term foreign liabilities.

Interest rates in the domestic banking system were initially raised in January 1980 (by 4–6 percentage points), but subsequently were reduced by an equivalent amount in order to shore up the financial position of the business sector. The interest rate reduction, together with an acceleration of consumer price inflation, sharply lowered real interest rates (relative to the rate of increase in consumer prices over the previous year). For example, the real interest rate on one-year time deposits fell from near zero in 1979 to negative 14 percent in the last quarter of 1980.

Exchange Rate Policy

During 1979 the authorities continued to peg the won to the U.S. dollar. This exchange rate regime, which had been in effect since December 1974, resulted in a loss of external competitiveness. During 1975–78, the effective exchange rate depreciated by 15 percent, in line with the movements of the dollar, but appreciated by 13 percent in real terms because prices rose faster in Korea than in its partner countries. In

1979 the divergence in price developments was compounded by a substantial appreciation of the dollar. As a result, the real effective exchange rate further appreciated by 18 percent.

In order to restore external competitiveness, the authorities devalued the won by 17 percent in January 1980 and simultaneously introduced a more flexible exchange rate regime. Under the new regime, the exchange rate of the won vis-à-vis the U.S. dollar was to be determined on the basis of movements of a currency basket and other factors affecting Korea's external position. Because of a surge in inflation, the won depreciated by only 8 percent in real effective terms in the first quarter of 1980. During the course of the year, the won declined further in relation to the U.S. dollar. Between the first and fourth quarters of 1980, the effective value of the won declined by 18 percent in nominal terms and by 7 percent in real terms.

Energy Policy

The main structural problem facing the Korean authorities in this period was the dependence on petroleum, which was Korea's major source of energy. In 1979 oil accounted for 63 percent of domestic energy consumption, coal for 27 percent, and firewood for 7 percent. All the oil consumed in Korea and about 10 percent of coal consumed were imported.

The authorities reacted to the rise in world oil prices during 1979–80 by taking prompt action to encourage energy conservation. The Government raised domestic energy prices in lockstep with increases in world oil prices and changes in the exchange rate. Domestic oil prices were raised by about 230 percent during 1979–80, electricity rates by 110 percent, and coal prices by 80 percent. Restrictions were set on energy use, both household and in the industrial and public sector. Reflecting these and other measures and the economic recession, domestic consumption of petroleum products actually fell by 1 percent in 1980, after rising by around 13 percent a year in the previous decade. Also, a long-term energy program was adopted with the objective of cutting the share of oil in energy consumption to 42 percent by 1991.

Economic Developments

The period 1979–80 was characterized by a severe weakening of economic activity. The growth of real GNP slowed from over 10 percent a year during 1977–78 to 6.5 percent in 1979 largely because of a decline in exports. In 1980 exports recovered somewhat, but agricultural output dropped precipitously, and domestic demand contracted sharply because of a steep decline in the terms of trade, the poor harvest, and tight financial policies. Domestic output fell for the first time in modern

Korean history. Adding the loss of income associated with a sizable increase in interest payments abroad, real GNP declined by over 5 percent.

The rate of increase in consumer prices rose from 16 percent in 1978 to 21 percent in 1979, reaching 35 percent in 1980. The two main factors affecting price developments were the oil price increases of 1979-80 and the depreciation of the won in 1980.

Korea's external current account deficit rose from $1.1 billion (2.2 percent of GNP) in 1978 to $4.2 billion in 1979 (6.4 percent of GNP). Although the volume of merchandise exports fell by 1 percent, export receipts increased by 16 percent because of price increases. Since 1977, export growth had weakened markedly, reflecting a gradual erosion of external competitiveness, as well as a deceleration of the growth of export markets and intensified protectionism. Furthermore, investment policies during this period had neglected the traditional light industries, making it difficult for these industries to face increased competition from other developing countries. Demand for imports decelerated throughout the year as restrictive financial policies took hold. Nevertheless, the value of non-oil imports rose by about 27 percent, reflecting equal increases in volume and prices. The oil import bill rose by 45 percent, owing almost entirely to price increases, and reached $3.1 billion (equivalent to 16 percent of total imports). The external terms of trade remained relatively stable.

With a sharp deterioration in the external terms of trade in 1980, the current account deficit widened to $5.3 billion (8.7 percent of GNP). Although the volume of exports rose by 12 percent, export receipts rose only slightly faster than in 1979 (17 percent), because the rate of increase in export prices decelerated from 17 percent to 5 percent. Owing to restrictive demand management policies, the volume of non-oil imports contracted by about 16 percent and offset an increase in prices of about equal magnitude. However, the oil import bill rose by over 80 percent to $5.6 billion, owing entirely to a doubling of oil prices. The volume of oil imports, responding to policy measures and to the economic downturn, rose by less than 1 percent.

The widening of the current account deficit was accompanied by a sharp increase in external borrowing during 1979-80. Net capital inflows (of which a minimal part were direct investment inflows) rose from $2.1 billion in 1978 to $5.3 billion in 1979 and to $6 billion in 1980. In particular, net short-term inflows jumped from a negligible amount in 1978 to over $2 billion in 1979 and $4 billion in 1980 (Table 2). As a result, Korea's external debt rose by 80 percent during 1979-80 to almost $27 billion (42 percent of GNP), and the maturity structure of the debt shortened significantly.

Table 2. Korea: External Debt, 1979–84[1]

	1979	1980	1981	1982	1983	1984
	(In millions of U.S. dollars)					
Total external debt (end period)	20,410	27,315	32,480	37,120	40,215	42,559
Medium- and long-term	14,954	17,939	22,253	24,693	28,100	31,134
Of which: use of Fund credit	138	713	1,246	1,259	1,354	1,570
Short-term	5,456	9,376	10,227	12,427	12,115	11,425
Of which: trade-related[2]	3,839	6,573	7,717	8,824	9,438	8,273
Debt service payments	**3,271**	**4,449**	**5,475**	**5,821**	**5,720**	**6,757**
Principal, on medium- and long-term debt[3]	1,917	1,840	1,999	2,201	2,533	3,013
Interest, including on short-term debt	1,354	2,609	3,476	3,620	3,187	3,744
	(In percent)					
Growth rate of external debt	37.6	33.8	18.9	14.3	8.3	5.8
External debt (in percent of GNP)	32.7	44.6	48.4	52.4	53.6	52.5
Debt service ratio (in percent of exports and goods and services)[3]	16.9	19.7	20.1	20.6	18.8	20.1
Share of short-term in total debt	26.7	34.3	31.5	33.5	30.0	26.5
Ratio of gross international reserves to short-term debt	108.5	73.2	70.4	57.9	61.8	72.0
Ratio of trade-related debt to imports	20.1	30.5	31.8	37.6	40.9	30.2

Sources: Korean authorities; and Fund staff estimates.
[1] Incorporates merchant banks and reclassification of interoffice accounts of branches of foreign banks. Excludes foreign borrowings of Korean branches and subsidiaries residing abroad; such borrowing amounted to $6 billion at the end of 1984.
[2] Trade credits, oil bill, and refinance.
[3] Excludes rollover on interoffice bank accounts.

Situation at End of 1980

At the end of 1980, the Government faced difficult economic problems: an unsustainable external imbalance, rapidly rising external debt, a weak economy, and entrenched inflationary expectations. The external environment contained distinctly adverse elements: high and rising interest rates, weak demand, and intensifying protectionism. However, the policy actions taken during 1979–80 favorably positioned Korea to launch a successful stabilization effort. In particular, the adjustment of domestic oil prices to the new level of international prices had been accomplished and external competitiveness had been restored. Financial restraint, although contributing to the weakness of the economy, had helped to contain inflationary pressures and reversed the gap between increases in real wages and gains in productivity. Therefore, the situation at the end of 1980 presented important policy achievements, which were to be of great value in the period ahead as the authorities moved to close Korea's external imbalance and restore growth and price stability.

III. The Years of Recovery (1981–82)

At the outset of 1981, the economic environment was characterized by relatively high unemployment, high levels of inventories, and excess capacity. The Government continued with its adjustment effort during 1981–82, but relaxed financial policies to counter the severe economic recession. Economic conditions improved significantly during this period as output rose by an annual average of about 6 percent, while the rate of inflation fell gradually to below 4 percent of GNP. Nevertheless, the adjustment process was by no means completed by the end of 1982. The economy still operated well below full capacity and the external financing requirements remained large—a particularly serious problem in light of the emerging international debt crisis.

Policies

The adjustment program for 1981–82 was designed to restore economic growth, while reducing domestic inflation and the external imbalance. This program continued to be supported with a stand-by arrangement with the Fund (March 1981–February 1982) and a structural adjustment loan from the World Bank. The authorities adopted a more stimulative financial policy to revive the economy. The public sector deficit rose to over 4 percent of GNP, while domestic credit expansion slowed only moderately despite a sharp decline in inflation. Exchange rate policy was managed flexibly, although the real effective exchange rate appreciated somewhat and contributed to a weakening of exports. The Government's structural policies focused on the public investment program, tax reform, and trade liberalization.

Fiscal Policy

Fiscal policy was used to stimulate aggregate demand in 1981. The budgetary impulse became expansionary as public sector expenditures were raised and taxes cut. Largely as a result of expenditure increases, the consolidated public sector deficit rose from 3.2 percent of GNP in 1980 to 4.6 percent in 1981. Increased expenditures resulted from higher central government spending, greater purchases of rice by the Grain Management Fund to replenish stocks used after the 1980 crop failure, and extraordinarily large capital outlays in telecommunications.

Expenditure policy focused initially on increasing the tempo of public spending on rural projects so as to cushion the loss in agricultural incomes. The structure of expenditure shifted toward public capital formation and housing, and much of the fiscal stimulus was provided through net lending operations. Several temporary tax changes reinforced these expenditure measures. The larger overall deficit in 1981 resulted in significant increases in both foreign and domestic financing. The ratio of domestic financing to GNP rose from 2.3 percent in 1980 to 3.4 percent in 1981, largely reflecting an increase in bank financing.

With the strengthening of the economy in 1982, fiscal policy was reined in so as to help correct the external imbalance and improve the price performance. Faced with large shortfalls in revenues, central government expenditure was cut to a level below the budgetary target—a step which was instrumental in reducing the public sector deficit to 4.3 percent of GNP.

Monetary Policy

The objective of monetary policy in 1981 was to support economic growth while securing a reduction in inflation and further external adjustment. Monetary policy accommodated increased bank borrowing by the public sector, which was associated with the stimulative stance of fiscal policy. Nevertheless, overall credit was sufficiently tight to help bring about a further reduction in domestically generated inflation and a decline in the current account deficit. The growth of domestic credit decelerated from 41 percent in 1980 to 31 percent in 1981. Credit to the public sector accounted for 19 percent of the overall increase in domestic credit, compared with 8 percent in 1980. With a substantial decline in net foreign assets, the growth of broad money slowed from 27 percent to 25 percent. However, as the rate of inflation fell sharply, the real stock of broad money rose by 12 percent in 1981, compared with a decline of 6 percent in 1980.

Monetary conditions in 1982 were dominated by a financial scandal in the unorganized money market (the curb market) in May, which forced two large corporations into default and threatened other firms with insolvency. Dishonored checks rose sharply; their value during May reached almost 8 percent of demand deposits. Confidence in nonbank financial intermediaries was shaken and the public withdrew large amounts of funds from nonbank financial markets. As a result, the ratio of bank deposits to currency rose by 11 percent in May 1982. Lending activities in nonbank markets were curtailed, creating severe liquidity problems for enterprises that depended heavily on these sources of finance.

To offset the contraction in nonbank lending and to avoid a generalized financial crisis, the Bank of Korea permitted a rapid expansion of bank credit and supported this expansion by sharply increasing reserve money. As the turmoil in financial markets subsided in the fourth quarter of 1982, expansion of domestic credit slowed to an annual rate of 18 percent (Table 3).

The reduced borrowing requirements of the public sector in 1982 considerably eased the burden of reserve money management. About 50 percent of the credit needs of the public sector was satisfied by the Bank of Korea in 1982, compared with about 85 percent in 1981. Credit to the private sector in 1982 grew at virtually the same rate as in 1981 (about 25 percent). For 1982 alone, broad money rose by 27 percent—slightly faster than the average rate of expansion for the period 1980–81.

Bank interest rates, which are under government control, were reduced during 1981–82, but these reductions were held to less than the decline in inflation so that real interest rates would become positive. After the sharp drop in inflation in 1981, real interest rates turned positive in the fourth quarter of 1981 and remained positive throughout 1982, averaging about 3 percent.

The monetary authorities, in early 1982, changed the instruments by which they conduct monetary policy. The Bank of Korea replaced direct credit control exercised through ceilings on individual banks with indirect control exercised through the instruments of reserve requirements, open market operations, and the rediscount mechanism. The system of preferential lending rates of commercial banks was eliminated in June 1982, and the rediscount rates of the Bank of Korea were unified.

Exchange Rate Policy

The authorities pursued a flexible exchange rate policy during 1981–82 to preserve the external competitiveness of Korean producers. The effective exchange rate remained relatively stable as the won was allowed to depreciate by about 13 percent against the U.S. dollar. However, because domestic inflation exceeded foreign inflation, the real effective exchange rate appreciated by about 6 percent, contributing to the weak performance of exports in 1982.

Structural Policies

During 1981–82, structural policies were aimed at increasing the productivity and efficiency of the economy. These policies encompassed public sector investment, a comprehensive tax reform, and trade liberalization. The investment program was designed to support an increasingly urban and industrial economy. An important objective of the investment plan was to reduce dependency on imported petroleum by expanding domestic coal production and constructing electricity-generating plants powered by coal, liquefied natural gas, and nuclear fuel. To reinforce energy conservation, the Government passed through to domestic consumers only 30 percent of the $5 per barrel reduction in world oil prices in 1982. About 40 percent of the savings from the decline

Table 3. Korea: Selected Monetary Aggregates, 1982
(Percentage change)[1]

	March	June	September	December
Domestic credit	21.0	31.6	30.0	18.1
Broad money	27.5	41.0	38.3	4.2
Reserve money[2]	−1.2	2.9	45.4	−5.8

[1] Quarterly change at seasonally adjusted annual rates.
[2] Adjusted for increase in reserve requirements.

in world oil prices was earmarked for a special multipurpose fund to finance projects primarily in the energy sector. The remainder of the savings was absorbed by an import duty. Because basic needs for clothing and food had been largely met, housing became the centerpiece of the Government's social development efforts. Housing construction was promoted by a combination of financial incentives to private investors and direct public sector investment.

Significant reforms of the tax system were introduced in 1981 as part of the overall policy of structural adjustment. These reforms included an increase in the separate tax for interest and dividend income, a simplification of the corporate tax structure, and an extension of the value-added tax. The 1982 tax changes were more sweeping and were aimed at both making the system more neutral with respect to resource allocation and increasing the tax effort. The new tax measures changed the tax status of corporations, modified certain deductions and tax incentives to favor small- and medium-size firms, introduced tax credits to promote development of technology, reduced the number of industries that received tax advantages, and introduced a minimum tax on public corporations.

With the improved economic situation during 1981–82, the import liberalization drive was resumed following its lapse during the previous two years. This drive was aimed at improving the structure of industry by enhancing competition, stabilizing prices by increasing supplies, and facilitating trade negotiations with trading partners which restricted imports from Korea. At the same time, to avoid major disruptions in domestic production, selective use was made of import tariffs. Import restrictions were lifted on a large number of items during 1981–82, raising the ratio of unrestricted imports to total from 69 percent to 77 percent.

Economic Developments

Economic growth resumed in 1981, as real GNP rose by 6 percent. The recovery of agriculture and rapid expansion of exports dominated developments in aggregate output during 1981. Following the disastrous harvest of 1980, agricultural production rose by 22 percent in 1981, returning to the 1979 level. The volume of exports rose by 17 percent in response to both the devaluation of the won in 1980 and buoyant foreign markets. Domestic demand revived on the basis of an upturn in consumption and stimulative financial policies, but accounted for only one third of the overall growth in aggregate demand. Investment remained weak.

During 1982, external demand weakened considerably as traditional export industries—textiles, shoes, wood, paper—suffered under the impact of the global recession and restrictive trade policies in the industrial countries, as well as some loss of external competitiveness. Nevertheless, the growth of real GNP remained at about 6 percent, as domestic demand continued to expand in response to stimulative financial policies. Consumption continued to rise by about 4 percent in real terms, as an acceleration in public consumption offset a slowdown in private consumption. With the return of agricultural output to normal levels, food grain imports were drastically reduced. The volume of non-oil imports rose by 6 percent, while the volume of oil imports declined by 1 percent, reflecting continued success of energy conservation policies.

Domestic inflation fell from a peak of 35 percent in 1980, to 12 percent in 1981, and 5 percent in 1982. The principal reasons for this fall were lower inflation abroad and a stable effective exchange rate. Prudent demand management, improved food supplies, wage moderation, and productivity gains also contributed to lower inflation. Price controls were eliminated in 1981 and replaced by a price monitoring system under which selected enterprises are required to report price increases to the Government.

The unemployment rate fell slightly in 1982, reflecting a more rapid expansion of nonagricultural output and a rise in domestic investment; manufacturing employment rose significantly.

The external position improved steadily during 1981–82. The current account deficit decline to $4.6 billion (6.9 percent of GNP) in 1981, as the vigorous expansion of exports (20 percent) more than offset the increase in imports (12 percent), the continued growth in interest payments, and a small deterioration in the external terms of trade. The moderate growth of imports represented a significant adjustment effort in view of the exceptionally large rice imports (equivalent to 1 percent of GNP) that were necessitated by the 1980 crop failure. In 1982 the current account deficit was almost halved to $2.6 billion (3.7 percent of GNP), despite stagnating exports. The main factors contributing to the improvement in the current account were a sharp decline in import prices (8 percent) and a further slowing of the volume growth of imports. The narrowing of the current account imbalance during

1981–82 reflected a gradual decline in the ratio of gross domestic investment to GNP. The ratio of gross national savings to GNP remained relatively stable.

With the gradual decline in external financing requirements, the growth in Korea's external debt, which had averaged about 35 percent a year during 1979–80, slowed to about 16 percent during 1981–82. Nevertheless, outstanding external debt rose by close to $10 billion, reaching $37 billion (52 percent of GNP) at the end of 1982; the associated debt service ratio rose from 20 percent to 21 percent. Short-term debt rose by 15 percent a year during 1980–82; its share in total debt remained at around 34 percent.

Situation at End of 1982

By the end of 1982, the Korean economy had made substantial headway in overcoming the economic crisis of 1980. The progress in reducing the rate of inflation and the current account deficit was particularly noteworthy. Korea's growth outcome of about 6 percent a year was satisfactory in comparison with the growth rates in other developing countries, but fell well below Korea's historical performance. The gradual weakening of the export sector was of particular concern in view of Korea's large external debt and the emerging crisis in the international capital market.

Notwithstanding the significant reduction in the current account deficit, Korea's borrowing during 1980–82 was substantial. Although Korea's debt-servicing obligations remained consistent with its capacity to earn foreign exchange, the level of its outstanding debt was high in an international context. Commercial banks became increasingly reluctant to raise their exposure limits, mainly because of the fallout from the financial crisis in Latin America as well as in Asia. In this environment, the high level of short-term debt, particularly in relation to international reserves, became an increasing source of concern.

IV. The Years of Adjustment (1983–84)

In early 1983, the Korean authorities stepped up their efforts to reduce the external imbalance by formulating an adjustment program which was supported by a stand-by arrangement with the Fund.[1] The program sought to reduce gradually the current account deficit during 1983–84 to 2.5 percent of GNP, while raising the growth of output to

---

[1] A stand-by arrangement in an amount of SDR 576 million was approved on July 9, 1983 for the period through March 31, 1985. The structural elements of the program also were supported by a second structural adjustment loan from the World Bank in the amount of $300 million.

7.5 percent a year and containing inflation to 5 percent. The program envisaged a sharp deceleration of the growth of external debt and a substantial improvement in its maturity structure. These objectives represented a significant departure from the development strategy pursued in the 1960s and 1970s, which had aimed at maximizing growth through substantial recourse to inflationary finance and external borrowing.

The actual performance of the economy during 1983–84 surpassed initial targets: the current account deficit fell to below 2 percent of GNP, while output rose by an annual average of over 8 percent and inflation was held to about 2 percent. With the improvement in the external position, foreign borrowing decelerated sharply and the maturity structure of external debt was lengthened significantly. Although a recovery in export markets and stable foreign prices contributed to this favorable outcome, the authorities deserve much of the credit. They implemented a strong adjustment program consisting of strict financial discipline, which sharply reduced the public sector deficit and the rate of monetary expansion, and a flexible exchange rate policy, which improved external competitiveness.

Policies

The major elements of the adjustment program for 1983–84 were a sharp reduction in both the public sector deficit and the rate of credit expansion and a real depreciation of the currency. The public sector deficit declined from about 4.5 percent of GNP during 1981–82 to 1.5 percent during 1983–84, while the rate of credit expansion was cut by more than half to about 13 percent. The effective exchange rate depreciated by about 7 percent in real terms during 1983 and remained stable subsequently. Structural policies continued to focus on trade liberalization and financial sector reform.

Fiscal Policy

Fiscal policy was tightened considerably in 1983. The public sector deficit declined from 4.3 percent of GNP in 1982 to 1.6 percent in 1983, a level markedly below the initial target.[2] While cyclical factors contributed to the improvement in the fiscal position, particularly on the revenue side, the major portion of fiscal adjustment was associated with discretionary measures. Higher indirect taxes were supplemented with a newly imposed 5 percent tariff on imported oil, resulting in an increase of 1.3 percentage points in the ratio of revenues to GNP. Expenditure measures accounted for slightly more than half of the fiscal adjustment.

---

[2] A comparison of the fiscal outcome for 1982 and 1983 must take into account the removal of the Civil Servants' Pension Fund and Special Account in 1983, which lowered both revenues and expenditures by close to 1 percent of GNP, without altering the deficit.

The ratio of central government expenditures to GNP declined by 0.7 percentage point, mainly because of a cut in capital outlays. Current expenditures on health, education, and public services rose broadly in line with GNP. The resulting shift in the composition of expenditure was in accordance with the fifth Five-Year Plan's objective of concentrating the development effort during 1982–86 on social infrastructure. The improved fiscal position in 1983 reduced the Government's recourse to all sources of financing. The public sector made net repayments to the banking system for the first time since 1979, while borrowings from both domestic nonbank and external sources were cut substantially.

With the substantial improvement in the public sector position in 1983, there was limited scope for further fiscal adjustment. Accordingly, the fiscal policy stance remained broadly unchanged in 1984: the ratio of the public sector deficit to GNP declined only slightly to 1.4 percent. The share of total revenues in GNP rose marginally to 20 percent. Aggregate expenditures rose in line with nominal GNP. The rise in current outlays of the Central Government was constrained, in part, by a freeze on wages and salaries of the public sector. The increase in government expenditure also was modest, although expenditure on public housing was stepped up somewhat in the face of an easing of private construction demand. The pattern of financing of the public sector deficit remained broadly unchanged, with the Government continuing to record a small surplus with the banking system and to rely on domestic nonbank and external sources of finance.

Monetary Policy

Monetary policy was tightened substantially during 1983–84. The implementation of monetary policy was hindered by two financial incidents, both in 1983, which forced the Bank of Korea to step in as lender of last resort and rescue the affected banks. The authorities successfully sterilized the monetary impact of these rescue operations by tightening rediscount policy and issuing additional stabilization bonds. The growth of domestic credit decelerated from 25 percent in 1982, to 16 percent in 1983, and 13 percent in 1984. With the lower level of domestic inflation, the deceleration in real credit was less pronounced (from 19 percent in 1982, to 14 percent in 1983, and 10 percent in 1984). Because the public sector recorded a surplus with the banking system in both years, there was adequate room for extending credit to the private sector to support growth without jeopardizing external or inflation objectives. Pressures on bank credit were also eased by measures designed to encourage firms to liquidate their speculative holdings of real estate and to increase their direct financing from the nonbank private sector. With the abolishment of credit ceilings in 1982, the authorities relied mainly on the control of reserve money for monetary management during 1983–84.

Monetary expansion, which had hovered around 26 percent throughout the previous three years, was reduced to 15 percent in 1983 and 11 percent in 1984. In real terms, broad money rose by 13 percent in 1983 and 8 percent in 1984. As a result, the velocity of broad money fell by about 6 percent in 1983 and subsequently remained relatively stable. The 1983 decline was associated with the continued progress made on the price front, which further reduced the public's inflationary expectations.

In order to enhance the role of market forces in the determination of interest rates, the authorities introduced, in January 1984, a narrow band for bank lending rates (10–10.5 percent), which permitted banks to charge different rates according to borrowers' creditworthiness. Also, a new term structure for deposit rates was established (ranging up to 9 percent for one-year deposits) to encourage a shift of financial savings into longer-term deposits. Long-term deposit rates and the upper limit of the bank on lending rates were further increased by 1 percentage point in November. Notwithstanding the rise in bank interest rates, the gap between these rates and those prevailing in the nonbank financial sector remained large. The high level of interest rates in the nonbank sector was partly attributable to inflationary expectations; after 20 years of relatively high inflation, the public was understandably slow in adjusting its expectations downward. With continued price stability, inflationary expectations gradually dissipated, and interest rates in the nonbank sector began to decline.

The Government took advantage of the favorable economic developments and, in April 1985, further widened the band on bank lending rates by increasing the maximum rate on term lending by 2 percentage points to 13.5 percent. In addition, two new deposit schemes were introduced which offered attractive interest rates (12–13 percent) to household savers.[3] Interest rates during this period were significantly higher than the rate of inflation. They remained below the rates prevailing in the nonbank financial sector, but the differential narrowed.

External Policies

External policies during 1983–84 were designed to further reduce reliance on foreign debt as well as to lengthen the maturity structure of such debt. The exchange rate policy was managed flexibly so as to improve external competitiveness and facilitate the recovery of exports. Both the nominal and real effective exchange rates depreciated by about 7 percent during 1983 and remained stable during 1984. There was a

---

[3] These schemes include a savings deposit with an annual yield of 12 percent for six-month deposits of less than W 30 million and a household installment account for three-year deposits of less than W 10 million (approximately $11,500).

substantial divergence, however, between movements in competitiveness vis-á-vis the United States and the other industrial countries, reflecting the sharp appreciation of the U.S. dollar against other major currencies.

An important element of the adjustment program during 1983–84 was the improvement in the maturity structure of external debt. While the overall level of Korea's debt had remained consistent with its debt-servicing capacity, the increase in short-term debt during 1979–82 had become a source of increasing concern. A large portion of short-term debt was trade related, but its sharp increases since 1979 in relation to both total debt and to international reserves had rendered Korea vulnerable to shifts in market sentiment.

To correct the situation, the authorities restricted their external borrowings during 1983–84 to only medium- and long-term maturities and took a number of measures to reduce short-term borrowing by the private sector.

Structural Policies

During 1983–84, the authorities accelerated their efforts to liberalize the trade system and introduced a number of important measures to reform the financial system. Trade liberalization efforts took place despite an adverse trade climate in export markets. Early in 1984, the Government announced its intention of following a five-year plan of import liberalization. Under this plan, the import liberalization ratio was raised to 85 percent in 1984, and it is expected to rise, by 1988, to 95 percent—the level presently prevailing in the industrial countries.

The Government also announced a five-year program of tariff reform. Under this program, the average (unweighted) tariff rate was reduced from 22 percent in 1984 to 21 percent in 1985, and it is expected to decline further to 18 percent by 1988. In addition to the reduction in the average tariff rate, the dispersion in the rates is also to be substantially narrowed.

In the area of financial sector reform, the Government initiated a long-term program of liberalization, an essential element of which was the gradual relaxation of interest rate ceilings. During 1984 and early 1985, the Government took the initiative to promote domestic savings by encouraging the introduction of a number of financial instruments. In addition, important institutional reforms were implemented to enhance competition within the financial sector and reduce the role of the Government in credit allocation. In early 1983, the Government divested itself of all nationwide commercial banks. Also, certain amendments to the General Banking Act were made so as to promote the managerial autonomy of banks and to increase their public accountability. Commercial banks were also authorized to undertake new activities to improve their profitability and their competitive position with the nonbank sector. To spur competition, two new nationwide banks, which are joint ventures with foreign banks, and numerous nonbank financial institutions were established. In addition, large security companies were allowed to participate in some money market activities that had previously been limited to commercial banks.

Consistent with the government policy of easing restrictions on foreign banks, these banks were granted access to the rediscount window of the Bank of Korea on the same terms available to local banks. Effective July 1985, the branches of foreign banks were also given permission to engage in trust business.

Economic Developments

By any conventional standard, Korea's economic performance during 1983–84 was outstanding. In 1983 output expanded by 9.5 percent, reminiscent of the growth experienced during the 1960s and 1970s. Economic growth decelerated in 1984, but the recorded rate of 7.6 percent was still unmatched by all except a few countries. Consumer prices rose by a mere 2 percent in both 1983 and 1984, while the current account deficit fell from 3.7 percent of GNP in 1982, to 2.1 percent in 1983, and 1.7 percent in 1984.

The rapid growth in 1983 was propelled by a rebound in manufacturing and the continued construction boom. Real gross investment increased by 14 percent, or nearly triple the pace of 1982, while the growth in real consumption nearly doubled to 7 percent. Real exports of goods and services increased by 14 percent, or more than twice as fast as in 1982. While both external and domestic demand contributed to the economic recovery in 1983, a comparison of developments in the first and second half of the year reveals a striking shift in the pattern of growth: the stimulus provided by domestic demand, which was the main expansionary force during 1982 and early 1983, gradually diminished as a result of tight financial policies and was replaced by foreign demand. The dampening of domestic demand and the recovery of foreign demand returned the Korean economy to its traditional pattern of export-led growth. Import growth was also very high (13 percent in volume terms), reflecting the rapid expansion of exports, investment, and economic activity in general.

The strong, albeit slower, growth of output in 1984 was supported by a buoyant manufacturing sector. Manufacturing output rose by 15 percent, and the real investment in machinery and equipment rose by 12 percent. Consequently, the growth of real gross investment decelerated only slightly (12 percent), despite a weakening in private construction that resulted from tight financial policies and measures to discourage speculation in real estate. The growth of domestic consumption also slowed slightly but, with a concomitant slowdown in imports, the contribution of domestic demand (for domestic products) to GNP growth remained high (about 4.7 percentage points). The contribution of real exports, on the other hand, fell, as export growth decelerated to 8 percent in real terms.

The rate of domestic inflation dropped further to 2 percent in 1983 and remained at this level during 1984. Appropriate demand management, stable prices of traded goods, plentiful supply of agricultural products, and moderate wage increases contributed to this favorable price development.

The current account deficit declined from $2.6 billion (3.7 percent of GNP) in 1982, to $1.6 billion (2.1 percent) in 1983, and $1.4 billion (1.7 percent) in 1984. With the recovery of export markets and improved external competitiveness, exports resumed their rapid growth, although at a slower pace than that observed during the 1970s. The volume of exports rose by 17 percent in 1983 and 15 percent in 1984. The slowdown of exports in 1984 reflected both the weak oil market that adversely affected exports to the Middle East and the rising protectionism against Korean exports in several markets. The composition of export markets during this period shifted in favor of the North American market, reflecting the strength of the recovery in the United States and Canada and the improvement in Korea's competitiveness vis-à-vis those countries. Imports also grew rapidly during this period because of the rapid expansion of exports, investment, and economic activity in general.

The improvement in the current account position during 1983–84 was associated with higher domestic savings—the ratio of national savings to GNP rose by 5 percentage points to over 28 percent, while the ratio of domestic investment to GNP rose by 3 percentage points to nearly 30 percent. The rise in the savings rate was attributable to both cyclical and more permanent factors. Following the recession of 1980, the savings rate plummeted from over 28 percent to below 22 percent, as the public apparently regarded the decline in its income as a transitory phenomenon and did not adjust its standard of living. During the subsequent economic recovery, the savings rate rose gradually and, by 1984, returned to the level prevailing in 1979. A contributing factor to the recovery of the savings rate was the reduction in domestic inflation and the emergence of high positive interest rates. The ratio of gross domestic investment to GNP also rose during 1983–84, but remained well below the peak levels of the late 1970s.

With the reduced current account deficit, Korea's external financing requirements fell sharply during 1983–84. The overall payments position strengthened. Gross international reserves rose by $0.5 billion and at the end of 1982 stood at $8.2 billion, or equivalent to 2.8 months of imports. The growth of external debt, which had decelerated continuously from 36 percent during 1979–80 to 16 percent during 1981–82, slowed further to 8 percent during 1983–84. Outstanding debt stood at $43.1 billion at the end of 1984. Notwithstanding the relatively high level of debt relative to GNP (53 percent), the debt service ratio remained moderate (20 percent).

In line with the Government's policy of restructuring the maturity profile of external debt, the level of short-term debt, which had increased by $9 billion during 1979–82, declined by $1 billion during 1983–84. Consequently, the ratio of short-term debt to total debt declined from over 34 percent at the end of 1982 to 26 percent at the end of 1984. With the concomitant increase in international reserves during this period, the ratio of reserves to short-term debt rose from 58 percent to 72 percent. These developments improved significantly the maturity structure of Korea's debt and bolstered its position in international capital markets.

V. Overview

This paper has described the severe economic crisis that Korea faced at the turn of this decade, and the highly successful adjustment effort undertaken by the Government in the subsequent years. The authorities introduced an adjustment program, which was supported by two one-year stand-by arrangements with the Fund (March 1980–February 1982). The main elements of the program were a substantial depreciation of the currency, tight financial policies, and adjustment of administered prices, particularly of energy. These policies were effective in sharply reducing the volume of imports and increasing the volume of exports in 1980. However, the favorable impact of these developments was overshadowed by severe external and domestic shocks, including further increases in oil prices, the hike in international interest rates, the worldwide recession, a disastrous harvest, and domestic political disturbances. Output, which had risen by an annual average of 10 percent during the 1960s and 1970s, actually fell by 5 percent, while inflation soared to 35 percent, and the current account deficit rose to a peak of nearly 9 percent of GNP.

Economic policies for 1981–82 were designed to revive economic growth, while reducing domestic inflation and the current account imbalance. Financial policies were relaxed to counter the severe domestic recession. The growth of exports accelerated during 1981 in response to improved competitiveness and, together with a recovery of agriculture and a fiscal stimulus, led to a resumption of growth. However, with the deepening of global recession in 1982 and a deterioration in external competitiveness, export performance weakened considerably. Output growth was sustained on the strength of domestic demand, but the economy continued to operate well below full capacity. At the same time, the rate of inflation was reduced gradually to 5 percent, while the current account deficit was more than halved to below 4 percent of GNP. The improved price and external performance, however, reflected mainly a sharp decline in import prices, and Korea still faced difficult problems by the end of 1982. The weak export performance was a major source of concern in view of Korea's large external debt and the emerging international debt crisis. A related problem was the short maturity structure of Korea's debt, which had increased the country's vulnerability to shifts in market sentiment.

With the resumption of growth, the focus of the adjustment program for 1983–84, which was supported by a stand-by arrangement with the Fund (July 1983–March 1985), shifted to achieving price stability and further reducing reliance on foreign borrowing. This reorientation of program objectives represented a significant departure from Korea's traditional development strategy, which had aimed at maximizing growth through substantial recourse to inflationary finance and external borrowing. The financial policies implemented during this period consisted of strict financial discipline, which sharply reduced the public sector deficit and the rate of monetary expansion, and a flexible exchange rate policy, which improved external competitiveness. The authorities also made considerable progress in liberalizing both the trade and the financial systems. These policies, together with a recovery in export markets and favorable foreign prices, led to a revival of export-led growth and a further improvement in domestic inflation and the external position. During 1983–84, output rose by an annual average of about 8 percent, inflation was contained to about 2 percent, and the current account deficit was reduced to below 2 percent of GNP. At the same time, the growth in external debt decelerated sharply and the maturity structure of debt was lengthened considerably.

Korea's impressive achievements in recent years have bolstered its standing in the international capital market. The country's outstanding level of external debt, although high in absolute terms, is consistent with its debt-servicing capacity: while Korea is the fourth largest debtor among developing countries, it ranks sixteenth in terms of its debt to exports ratio and fifteenth in terms of its debt-service ratio. Nevertheless, in view of the tight conditions in the international capital market, the Government is committed to pursuing strong adjustment policies so as to limit its recourse to external financing. The 1985–86 economic management plans, which were supported by a new stand-by arrangement with the Fund (July 1985–March 1987), aimed at consolidating the recent economic gains and effecting further external adjustment. The Government's policies met with great success. In 1986 real GNP rose by about 12 percent, inflation remained low, and the external current account swung into surplus. By adopting an export-led growth strategy, Korea has succeeded in exploiting its comparative advantage and overcoming the constraint imposed by the size of its domestic market. The rapid growth of Korean exports and imports over the last two decades has generated sizable benefits for both Korea and its trading partners. The Korean success story, however, should not obscure the fact that Korea is still a developing country with a relatively low level of income: its per capita income in 1986 was about $2,300, or about one third the per capita income in Singapore, and about one seventh that in Japan and the United States. The authorities are making an admirable effort to elevate Korea to the ranks of industrial nations. But the specter of protectionism casts a shadow over Korea's prospects for meeting its growth potential and its debt-servicing obligations. It would be unfortunate if the attainment of Korea's development objectives were to be obstructed by the imposition of trade barriers in its export markets. For their part, the Korean authorities are making commendable progress in liberalizing imports.

References

Bank of Korea, *National Accounts* (Bank of Korea: Seoul, 1984).

Cole, David C., and Yung Chul Park, "The Unregulated Financial Institution and Markets," Chap. 4 in *Financial Development in Korea, 1945-78* (Cambridge, Massachusetts: Harvard University Press, 1983).

International Monetary Fund, *International Financial Statistics* (Washington: International Monetary Fund, various years).

———, *World Economic Outlook, April 1985: A Survey by the Staff of the International Monetary Fund* (Washington: International Monetary Fund, April 1985).

Suh, Sang Mok, "The Pattern of Poverty," in *Human Resources and Social Development in Korea*, ed. by Chong Kee Park (Seoul: Korea Development Institute, 1980).

Comment

Sang Woo Nam

I. Introduction

The most distinctive features of Korea's economic policies in the 1980s are price stabilization and institutional reform in the interest of achieving higher economic efficiency. The paper by Aghevli and Márquez-Ruarte described Korean adjustment efforts in such an effective and balanced manner that I have few things to add or disagree with. I shall therefore mainly supplement the paper by trying to evaluate Korean macroeconomic policies in more quantitative terms. While focusing on stabilization efforts, I shall also try to identify the costs and beneficial consequences of Korea's anti-inflation policy. Finally, I will discuss some of the difficulties we have faced in pursuing structural policies.

II. Evaluation of Korea's Stabilization Efforts

Sources of Stability

While most people are impressed by the sharp decline in Korea's inflation rate during 1979–85, they do not necessarily agree on the major sources of price stability. The annual inflation rate in terms of the gross national product (GNP) deflator dropped from 23 percent during 1979–80 to about 3 percent during 1983–85. Although some observers have attributed most of this decrease to the favorable external environment, a breakdown by source shows that only one third of the deceleration was directly due to stable unit import prices, while almost half came from a slowdown in unit labor costs (Table 1).

Beneficial Effects of Stability

What good has the price stability done for the economy? Above all, stable domestic prices and wages kept the manufacturing unit labor cost in terms of the U.S. dollar unchanged during 1980–84, in sharp contrast to the average annual rise of 23 percent during 1976–79. This stability probably also contributed to the accompanying improvement in the bal-

**Table 1. Korea: Decomposition of Inflation by Source
(Contribution to Annual Average Increase in GNP Deflator)**
(In percent)

	1976-78	1979-80	1981-82	July 1982-June 1985
Cost approach				
Import cost	0.5	8.7	3.7	0.6
(Unit import price)	(0.1)	(6.2)	(0.4)	(−0.9)
(Exchange rate)	(0.4)	(2.5)	(3.3)	(1.5)
Unit labor cost	18.0	16.4	10.8	6.5
Demand pressure	0.7	−1.4	−0.6	0.6
Inflationary expectation and capital cost	−0.3	0.6	−1.4	−4.0
Others	0.5	−1.0	−1.1	−1.0
Actual inflation rate	**19.4**	**23.3**	**11.4**	**2.7**
Monetary approach				
Money supply (M1) relative to real GNP	18.7	16.2	14.9	13.2
Real interest rate	1.0	3.4	−6.0	4.4
Inflationary expectation	−0.5	0.4	−1.7	−9.2
Others	0.2	3.3	4.2	−5.7
(Institutional changes affecting demand for M1)			(5.6)	(−3.7)

Note: The decomposition in this table is based on the author's calculations.

ance of payments. Between 1980 and 1984, the annual current account balance improved by $3.9 billion, of which $1.3 billion was due to changes in the terms of trade. As these changes were wholly offset by increased interest payments on Korea's foreign debt, all the improvement in the current account balance came from the growth of real exports in excess of real imports.

Price stability has brought other desirable results as well. The domestic savings ratio increased from 22.4 percent in 1982 to 27.3 percent in 1984. The corporate capital structure is also much healthier: the average equity ratio of manufacturing firms rose to 22.6 percent in 1984 from 17.0 percent four years before. Income distribution also showed a considerable improvement over the 1976-82 period.[1] While these developments must have been the result of a variety of factors, price stability seems to have been a particularly critical one.

---

[1] The income share for the richest 20 percent of the population dropped from 45.3 percent in 1976 to 43.0 percent in 1982. During the same period, the income share for the poorest 40 percent of the population increased from 19.9 percent in 1976 to 18.8 percent in 1982.

Costs and Side Effects

Was the stabilization policy accomplished without any costs? Answering this question requires a review of the major policy tools employed in Korea's stabilization efforts. Anti-inflation policy in Korea has relied on both incomes policy and demand management.

Incomes policy was intended to keep people's inflationary psychology from creating a bottleneck in the stabilization process. It included imposition of informal wage guidelines or jawboning efforts to moderate wage increases, control of interest rates and dividend yields, as well as adjustments of the government purchase price of rice. Empirical evidence indicates that actual wage hikes in the 1980s were roughly what could have been expected without any guidelines. The government-imposed wage guidelines only resulted in a large wage drift, widening the wage gap between public servants and private employees, and creating an environment detrimental to the development of healthy labor relations.

The drastic reduction of nominal interest rates also gave rise to instability in the financial market. During 1982 and 1983, there was a strong disintermediation phenomenon, creating a shift out of financial assets into the real estate market and a shortening of maturities for financial assets. In sum, although the incomes policy might have quickened price stabilization somewhat, it produced many unfavorable side effects. Lack of consensus has deepened the dissatisfaction of wage workers and farmers and undermined public trust in the government.

As discussed below, restrictive demand management has been the key ingredient in Korea's stabilization efforts, particularly since 1973. Given the short-run trade-off between growth and price stability, restrictive demand management entails a slowdown in income growth. However, we were prepared to accept this slowdown, as our experiences in the 1970s had shown that stable prices are a precondition for sustained economic growth. Nevertheless, a case might be made for a stabilization program that has a longer time horizon, thereby minimizing the short-run sacrifice of growth or other disruptive effects.

Assessment of Major Macropolicies

A fiscal impulse analysis (Table 2) shows that the Korean fiscal policy stance was restrictive in 1979; as the economy was in a deep recession, fiscal reaction was not prompt enough. In 1981 a strong fiscal stimulus was applied, and the public sector deficit peaked at 4.6 percent of GNP. As the economy regained its growth momentum in 1983, the fiscal stance again turned restrictive, and the public sector deficit dropped to 1.6 percent of GNP.

An analysis of the monetary stance from 1979 to 1985 based on an estimation of demand-for-money equations indicates that monetary pol-

Table 2. Korea: Fiscal Impulse—Public Sector[1]
(In percent)

	Real GNP Growth	Actual Deficit (percent of GNP)	Change	Fiscal Impulse[2]			
				IMF measure		OECD[3] measure	
				(A)	(B)	(A)	(B)
1971	8.8	2.3	1.4	0.7	1.3	0.7	1.3
1972	5.7	4.6	2.4	1.6	1.7	1.6	1.7
1973	14.1	1.6	−3.0	−2.2	−2.2	−2.2	−2.3
1974	7.7	4.0	2.4	2.1	2.1	2.1	2.1
1975	6.9	4.6	0.6	0.4	0.2	0.4	0.2
1976	14.1	2.9	−1.8	−1.0	−1.2	−1.0	−1.3
1977	12.7	2.6	−0.2	0.1	−0.1	0.1	−0.1
1978	9.7	2.5	−0.1	−0.1	−0.0	−0.1	−0.0
1979	6.5	1.4	−1.1	−1.6	−1.1	−1.7	−1.1
1980	−5.2	3.2	1.7	−0.4	−0.1	−0.8	−0.4
1981	6.2	4.6	1.5	1.7	1.6	1.6	1.5
1982	5.6	4.3	−0.3	−0.3	−0.5	−0.4	−0.6
1983	9.5	1.6	−2.7	−1.9	−2.1	−1.8	−2.0
1984	7.6	1.4	−0.2	0.2	0.1	0.3	0.1

[1] Public sector includes central government (general account, 12 special accounts, and 21 funds) and five public enterprise accounts (grain management, monopoly, railways, communications, and supply), together with two related funds (grain management and supply).

[2] Fiscal impulse measure A uses potential GNP (Y^p) obtained from a regression equation; measure B uses peak-through interpolated Y^p.

[3] Organization for Economic Cooperation and Development.

icy was not restrictive until around the first half of 1982. The annual rate of growth of broadly defined money (M2) was as high as 26–28 percent during 1980–82, when a series of reflationary policy packages were adopted in the situation of delayed recovery. Since late 1982, however, monetary expansion has fallen short of demand for money, which has grown much faster than nominal GNP due to declining inflationary expectations. M2 grew at only 11–12 percent during 1984–85.

At the beginning of the adjustment period, management of the exchange rate was somewhat rigid, in particular during 1981–82. Although the real effective exchange rate was supposed to be maintained roughly constant, it was overvalued by about 5 percent during this period, compared with 1980. Furthermore, the interest subsidy given to export financing vis-à-vis general loans, which is equivalent to an additional 4–5 percent overvaluation for exporters of the real effective exchange rate, was eliminated in June 1982. Thus, exporters' competitive disadvantage was much more substantial than suggested by the real effective exchange rate indicators. However, since 1983 the currency overvaluation has been corrected, and the won actually depreciated by 10 percent in 1985 from the 1980 level on a real effective basis.

In sum, the deceleration of inflation during 1981–82 is mainly attributable to the decline in unit import prices, the slowdown of wage increases in connection with weak labor demand, and the overvalued exchange rate. The further drop in the inflation rate during 1983–85 was helped by the restrictive stance of fiscal and monetary policy and declining inflationary expectations, while exchange rate management became flexible enough to give exports some competitive stimuli.

III. Constraints in Structural Policies

The two most important structural policies in the 1980s were financial reform and liberalization of external transactions. Though a great deal of progress has been made in these areas, some fundamental hindrances persist.

Financial Liberalization

Financial reform in the 1980s included divesting government equity shares in the major city banks, lowering entry barriers into the financial market, introducing institutional changes toward a more universal banking system, and achieving some progress in interest rate liberalization. Still, most interest rates in the organized financial markets remain closely regulated by the monetary authorities. Moreover, the share of policy loans in deposit money bank credit has not declined noticeably.

Further financial liberalization seems to be hindered by complications arising from the excessive government intervention in private resource allocation during the 1970s. The overseas construction and shipping authorities, whose promotion was heavily supported by the government, are known to have accounted for most of the nonperforming bank loans. Neither banks nor the Government could afford to let troubled firms go bankrupt, not only because the value of their collateral was far below their loan amount, but also because the cost of the social and economic repercussions would be too high. In the meantime, bailout credit has snowballed and managerial autonomy for commercial banks has become even more remote.

Recently, the Government sought to rectify this situation. Measures included helping the banking institutions, the major victims of government intervention, by allowing attractive deposit rates compared with nonbank institutions and providing subsidized central bank credit, and exempting capital gains tax on collateral supplied by the troubled firms.

In other words, the cost of imprudent government intervention was paid for by consumers, taxpayers, and continued financial repression.

Another aspect of this problem is industrial adjustment. In order to further streamline the existing industrial incentive system and to deal with both the declining industries and the promising infant industries, the Industrial Development Law was recently passed. It is hoped that, under this law, industrial restructuring will be effectively supported.

External Liberalization

In evaluating Korea's external liberalization efforts, I fully agree with the authors of the paper. Korea has pursued import liberalization and tariff reductions as rapidly as feasible on its own initiative. The environment for direct foreign investment has also improved significantly over the past few years. Moreover, the Government has already announced schedules for further liberalization up to 1988 when the degree of Korea's market openness will almost reach the level of developed countries.

While most Koreans seem to be convinced that free trade is desirable, they are concerned about the speed at which their market is opening at a time when advanced nations are raising an increasing number of barriers against Korean export goods. However, despite the unfavorable trade environment and domestic pressure to slow down external liberalization, Korea's open-door policy is likely to continue, although we may have to depreciate our currency more than would otherwise be necessary in order to pay back foreign debts. A depreciation will most likely aggravate Korea's terms of trade and, to that extent, will reduce the standard of living of the Korean people.

Developed countries should be aware of the consequences of their protective actions against newly industrialized countries (NICs), including Korea. NICs may find it difficult to repay their foreign debts and will no longer be able to play a dynamic role in the world economy. Furthermore, many developing countries, drawing the wrong lesson from the Korean experience, may turn to a more inward-oriented policy stance.

4

The Role of Aid and Private Capital Inflows in Economic Development

Helen Hughes

I. Introduction

The role of foreign capital in economic development has been a subject of international debate for as long as development itself has existed. In the 1950s and 1960s the discussion centered on aid flows, direct foreign investment, and export credits. Since the mid-1970s attention has shifted to private banking flows and developing country debt problems.

In absolute terms the developing countries' capital needs, say to the year 2000, are enormous. Achieving even moderate living standards in the poorer and more populous countries, notably India and China, will require very large absolute capital amounts. But, year by year, in relation to the developing countries' savings and absorptive capacities for investment, their capital needs are both measurable and manageable.

Except for very small countries, the contribution that foreign capital can make to development can only be marginal; but it is, of course, at the margin that capital inputs matter, particularly in association with the technical inputs that aid and private capital bring. The policy issues of concern to developing countries are centered on the quality of the technological and management components of the capital inflow "package," the optimal levels of flows, the real economic as well as financial costs of flows, and the benefits arising from the uses to which the imported capital is applied. But in small countries, and in large doses even in medium-sized countries, aid can have "Dutch Disease" effects that are difficult to neutralize. Private capital flows that are large in relation to an economy can also undermine rather than strengthen economic performance. Excessive foreign capital flows have proved costlier to development than insufficient ones.

The volume of capital flows to any developing country is largely demand-determined. All developing (and East European) countries still account for less than 10 percent of total world borrowing. Their solvency and liquidity are of concern to international capital markets because lending is highly concentrated in some 30 banks and a dozen or so debtor countries that have borrowed excessively. Unfortunately, there is no developing countrywide solution to such excessive lending and borrowing. Each excessive lender and borrower must set its own house in order. The schemes put forward to help developing countries overcome their indebtedness and to safeguard international capital markets would be likely to lead to more problems than they remedy, because they would add new "moral hazards" to those already created by the guarantees, subsidies, and other distortions that have contributed to excessive borrowing and lending in the past.

The range of development experience since 1945 has been very broad. In some countries living standards of the majority of the population have changed little. In a few they have even deteriorated. But in other countries, including some that were very poor at the end of World War II, living standards are rising appreciably, and a few countries are catching up with and bypassing the more slowly growing industrial countries.

There are many hypotheses as to why some countries have grown faster (and at the same time more equitably) than others (Riedel (1986)). But three old verities about the relationship of capital to growth have stood the test of time. First, the investment of capital is necessary, but not sufficient, for growth. Second, the degree to which investment stimulates growth depends on the efficiency with which it is used, and such efficiency is determined by a country's own policies. Third, capital tends to flow from higher-income (industrial and small population, natural resource-rich) countries, where capital is relatively plentiful and has a low marginal productivity, to lower-income countries, where capital is relatively scarce and has a high marginal productivity.

All countries face the same international conditions. These conditions affect their ability to raise their productivity and competitiveness through trade, and hence their capacity to absorb aid and to borrow abroad. Supply conditions in national and world markets are, of course, also important in the determination of capital inflows, but developing countries are still marginal users of the capital that flows internationally. The extent to which a country saves, invests, and obtains capital abroad, and whether or not it does so optimally, depends principally on its domestic policy framework. That is, the mix, interconnections, and consistencies of a country's financial, monetary, trade, fiscal (and public ownership), exchange rate, manpower, and other policies determine the level of capital inflows and their impact on growth.

The next section of this paper reviews the relationship between foreign capital inflows and development. Section III presents a stylized model of capital flows to developing countries. Section IV concludes with a consideration of the relationship of debt to development.

II. Foreign Capital and Development

Although the Harrod-Domar model placed (physical) capital investment firmly at the center of development economics, the intellectual foundations of the role of foreign capital in development were only developed in the mid-1960s, largely through the work of Hollis Chenery for the U.S. Agency for International Development (AID). The two-gap model (Chenery and Strout (1966)) held center stage for a decade and more: in crude terms it was argued that developing countries in the early stages of development could neither save enough nor import enough capital goods from abroad to satisfy their investment requirements. Aid flows were needed to bridge these two gaps, mainly in the form of concessional loans. This philosophy suited Robert McNamara's drive to expand the activities and influence of the World Bank, particularly during the early and mid-years of his presidency. With soaring global liquidity after 1974 increasing the global supply of capital while the demand for capital faltered in industrial countries, the two-gap theory of development was extended to apply to private capital flows as well as to aid, intellectually underwriting the expansion of private as well as official capital flows to developing countries.

There was no dearth of critics of the two-gap theory, but their analysis was muted lest they be thought to be opposed to aid. However, at the end of the 1960s three types of empirical evidence cast serious doubt on the two-gap theory. Savings rates were clearly not a function of a country's "poverty" (as measured by per capita income), but of economic policies and administrative capability. Countries could—and some did—overcome their balance of payments difficulties by "unshackling" exports (Riedel (1986)). There was clearly no fixed relationship between imports and growth. Marginal import to growth ratios were often twice as high in Latin America as in East Asian countries. Capital inflows did not necessarily lead to growth. Economies such as the Republic of Korea and Taiwan Province of China did not grow rapidly in periods of high aid inflows. Arguments that such aid created preconditions for growth were weak. At best, there was some contribution to the building of a human and physical infrastructure. Capital inflows were often inversely correlated with growth. The poorest, least developed and least development-oriented countries attracted the most aid. Banks proved unable to "pick the winners" among developing countries. Although some countries, notably in East Asia, borrowed well for growth, their experience was swamped by the major borrowers that did not have appropriate domestic policies for borrowing.

The increasing weight placed on human capital is an important factor in explaining the failure of foreign capital inflows to lead to growth. Foreign expertise cannot substitute for local skills, notably in policy formulation and administration, both of which are essential to prudent borrowing and the productive use of borrowed funds. Ideology and political insecurity can exacerbate the lack of human capital, leading to relatively low savings and investment rates and higher incremental capital output ratios than per capita income levels alone would imply.

Capital inflows, particularly of aid funds, can create economic rent effects similar to those of the Dutch Disease (Corden (1984)). Public administration can become the "booming" sector. It can be argued that such effects are even more virulent than those of mineral rents because, instead of percolating from goods to services, they immediately swell government employment. Resources are drawn to government where they receive excessive remuneration; the private sector is correspondingly denied human and physical capital and is burdened by high wages and other costs. With high capital inflows, the rate of exchange becomes overvalued in relation to domestic costs. With high aid to national income ratios, which are typical of small, poor countries, aid flows can become counterproductive if they are not offset by appropriate national policies. This is the case in some low-income sub-Saharan African and small island countries. Foreign capital inflows in "low income sub-Saharan Africa," for example, represent nearly two thirds of the low investment that takes place (Table 1).

Private capital inflows can also have associated Dutch Disease costs. If policies lead to a misallocation of resources among sectors, for example, biasing investment toward protected manufacturing industries, capital inflows can exaggerate the high costs of inappropriate policies. Where private capital inflows are used to bolster government budgets so that fiscal reform can be avoided, the effects are also counterproductive.

In a well-run economy, where capital inflows are marginal, their stimulus to growth can be substantial, particularly if they carry substantial human capital and technical inputs that are otherwise difficult to obtain. The technology-management package that accompanies private direct foreign investment is well known for its positive values, but aid and banking flows can have similar effects.

In contrast, the rents associated with capital inflows cannot be laundered out of a national economic system by being invested abroad. The only effective way in which the Dutch Disease associated with high

Table 1. Gross Domestic Investment in Gross Domestic Product and Net Capital Inflows in Gross Domestic Investment, 1970–80
(In percent)

	Gross Domestic Investment as a Share of Gross Domestic Product		Net Capital Inflows as a Share of Gross Domestic Investment	
	1970	1980	1970	1980
Low-income countries[1]				
Asia	24.4	27.5	2.8	6.8
Africa, south of Sahara	15.6	15.5	28.7	62.9
Middle-income countries[1]				
Oil importers	23.5	25.9	14.9	17.5
Oil exporters	20.5	29.7	13.3	10.8
All developing countries	**22.9**	**27.2**	**10.7**	**13.5**

Sources: World Bank (1983), and Poats and Organization for Economic Cooperation and Development (1985).
[1] For definition of country groups, see World Bank (1985a).

capital inflows can be avoided is through policy reform, but this is often difficult to implement. Political realities then indicate that conditions have to be laid down by donors or lenders if negative Dutch Disease effects are to be avoided.

Where essential policy changes are difficult to achieve for political reasons, bureaucrats and politicians can often use "conditionality" as a scapegoat. But the technical components of capital inflows and conditionality are not always appropriate. Suppliers' credits, for example, can have very distorting effects, despite low costs. Policy conditions imposed by donors may be wrong. A country must give itself the room, by its long-term policies, to be able to do without foreign capital if it judges the conditions that accompany it to be unwise. However, for well-run developing countries, foreign capital, at the margin, can contribute markedly to growth by adding to capital, technological, and management resources at an affordable cost.

III. Evolution of Capital Flows to Developing Countries

Aid, private direct foreign investment packages (with entrepreneurial and technical components), export credits, syndicated bank loans, and other forms of capital flows form a continuum of complementary and substitutable international capital transfer instruments. The essential homogeneity of capital makes it very difficult to distinguish among the various flows. Borrowers and lenders move among the capital instruments available to them in response to relative prices (including such nonmonetary aspects as conditionality and risk). The prices of capital, in turn, reflect the demand and supply schedules of the borrowers and lenders (Hughes (1979, 1984)).

In stylized form, the evolution of capital flows in developing countries may be described as follows. A low-income developing country initially has two main sources of external finance: trade credit and official flows. The latter includes technical assistance, aid in kind, grants, the concessional component of bilateral loans, official export credits, military aid, and the concessional component of multilateral drawings and loans. Some aid flows, such as concessional loans, have a monetary cost, and almost all aid is conditional and hence has costs in some sense (Ohlin (1966) and Wall (1973)).

As a country develops, official inflows continue, and more private capital generally becomes available (Hope and McMurray (1984)). Even relatively undeveloped countries can attract some private direct foreign investment, notably in natural resources (mining, timber, plantation agriculture), in the processing of natural resources, in manufacturing (for the domestic market and for export), and in service industries. Export credits, too, usually become available at very early stages of development for both private and public investment. But because export credits are frequently subsidized by the lender's government, they often lead to excessive borrowing and debt difficulties. A country can therefore acquire relatively high capital servicing liabilities in relation to both its gross domestic product and its exports at an early stage of development.

In later stages, a country's private and public borrowers are regarded as "creditworthy" for bank borrowing and ultimately for bond issues, though the latter have been little used, in contrast to the nineteenth century. The country can then shift from direct investment and export credits to bank sources, thereby avoiding drawbacks that may be associated with foreign investment and supplier's credits. Countries generally continue to take some advantage of the direct investment "package," and they may still find export credits attractive, but they no longer have to depend heavily upon these sources. Thus far, developing country access to bond markets has been largely indirect, channeled through the multilateral banks. Some countries, however, have successfully launched bond issues, principally to prove their creditworthiness to banks. By this stage of development, official flows, even from multilateral banks, are usually declining.

Because of domestic policy distortions, political ties and fluctuations in capital markets, the evolution of capital inflows has not always followed this stylized pattern. During periods of high international liquidity, some countries still in very early stages of development have obtained bank loans, notably to replace equity in natural resource development. On the other hand, some relatively high-income countries have chosen not to borrow a great deal from private sources.

Official sources dominated capital flows to developing countries in the 1950s and early 1960s, when many developing countries were gaining independence and more industrial countries became interested in assisting development. Both official and private flows continued to grow in the 1970s (Tables 2 and 3). The industrial countries increased the concessionality of their aid at the same time as they were increasing its volume. Net aid from members of the Organization of Petroleum Exporting Countries (OPEC) rose rapidly in the 1970s to a peak of about $8 billion in 1980. Total aid flows thus also peaked in the early 1980s, although industrial countries have continued to maintain and even increase aid flows, particularly in recent years. But net private flows rose even faster from about $8 billion in 1950–55 to nearly $70 billion in 1981 as countries attained creditworthiness in highly liquid markets. Thus, even in real terms the increases in total capital flows to developing countries have been impressive.

Developing Countries' Demand for Foreign Capital

Three principal demand characteristics broadly corresponding to the term structure of lending and borrowing affect the developing countries' demand for external capital.

First, developing countries have a demand for short-term capital. This is largely synonymous with the demand for trade credit by the public and private enterprises that make up the production and service sectors. Developing countries may also borrow to offset seasonal and other short-term fluctuations in output and, hence, in public revenue income and foreign exchange earnings. The funds are characteristically supplied from private sources (banks and exporters).

True short-term debt is self-liquidating as imported goods are sold or as seasonal cycles are completed. Even low-income countries can contract short-term debt, provided they have stable and effective economic management. Typically, short-term borrowing increases with a developing country's growth and participation in the international economy, but its size relative to gross national product (GNP) and to exports stays roughly constant.

Some short-term borrowing, of course, is not for short-term purposes. Given particularly good balance of payments and debt management, this may not cause difficulties. A country or enterprise will eventually get into trouble, however, if it borrows to avoid dealing with underlying problems. In time, short-term borrowing then has to be transformed into medium- to long-term borrowing.

Second, medium-term capital from abroad may be used to provide liquidity for a "stretching-out" of costs, while an enterprise, a province, or even the national economy is correcting basic structural problems. Such borrowing may facilitate adjustment to changes in demand, supply, or other factors, the correction of past policy mistakes, or reconstruction after earthquakes or other "acts of God."

The International Monetary Fund (IMF) has long recognized the need for medium-term financing for nation states. IMF drawings for medium-term adjustment were made subject to policy conditions to ensure that they were not used to avoid adjustment, so that borrowing countries would be able to liquidate their medium-term debt on schedule. To permit complex policy responses, the maximum period of such lending has gradually been lengthened to ten years. IMF drawings are available to all IMF members, but they have been used primarily by the developing countries, particularly in recent years.

Since the 1960s enterprises and governments of the more advanced developing countries have been able to borrow from private sources (principally through syndicated bank loans) for medium-term purposes. As long as enterprise or public policies ensure that the necessary restructuring actually takes place, the use of borrowed funds is irrelevant. As in short-term borrowing, if restructuring is not undertaken, the medium-term borrowing will need to be transformed into longer-term borrowing.

Because major investments usually have gestation periods of more than ten years, the third, and principal, demand for foreign capital is for long-term investment. Development takes time. A country's need for investment grows as capital intensity increases with development. Capital for long-term investment may come in the form of official or private flows. It is usually used for expenditures on capital equipment, buildings, or infrastructure. But an enterprise may also use it for working capital, and a government may properly use it for recurrent expenditures in some instances. For example, the education sector may require expenditures that appear as recurrent items in the budget even though, in fact, they are an investment in human capital.

Each type of capital flow has its own demand schedule. Political as well as economic factors enter the calculus. For example, the effective demand for aid reflects both the developing country's ability to demonstrate how much aid it can absorb (aid diplomacy) and its social, political, and economic ties to the donors. As a country becomes increasingly able to service private capital flows, demand schedules for various types of private capital evolve. The demand for direct investment varies considerably by sector, and is associated with that for advanced technology, management, and access to foreign markets. Thus, demand for direct investment in natural resource exploitation differs from the demand for

Table 2. Total Resource Flows to Developing Countries by Type, 1950-84
(In billions of U.S. dollars at 1983 prices and exchange rate)

	1950-55	1960-61	1970	1980	1981	1982	1983	1984
Official development assistance	(8.35)	19.54	22.18	36.05	36.23	33.69	33.80	35.75
Flows from bilateral sources	8.35	18.60	19.38	28.75	28.52	26.21	26.23	27.35
DAC countries[1]	8.35	15.87	14.82	16.99	17.71	18.35	18.53	20.10
OPEC countries[2]	—	—	1.02	8.19	7.46	4.56	4.33	3.79
CMEA countries[3]	...	1.80	2.60	2.48	2.88	2.86	2.94	2.95
Non-DAC/OECD[4]	...	0.02	0.01	0.81	0.21	0.18	0.07	0.10
LDC donors[5]	...	0.91	0.93	0.28	0.26	0.26	0.26	0.41
Flows from multilateral agencies	...	0.94	2.80	7.30	7.71	7.48	7.57	8.40
Grants by private voluntary agencies	...	...	2.25	2.17	1.97	2.30	2.34	2.50
Nonconcessional flows	7.54	15.29	28.66	55.66	68.56	60.10	82.12	54.00
Official or officially supported	...	6.57	10.36	22.91	21.55	21.90	19.82	20.00
Private export credits (DAC)	...	2.03	5.47	10.43	10.99	7.06	5.50	5.00
Official export credits (DAC)	...	2.80	1.54	2.31	1.95	2.65	2.10	2.50
Multilateral	...	0.80	1.86	4.55	5.57	6.58	7.22	7.50
Other official and private flows (DAC)	0.94	0.65	0.68	1.91	2.62	3.00	3.00	3.00
Other donors	...	...	0.84	3.52	1.13	2.99	2.00	2.00
Private	...	8.72	18.30	32.75	47.01	38.21	62.30	34.00
Direct investment	...	6.54	9.66	9.89	16.77	11.81	7.80	9.50
Bank sector[6]	...	2.18	7.85	21.57	29.19	25.89	54.00	24.00
Bond lending	...	...	0.79	1.29	1.05	0.51	0.50	0.50
Total resource flows	**(15.89)**	**34.83**	**53.09**	**93.88**	**106.76**	**96.09**	**118.26**	**92.25**

Total bank lending	...	...	45.96	50.59	40.83	35.00	18.00
of which: Short term	...	...	24.39	21.40	14.94	−19.00	−6.00
IMF purchases, net[7]	...	0.89	2.45	6.01	6.38	12.48	5.50

Source: Poats and Organization for Economic Cooperation and Development (1985).

[1] Development Assistance Committee.
[2] Organization of Petroleum Exporting Countries.
[3] Council for Mutual Economic Assistance.
[4] Non-Development Assistance Committee/Organization for Economic Cooperation and Development.
[5] Less-developed country.
[6] Bank sector includes, for 1983 and 1984, significant amounts of rescheduled short-term debt. The real evolution of bank lending is best reflected in the line showing "Total Bank Lending" at the bottom of the table.
[7] International Monetary Fund.

Table 3. Resource Flows to Developing Countries, 1950-84
(Percentage shares of total flows)

	1950-55	1960-61	1970	1980	1981	1982	1983	1984
Official development assistance	(52.5)	55.9	41.8	38.4	33.9	35.1	35.9	41.9
Flows from bilateral sources	52.5	53.6	36.5	30.6	26.7	27.3	27.8	32.0
DAC countries[1]	52.5	47.7	27.9	18.1	16.6	19.1	19.7	23.6
OPEC countries[2]	—	—	1.9	2.6	2.7	3.0	4.6	4.4
CMEA countries[3]	...	5.2	4.9	2.6	2.7	3.0	3.1	3.5
Non-DAC/OECD[4]	...	0.1	—	0.9	0.2	0.2	0.1	0.1
LDC donors[5]	...	2.6	1.8	0.3	0.2	0.3	0.3	0.5
Flows from multilateral agencies	...	2.3	5.3	7.8	7.2	7.2	8.0	9.9
Grants by private voluntary agencies	...	...	4.2	2.3	1.8	2.4	2.5	2.9
Nonconcessional flows	47.5	44.1	54.0	59.3	64.2	62.5	61.6	55.2
Official or officially supported	...	18.9	19.5	24.4	20.2	22.8	21.0	23.5
Private export credits (DAC)	...	5.9	10.3	11.1	10.3	7.3	3.8	5.9
Official export credits (DAC)	...	8.1	2.9	2.5	1.8	2.8	2.2	2.9
Multilateral	...	2.3	3.5	4.8	5.2	6.8	7.7	8.8
Other official and private flows (DAC)	...	2.7	1.2	2.2	1.8	2.7	3.2	3.5
Other donors	...	...	1.6	3.7	1.1	3.1	2.1	2.3

Private	...	25.1	34.9	44.0	39.8	40.6	31.7
Direct investment	...	18.8	10.5	15.7	12.3	8.3	11.2
Bank sector[6]	...	6.3	23.0	27.3	26.9	31.8	20.0
Bond lending	...	...	1.5	1.4	1.0	0.5	0.5	0.6
Total resource flows	**100.00**	**100.00**	**100.00**	**100.00**	**100.00**	**100.00**	**100.00**

Source: Development Assistance Committee (1985).
[1] Development Assistance Committee.
[2] Organization of Petroleum Exporting Countries.
[3] Council for Mutual Economic Assistance.
[4] Non-Development Assistance Committee/Organization for Economic Cooperation and Development.
[5] Less-developed countries.
[6] Percentages for 1983 and 1984 have been calculated using a baseline figure for ordinary bank sector lending business, i.e., US$30 billion and US$17 billion after excluding from long-term flows estimated amounts rescheduled from short-term flows in those years.

investment in import-substituting manufacturing and from that in export-oriented manufacturing. Export credits, banking flows, and bond issues also have their own demand schedules.

A country's total external borrowing—official plus private—can be expected to expand for 30, 50, or more years until productivity and living standards approach those of the most advanced countries. When the development process is essentially completed, a country will cease to be a major net borrower abroad. A country may become a net lender as its savers and entrepreneurs find that their capital can earn a higher income in other, less developed countries than at home. However, while international borrowing and lending transactions by private and public entities continue, over time they will tend to come into balance.

In a competitive environment without major policy distortions—where prices reflect costs, and costs reflect productivity—the demand for external capital is related to marginal socioeconomic costs and returns. These, in turn, are close to marginal private costs and returns over a wide range of activities. The demand for foreign capital is then optimal. An adequate capital servicing capacity is created automatically. Short-term liquidity problems may occur from time to time, with abrupt demand or supply changes or in periods of serious international recession. But these do not reflect underlying solvency problems. Savings, investment, and foreign borrowing march together, in step with the growth of exports and national product. In a formal sense, the marginal socioeconomic return on domestic and on foreign capital will be the same, and it will be equal to the real marginal cost of total borrowing. The real world is, of course, more complex than this theoretical construct. Market imperfections exist. In many developing countries poor domestic policies have created an excessive demand for foreign capital. The principal distortions originate in financial, trade, and fiscal policies.

In countries with "repressed" financial systems, savings tend to flee the country or remain outside the monetary system. Those savings that do remain in the country are usually poorly distributed. Domestic capital is thus difficult to obtain. Rationing has to substitute for market mechanisms. Only a few privileged enterprises can obtain domestic capital through the banking system; all others must pay very high "curb" interest rates. As a result, most firms seek financing abroad.

If the developing country has highly protectionist trade policies, incentives to invest in the protected domestic market will be strong. Foreign direct investors—as well as local investors—will wish to enter into production in such countries. Capital inflows will be further encouraged if the developing country guarantees the repayment of private debt. Even if the protection is at least partially offset by export incentives, resource allocation is likely to be distorted. Private returns on foreign borrowing will probably exceed social returns. But protection undermines the country's foreign debt servicing capacity by discriminating against its exports. Thus, liberalizing access to foreign capital without also liberalizing trade is particularly conducive to excessive borrowing abroad (McKinnon (1982)).

Inappropriate fiscal policies also often encourage excessive foreign borrowing. Developing countries frequently give tax holidays to investors in "essential" industries, thereby not only forgoing government revenue, but also attracting inappropriate direct foreign investment (particularly if there is protection) and encouraging foreign borrowing by local investors. If a country does not have a strong taxation base, there will also be intense pressure to borrow abroad for public investment, particularly if the government has taken over "basic industries" to bring them under national and/or indigenous control (Freeman (1985)). Moreover, the lack of a strong tax base usually leads to inflation, which together with restricted financial policies and protective trade policies contributes to the overvaluation of the exchange rate. And an overvalued exchange rate further increases the demand for borrowing abroad.

Dutch Disease encourages excessive external borrowing in mineral-rich countries. Mineral rents tend to encourage highly protectionist, financially distorted, fiscally inappropriate government policies. Excessive expectations of growth in times of high mineral prices have often caused borrowing to increase much more rapidly than future income could possibly grow. Then, if mineral prices fall (cyclically or because supply is increased or demand falls), public and private revenues and savings fall; the demand for capital increases to sustain investment and even consumption. Many mineral-rich countries have, therefore, become high borrowers.

Policies that lead to excessive borrowing also result in low returns on investment because of distorted resource allocation, low factor utilization, and a low propensity to export. The ability to service borrowing is thus much lower than in countries with more appropriate policies. Since most individual developing countries represent so small a component of demand that they are largely able to determine the amount they borrow (Riedel (1983)), their domestic policies are the principal determinants of borrowing levels.

Overall, the share of net capital inflows in gross domestic investment increased in the 1970s (Table 1). In sub-Saharan Africa and Latin America this reflected low domestic savings rates and, respectively, rising aid and rising private inflows. But in the other regions, capital inflows grew side by side with ratios of savings and investment to GNP.

Supply of Foreign Capital

Political as well as economic factors affect not only the demand for external capital, but also its supply. Concessional and nonconcessional official flows, for example, are often largely politically motivated; military/strategic issues often loom large in the determination of recipients and volumes of flows. They usually also have an economic component: donors expect future trade or investment gains. Humanistic factors are clearly also important, particularly in the allocation of aid to small, poor, and distant countries.

Savers—individuals, institutions, and governments—are the ultimate source of capital flows to developing countries. They seek high returns and liquidity. Borrowers seek precisely the opposite: namely, low costs and long maturities. Financial intermediaries intervene to reconcile these widely diverging requirements (Llewellyn (1984)).

Transnational corporations invest directly through their subsidiaries and associated companies or through management contracts and similar arrangements. The savers in this case are interested not only in returns on capital, but also in returns to entrepreneurship, in mineral and other resource rents, and in quasi-rents associated with new technology, trademarks, and so on—all subject to prudential considerations.

Financial intermediaries proper, notably banks, transform savings into loans. Their fee is the difference between deposit and lending rates, plus management, commitment, agency and other fees, and profits on ancillary business such as foreign exchange transactions. They arrange capital flows and associated services from the ultimate lenders to the ultimate borrowers such as private and public enterprises, including other banks and governments. However, they are not simply brokers in a perfectly informed and otherwise perfect market. They are also profit maximizers, so that in transforming short-term lending into long-term borrowing they must ensure their own liquidity. They have to trade off spreads and fees against the volume of business, and volumes and spreads against risk. Failure of their clients to service loans on time, ultimately becoming bankrupt or defaulting, is a critical element in the banks' profitability.

Creditworthiness—be it of an enterprise or a country—is a highly subjective concept, particularly ex ante. Therefore, all lending is risky. But lending abroad entails special additional risks. Some of these risks are "systemic;" that is, they apply to all the loans in a country or groups of countries. "Transfer risk" represents the danger that a debtor country will not make sufficient foreign exchange available for servicing debt. "Country risk" encompasses those dangers to which a lender is exposed because of unique legal and other institutional obstacles to the collection of debt service in the debtor country. "Sovereign risk" is associated with lending to a government rather than a private borrower (Heller (1982)). Other risks can be offset if lenders diversify their lending within or across countries.

Lending abroad thus has prudential considerations in addition to those of matching capital and liabilities to assets, and of distributing loans among individual enterprises and between public and private borrowers. Moreover, like private direct investment, it has long-term perspectives; it looks to the borrower's future as well as current economic position.

The supply schedules of capital are globally determined. Lending to developing (and centrally planned) countries is part of a continuum encompassing capital flows within a particular industrial country, other industrial countries, and the rest of the world. The basic price of capital is decided in the industrial countries by their supply and demand for capital, both of which are affected by these countries' financial and monetary policies. Margins over this basic price (including spreads and fees), however, are loan-specific, varying both across countries and over time. Some developing countries (such as Malaysia) have, on occasion, paid less for foreign capital than some industrial countries (such as Italy).

Because there is essentially only one global supply schedule for each type of capital instrument, the macroeconomic policies in the industrial countries that affect their own various demands for capital also affect the supplies of capital available to developing countries. Thus, the industrial economies' failure to deal with the problems that beset them from the late 1960s (inflation, price inflexibility, unemployment), followed by their failure to adjust to increased petroleum prices in the mid-1970s, led to their low demand for capital for domestic investment. This occurred at the same time the low capital absorbers among the petroleum exporters were placing their savings in financial intermediaries in industrial countries, making the international capital markets very liquid. The Eurodollar markets were thus able to respond very readily to the increased developing country demand for private capital in the mid-1970s and to sustain it into the 1980s. Then petroleum export volumes declined and real petroleum prices sagged. The industrial countries again became net savers and substantial capital exporters from the later 1970s (Watson, Keller, Mathieson, et al. (1984)). Their policies—or lack thereof—were not conducive to domestic investment. Large capital inflows into international capital markets, together with a general lag in the perception of inflation and permissive monetary policies in industrial countries, led to low and even negative real interest rates, encouraging developing country borrowing. Thus, from a global and long-term perspective, too much capital probably flowed to developing countries during the mid- and late-1970s. The pro-cyclical policies of the

World Bank and the IMF contributed to excessive borrowing. Both organizations, though the IMF less so than the World Bank, increased lending, competing with each other and the commercial banks and forgoing conditionality in the process.

Nation states have established central banks to safeguard borrowers and lenders against market imperfections and disruptions. They also have expanded their regulatory systems to control financial intermediation associated with international capital flows. These regulations were considered excessive by private financial institutions and, hence, led to the establishment of offshore banking centers and the Eurodollar markets in the late 1950s and 1960s and other developing country centers such as Bahrain and Singapore in the 1970s.

Some country-related prudential rules, such as "country exposure" limits, have had only very limited intended effects, and have, instead, further pushed business into offshore markets. Tax holidays and other benefits to direct investors abroad have helped encourage direct investment at the expense of bank lending, whereas official guarantees and subsidies for export credits have expanded export credits (and associated bank lending) at the expense of direct investment. Industrial countries also provide guarantees and political risk insurance, particularly for export credits, but also for some other loans to developing countries; in shifting the cost of nonpayment from financial institutions to taxpayers, this has introduced "moral hazard" and encouraged lending beyond levels that would otherwise have taken place. The motivations and the design of the policies that attempt to regulate capital movements to developing countries have been too vague, contradictory, and complex to have had much intended effect, but they have substantially weakened the analysis of creditworthiness by lending institutions and therefore led to excessive lending.

An optimal level of borrowing from a country's point of view is far from synonymous with creditworthiness from a banker's point of view. A country may be able to continue to service its debt by taxing its population (at least, for a time), although it has borrowed excessively and/or used its borrowed funds for purposes with low socioeconomic returns. That is, it may be creditworthy, though it has borrowed excessively. While in a loose, arithmetic sense a country can afford to borrow as long as the growth of income exceeds real interest costs (Avramovic (1958)), or even as long as borrowing covers service payments (Kharas (1981)), in economic terms a country has to earn more on its borrowing than the inflows of capital cost if the borrowing is to be worthwhile.

International Capital Market Trends

A growing number of banks entered into international lending from the mid-1970s as its relatively high profitability became recognized, first in the United States and then in Europe, Japan, and the expanding developing country money markets. This led to highly competitive conditions, driving down margins over the London interbank offer rate (LIBOR) and fees to very low levels from 1976 onward (after recovery from the Herstatt and Franklin banking failures).

A number of new instruments were developed to facilitate international lending and borrowing. International bank syndications, following U.S. domestic lending practices, were introduced to facilitate risk-spreading and to finance very large projects and large loans to governments. Small and inexperienced banks were able to enter international business gradually. The London interbank market helped the individual banks to handle short-term liquidity changes. Variable interest rates were introduced to offset the risks associated with fluctuations in inflation. The interbank market also dealt with currency fluctuations caused by floating exchange rates when these were introduced in the 1970s. As banks wanted to continue to expand lending to clients once they established a good business relationship, rollover or refinancing practices became commonplace. This reduced the importance of loan maturities and facilitated planning for both lenders and borrowers. The ease of rolling over private loans contrasted markedly to the cumbersome rescheduling of official loans through the administrative channels of the Paris Club of donor governments.

Extremely low real interest rates transferred income from savers to borrowers. To the extent that petroleum exporters were savers and petroleum importers were borrowers, this income transfer helped offset the increase in petroleum prices. Bank profitability was maintained by the high front loading of fees and by high nominal interest rates, which in effect led to the prepayment of amortization (Nowzad, Williams, et al. (1981)). Overall, borrowing was shifting from direct investment to bank loans and private export credits (Tables 2 and 3). Taxation policies in developing countries also encouraged this shift; dividends were taxable as profits, while interest payments on loans were deductible as costs. There was little conditionality in private bank lending, so that the IMF's and multilateral banks' loss of leverage was not compensated. The only discipline that was imposed was largely that of the borrowing countries themselves. For example, since the mid-1970s, East Asia has used IMF facilities twice as intensively relative to GNP as has Latin America and the Caribbean. For the period 1971–81, East Asia, Latin America, and the Caribbean made the same amount of IMF purchases, with East Asia making most of its purchases in 1980–81. However, East Asia's purchases (net of the reserve tranche) represented a 0.25 percent share of GNP, whereas Latin America's was only 0.10 percent.

Very low, and sometimes even negative, real interest rates could not last. The Federal Republic of Germany, Japan, and a few other industrial countries had begun to use a combination of fiscal, income, and monetary policies in the mid-1970s to fight inflation. In the other industrial countries, the problems of low growth with increasing unemployment and high inflation came to a head after the second petroleum price increase. Only then did the United States act, largely relying upon monetary policy (because it was unable to control fiscal deficits for political reasons) to bring down inflation. This, together with a new appreciation of the costs of worldwide inflation, raised real interest rates even faster than they had fallen in the mid-1970s. The tight monetary policies deepened and prolonged the post-1978–79 recession (in contrast to the short, sharp trough of 1975), catching the developing countries in a scissors movement; their interest payments rose sharply just as the recession, exacerbating a cyclical downturn in raw material prices, slashed their export earnings. Many countries were now much more "borrowed up" than they had been in 1975, and they accordingly slowed their rate of borrowing. At the same time, some lenders became concerned with the liquidity and solvency of the high borrowers, and further raised the cost of borrowing from 1978. Savings in management and other fees and in spreads over LIBOR only slightly compensated for high interest rates, with a resulting move back to direct investment and export credits. At an 8 to 10 percent nominal interest rate, export credits became very economical as industrial countries strove to sell abroad in a mercantilist reaction to higher petroleum prices. Net transfers less interest payments to developing countries declined sharply as their interest service on debt rose; in some instances they even became negative. When nominal interest rates again began to fall in 1982, the savings on debt service were considerable. Borrowing, nevertheless, declined in 1982, mainly because of the difficult position of the principal Latin American countries.

Borrowing from private sources (including short-term as well as medium- and long-term) was highly concentrated. Three countries (Mexico, Brazil, and Argentina) accounted for more than 50 percent of the developing countries' borrowing. Another four countries (Venezuela, the Republic of Korea, Chile, and the Philippines) accounted for another 20 percent. The low-income countries of Asia have participated little in the international markets thus far, particularly in comparison to the low-income countries of sub-Saharan Africa. India, for example, has argued that its financial structure and protection of domestic industries do not permit the entry of private direct investment or other private capital. China has similarly maintained a very cautious stance to foreign borrowing.

Capital Flows to Developing Countries and Current Account Deficits

The connection between foreign financing for development and current account deficits and surpluses is tenuous. Current account balances reflect the working out of trade, remittance, and capital service flows. Deficits can occur only if they can be financed. The current account data used here exclude grant aid, so they cannot in any case be used as proxies for the financing needs of developing countries. Developing country deficits remained fairly small as a share of GNP (Table 4) until the recession of 1975, reflecting the limited absorptive capacity of most developing countries for foreign borrowing. The high deficits from 1980 reflect several factors: the unintended prepayment of amortization through high nominal interest rates shifted payments from the capital to the current account; the tropical beverage boom of 1977-78 and high private and official flows to 1978 led to (lagged) high import flows in 1979 to 1981; primary product prices, which had been falling since the 1972-73 primary product boom, bottomed out in 1981-82; the recession reduced the volume of demand for developing country exports; and real interest rates rose. When the possibility of a liquidity problem was predicted (Long (1980)) in the late 1970s, it was ignored. When the problem did arise, the World Bank, in particular, found that it had overextended its lending. Not only did it have institutional difficulties in terms of its capital base in maintaining borrowing, but many of its client countries could not support local funding for the projects on which they had embarked. The lack of effective conditionality in countries, such as Tanzania and the Philippines, had weakened rather than strengthened developing economies through structural assistance loans. Difficult as these conditions were to handle in the short run, they should not be equated either with long-run external financing requirements for all developing countries or with general developing country solvency. However, for countries that had not adopted sound growth and develop-

Table 4. Current Account Balances[1] as a Share of Gross National Product, 1960-84
(In percent)

Country Group	1960	1970	1975	1980	1983	1984
Low-income countries	−1.6	−1.1	−2.1	−2.2	−1.0	−1.3
Asia	−1.4	−0.9	−1.2	−1.4	−0.2	−0.6
Africa, south of Sahara	−3.3	−3.4	−10.2	−9.8	−10.0	−9.4
Middle-income countries						
Oil importers	−2.9	−3.2	−5.3	−4.1	−4.4	−2.7
Oil exporters	−2.7	−3.2	−5.5	−3.6	−3.1	−1.3
All developing countries	−2.2	−2.3	−3.9	−2.3	−2.8	−1.8

Source: World Bank (1985a).
[1] Excluding official transfers.

ment policies in the 1960s and 1970s, the early 1980s did result in serious solvency as well as liquidity problems.

IV. External Debt and Creditworthiness

Borrowing leads to the accumulation of debt as surely as night follows day, though in some international circles the earlier cry for better developing country access to private capital markets (Avramovic, et al. (1964)) has now been replaced by astonishment at the size of the developing countries' debt! In constant price terms, medium- and long-term debt grew at about 24 percent a year from the mid-1960s to 1972 and at 18 percent from 1973 to 1983 (Table 5). The 1965 to 1972 growth rate partly reflects the low initial base, the progressive addition of countries to the data base throughout the period, and the inclusion of private nonguaranteed debt in the data from 1970. Nevertheless, the growth of total indebtedness in the 1970s was not as rapid, either in real terms or in relation to the experience of the 1960s, as is frequently thought. Access to and the use of international banking flows and the relative shift in recent years from direct investment to bank borrowing have increased debt (while slowing the increase in the stock of investment held in developing countries by transnational corporations). Rising shares of debt are, of course, owed to private sources, on nonconcessional terms and at variable interest rates.

Debt, as a share of developing country GNP, grew as countries

Table 5. Growth of Medium- and Long-Term Debt of Developing Countries, 1965-83[1]

	Total Disbursed Debt End of Year			Average Annual Growth Rate	
	1965[2]	1973	1983	1965-72[2]	1973-83
	(In billions of U.S. dollars)			(In percent)	
Low-income countries					
Asia[3]	5.8	15.9	39.9	13.8	9.6
Africa, south of Sahara	1.2	5.0	27.1	19.2	18.4
Middle income countries					
Oil exporters	10.8	30.6	321.3	25.6	26.5
Oil importers	3.9	57.8	209.3	29.4	13.7
All developing countries	21.6	109.2	597.6	23.6	18.5

Source: World Bank (1984, 1985b).
[1] Data prior to 1970 exclude private nonguaranteed debt.
[2] Author's estimates.
[3] Includes China.

began to borrow (Table 6). But the ratio of reserves to debt also rose for most groups of developing countries until 1981, and the ratio of debt to exports declined until the world recession became fully felt in 1982. Countries that wanted to borrow needed a more rapid growth of exports and had to maintain higher ratios of reserves to imports. Thus, their borrowing was a force for outward-looking policies, often overcoming domestic protectionist pressures. In this sense, at least, debt has been an engine of growth; countries with rapid export growth have grown faster than others; several have taken advantage of international capital flows to achieve high export growth. Industrial country lending to developing countries also damps protectionism; the lenders want to get paid.

Given the increasing reliance on market financing, plus the general rise in interest rates, debt service has grown faster than debt. Debt service growth, however, was offset in part by a slowed growth of dividends and capital repayments on private investment. Total debt service ratios (interest plus amortization divided by exports of goods and services) have thus grown less than bank borrowing service ratios imply (Table 7). Even bank debt service ratios remained stable in East Asia and the Pacific, although they rose markedly in all other regions. The interest service ratio (interest payments divided by exports of goods and services), highly relevant in a market in which refinancing is a routine operation, grew more rapidly than total debt service with the adoption of variable interest rates, particularly for Latin America. Despite the coincidence of high interest rates with a more prolonged recession than any since the 1930s, most developing countries have been able to service their debt without interruptions; only those that have borrowed excessively because of their inappropriate domestic policies have run into trouble.

Table 6. Debt Indicators, 1973-83
(In percent)

Country Group	Debt/Exports 1973	Debt/Exports 1983	Debt/GNP 1973	Debt/GNP 1983	Reserves/Debt 1973	Reserves/Debt 1983
Low-income countries						
Asia	274.1	572.0	17.1	16.6	17.0	30.4
Africa, south of Sahara	104.13	612.4	15.9	38.0	28.9	6.9
Middle-income countries						
Oil importers	98.5	161.4	18.6	40.3	55.5	19.8
Oil exporters	103.5	158.5	20.2	38.2	38.5	19.3
All developing countries	110.6	174.5	18.6	36.5	43.9	19.7

Source: World Bank (1984, 1985b).

Table 7. Debt Service and Interest Ratios, 1973–83

Country Group	Debt Service Ratio 1973	Debt Service Ratio 1983	Interest Service Ratio 1973	Interest Service Ratio 1983
Africa, south of Sahara	9.9	23.6	2.8	10.1
East Asia and the Pacific	11.3	12.5	3.2	5.8
Latin America and the Caribbean	24.2	36.1	7.8	23.5
North Africa and the Middle East	16.1	28.7	2.9	7.7
South Asia	17.2	38.5	6.5	15.2
Europe and the Mediterranean	12.3	25.6	3.5	12.4
All developing countries	16.2	24.9	4.9	13.1

Source: World Bank (1984, 1985b).

As a group, the developing countries hold substantial assets in the industrial countries and earn income on them. Table 8 indicates the official and declared funds that developing countries hold in industrial country banks (including certain offshore branches of U.S. banks). A high proportion of privately held assets are excluded from the table, because such assets are registered as domiciled in the industrial coun-

Table 8. Developing Country Assets and Liabilities with Industrial Country Banks, End-September 1984[1]
(In billions of U.S. dollars)

Country Group	Assets	Liabilities
Low-income countries		
Asia	27	9
Africa, south of Sahara	4	3
Middle-income countries		
Oil importers		
East Asia and Pacific	29	70
Middle East and North Africa	21	20
Africa, south of Sahara	3	8
Southern Europe	14	39
Latin America and Caribbean	43	212
Oil exporters	163	178

Source: Bank for International Settlements (1985).
[1] The figures exclude all centrally planned developing economies. Also excluded are the following offshore banking centers: The Bahamas, Bahrain, Barbados, Cayman Islands, Hong Kong, Netherlands Antilles, Panama, and Singapore. The industrial country banks include certain U.S.-owned offshore affiliates.

tries. Some offshore banks that are major depositories for private developing country assets abroad are not included (World Bank (1985b)).

Debt Problems

The largest number of countries with debt problems are low-income countries, most of them in sub-Saharan Africa. Their debt difficulties are linked with their extreme poverty and development problems. For a number of years, their income growth has lagged behind their population growth; in some cases it has even been negative. The 1981-82 recession with its low primary product prices was for many the last straw. These countries still owe debt mainly to official lenders on concessional terms, though they have also done some borrowing from private sources, particularly in the form of subsidized export credits. These countries were never creditworthy. In nonguaranteed markets they would not have been able to borrow commercially and would have encountered serious problems. Some of these countries, despite debt service ratios of less than 10 percent, have repeatedly fallen in arrears. A dozen or so have had their official debt either forgiven or rescheduled and their private debt refinanced, often several times, usually with IMF assistance. Although these countries are numerous, their total population is small and they represent less than 5 percent of total developing country debt.

A second group of countries with debt problems is made up primarily of middle-income countries. It includes several mineral-rich and relatively advanced countries, notably Brazil, Mexico, and Argentina, which ran into serious liquidity problems in the 1980-82 recession, requiring large IMF drawings and refinancing arrangements with private banks. These countries vary quite widely in debt to GNP ratios and in debt service and capital service liabilities. However, they share an ineptitude in economic policy that led them to borrow heavily. When they subsequently fell into economic difficulties, domestic crises turned into debt problems. In Brazil and Argentina, particularly, serious solvency difficulties arising from inappropriate economic policies also underlie liquidity problems.

Despite the difficulties created by some of the large borrowers, a generalized debt crisis involving widespread developing country default (though predicted regularly since the mid-1960s) has been avoided. However attractive individual default may have seemed to some countries in the short run, it would have cut such countries off from all credit for a long time, and thus represented a very high-cost strategy. The costs of individual default would also be very high in terms of sequestration of assets. Cuba, which took this route, is advising fellow socialist countries against such a course of action. Mass default would severely constrain the institutions lending in the international capital markets, but would not cause their collapse (c.f., Eaton and Gersowitz (1981)).

As export markets have picked up and real interest rates stabilized, most developing countries have been able to continue to be net borrowers. The developing countries thus do not present a threat to international financial intermediaries. Despite some arrears and nonpayment situations that have sometimes led to the writing-off of bad loans, developing country lending remains more profitable than domestic lending. Many developing countries are still growing faster than the industrial countries and are likely to continue to do so. Another group is likely to graduate to borrowing from commercial markets on a significant scale by the end of the 1980s. Failures of large corporations in the industrial countries, where more than 90 percent of their lending lies, pose a greater threat for international banks than do the developing countries.

The IMF was established to be the world's international central bank. It has fulfilled part of this function through its financial operations, national consultations, and international surveillance over trade restrictions and monetary policies. It has not picked up all the responsibilities of a world central bank, and the Bank for International Settlements, therefore, also plays a major role in international finance, by providing a forum for consultations among the central banks of the industrial countries in which the headquarters of most major international financial intermediaries reside. The new money market centers in developing countries should now be brought into these consultations. Paradoxically, however, most of the prescriptions for improving the international debt situation, such as proposals for moratoria on existing debt, buying out private debt by multilateral public institutions (so that private banks could start lending to developing countries again), and other safety nets are inappropriate. They would subsidize and even encourage wasteful national managers, and in the long run they would penalize the careful ones. Like other additional national or international guarantees, they would exacerbate the already high moral hazard that has led to excessive borrowing and lending (Dorrance (1981)). Attempts to "privatize" the profits of international banking and "socialize" the losses would jeopardize the continued use of foreign capital for growth. There are no quick fixes for development problems. If external capital is to continue to flow to developing countries, many of them will have to improve their domestic policies, and financial intermediaries will have to learn to be more discriminating than they have been in the past.

References

Avramovic, Dragoslav, *Debt Servicing Capacity and Postwar Growth in International Indebtedness* (Baltimore: Published for the International Bank for Reconstruction and Development by Johns Hopkins Press, 1958).

_____, et al., *Economic Growth and External Debt* (Baltimore: Published for the International Bank for Reconstruction and Development by Johns Hopkins Press, 1964).

Bank for International Settlements, *International Banking Developments, Third Quarter, 1984* (Basle: Bank for International Settlements, February 1985).

Chenery, Hollis B., and A.M. Strout, "Foreign Assistance and Economic Development," *American Economic Review* (Nashville, Tennessee), Vol. 56 (September 1966), pp. 679–733.

Corden, W.M., "Booming Sector and Dutch Disease Economics: Survey and Consolidation," *Oxford Economic Papers*, n.s., Vol. 36 (November 1984), pp. 359–80.

Dorrance, Graeme S., "Would Loan Guarantees Undermine International Capital Markets?" *The Banker* (London), Vol. 131 (December 1981), pp. 39–41.

Eaton, Jonathan, and Mark Gersovitz, "Poor Country Borrowing in Private Financial Markets and the Repudiation Issue," Princeton Studies in International Finance, No. 47 (Princeton, New Jersey: International Finance Section, Department of Economics, Princeton University, 1981).

Freeman, John R., "The Politics of Indebted Economic Growth," Monograph Series in World Affairs, Volume 21, No. 3 (Denver, Colorado: Graduate School of International Studies, University of Denver, 1985).

Heller, H. Robert, "International Lending and the Debt of Developing Countries," paper presented at the National Science Foundation Conference on International Stability and Cooperation (Minneapolis, Minnesota: University of Minnesota, October 13–15, 1982).

Hope, Nicholas C., and David W. McMurray, "Loan Capital in Development Finance, the Role of Banks and Some Implications for Managing Debt," in *Problems of International Finance: Papers of the Seventh Annual Conference of the International Economics Study Group*, ed. by John Black and Graeme S. Dorrance (New York: St. Martin's Press, 1984), pp. 93–139.

Hughes, Helen, "Debt and Development: The Role of Foreign Capital in Economic Growth," *World Development* (Oxford), Vol. 7 (February 1979), pp. 95–112.

_____, "External Debt Problems of Developing Countries," in *Energy and Structural Change in the Asia-Pacific Region: Papers and Proceedings of the Thirteenth Pacific Trade and Development Conference, January 24–28, 1983*, ed. by Romeo M. Bautista and Seiji Naya (Manila, Philippines: Philippine Institute for Development Studies/Asian Development Bank, 1984), pp. 469–96.

Kharas, Homi, "The Analysis of Long-Run Creditworthiness: Theory and Practice," Domestic Finance Studies, No. 73 (Washington: World Bank, Development Economics Department, 1981).

Llewellyn, David T., "Modelling International Banking Flows: An Analytical Framework," in *Problems of International Finance: Papers of the Seventh Annual Conference of the International Economics Study Group*, ed. by John Black and Graeme S. Dorrance (New York: St. Martin's Press, 1984), pp. 35–76.

Long, Millard, "Balance of Payments Disturbances and the Debt of Non-Oil Less Developed Countries: Retrospect and Prospects," *Kyklos*, Vol. 33, No. 3 (1980), pp. 475–98.

McKinnon, Ronald I., "The Order of Economic Liberalization: Lessons from Chile and Argentina," in *Economic Policy in a World of Change*, Carnegie-Rochester Conference Series on Public Policy, Vol. 17, ed. by Karl Brunner and Allan H. Meltzer (Amsterdam: North Holland, 1982), pp. 159–86.

Nowzad, Bahram, Richard C. Williams, et al. *External Indebtedness of Developing Countries*, Occasional Paper No. 3 (Washington: International Monetary Fund, 1981).

Ohlin, Goran, *Foreign Aid Policies Reconsidered*, Development Center Studies (Paris: Organization for Economic Cooperation and Development, 1966).

Poats, Rutherford M., and Organization for Economic Cooperation and Development, *Twenty-Five Years of Development Cooperation: A Review* (Paris: Organization for Economic Cooperation and Development, 1985).

Riedel, James, "Determinants of LDC Borrowing in International Financial Markets: Theory and Empirical Evidence," (unpublished, School of Advanced International Studies, Johns Hopkins University, 1983).

─── , "Economic Development in East Asia: Doing What Comes Naturally?" National Center for Development Studies Working Paper No. 86/1 (Canberra: National Center for Development Studies, 1986).

Wall, David, *The Charity of Nations: The Political Economy of Foreign Aid* (New York: Basic Books, 1973).

Watson, Maxwell, Peter Keller, Donald Mathieson, et al., *International Capital Markets: Developments and Prospects, 1984*, Occasional Paper No. 31 (Washington: International Monetary Fund, 1984).

World Bank, *World Tables*, the Third Edition, Vol. 1 (Baltimore, London: Published for the World Bank by Johns Hopkins University Press, 1983).

─── , *World Debt Tables: External Debt of Developing Countries, 1983–84* (Washington: World Bank, 1984).

─── , (1985a), *World Development Report* (New York: Published for the World Bank by Oxford University Press).

─── , (1985b), *World Debt Tables: External Debt of Developing Countries, 1984–85* (Washington: World Bank).

Comment

Christopher Findlay

I. Introduction

Helen Hughes' theme is that external capital flows can contribute markedly to growth, even though such flows might be a marginal component of total investment, as long as the host country is "well run," or in other words, as long as the policy environment in the host country causes the capital inflow to be used efficiently. I would like to comment on two topics: first, the forms in which capital flows into developing countries; and second, the problem of creating the correct policy environment.

II. Forms of Capital Flows to Developing Countries

Hughes presents a model of the evolution of capital flows, which I characterize in the figure below (Chart 1). In the first stage of very low income, the developing country has two main sources of external funds—trade credits and official development assistance (ODA)—since at this stage the country appears unattractive as a place to invest in (unless it is relatively resource-rich) or to lend to in the absence of tangible security, like exportable products. The availability of private capital increases in the second stage and direct investment becomes more important, but the original sources also remain significant. At later stages of development, as the creditworthiness of the country increases, there is a shift in this model away from direct investment and "tied" funding such as aid to bank borrowing and, indirectly through the banks, bond finance.

This description of the model stresses the role of growth in determining the mix of capital inflow. However, as Hughes also points out, these forms of capital inflows are not all perfect substitutes and there will be a demand and supply schedule for each type of finance. The precise mix of sources of funds will also vary with their relative prices, and with specific supply and demand factors. For example, an increase in the liquidity of the banking system, new financial instruments,

Chart 1. Shares of Capital Inflow by Stage of Development
(percent)

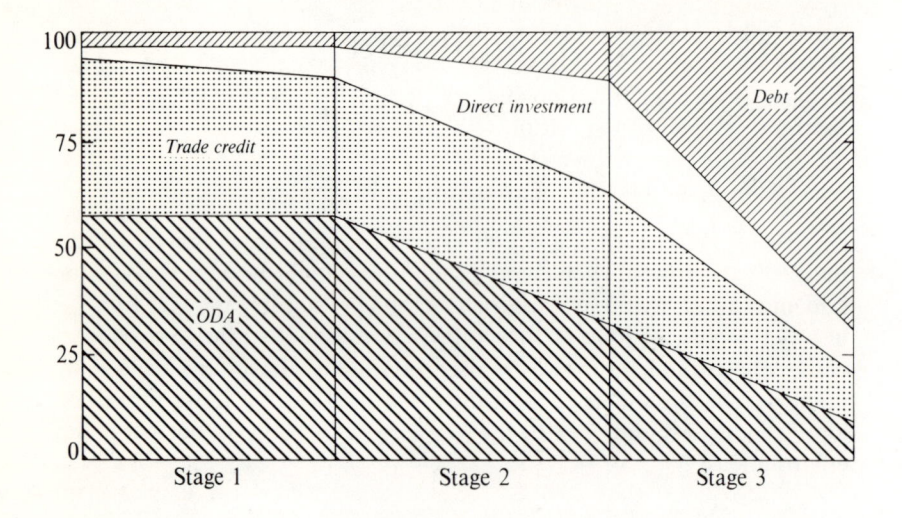

increased efficiency in banking, and changes in the regulatory environment could lower the cost of debt relative to other forms of inflow and increase its share at all stages. ODA also has a "price," as Hughes also stresses, which could change over time. To be more precise in predictions about the composition of the capital flows, the specification of those schedules and the time periods involved in each stage would have to be considered in more detail.

Hughes argues that on the supply side, there is essentially one global supply schedule for each type of capital instrument. However, there is evidence that capital flows, like trade flows, tend to be regionally concentrated. This is intuitively plausible for trade finance, direct investment, and aid, although perhaps less so for debt. Even there, risk assessment will depend on familiarity with the borrowing country, which will be greater for borrowers in the same region, or for borrowers with whom the lender has a longer history of economic contact (e.g., ex-colonies, members of the Commonwealth). Hence, the supply schedule facing a developing country might depend more on forces operating in the developed countries in its region (e.g., Japan in East Asia) than in such countries further away. (See Pangestu (1980) for evidence of the tendency for Japanese direct investment to be concentrated in the region.)

Hughes presents data on the composition of capital flows to developing countries (Tables 2 and 3, pp. 128–29 and 130–31). It might be tempting to use these data to attempt to infer whether the Hughes cross-section model of the composition of capital flows is a useful description

COMMENT   149

of changes in the resource flows to developing countries (DCs). But there are problems in doing so because the time series reported contain data from a number of countries at different stages. Also, the data reflect changes in the relative costs of various sources of funds, whatever the level of development, that is, vertical movements in the boundaries at *all* stages of development as depicted in Chart 1, which ideally should be separated from the composition of countries in the sample.

The data reported by Helen Hughes are reproduced in summary form in Chart 2. The bar charts show the volumes of various private

Chart 2. Resource Flows to Developing Countries
(1960–84)

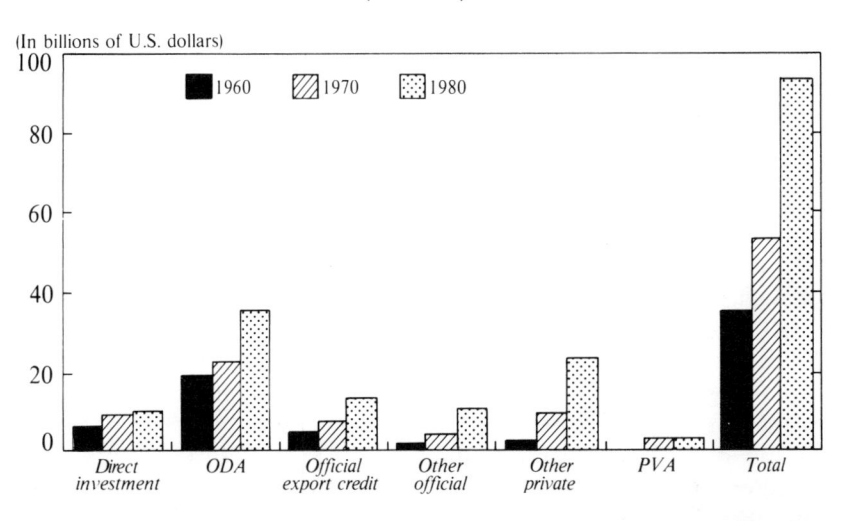

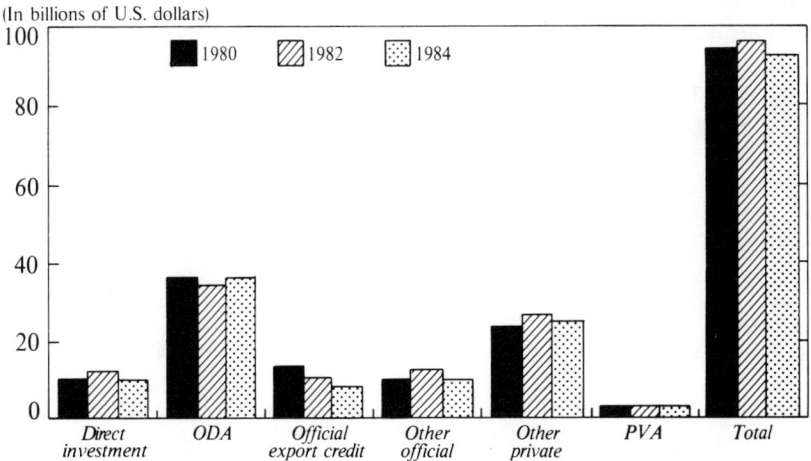

flows, aggregated into direct investment and "other private," which is mainly bank lending, as well as private voluntary assistance (PVA). The official flows are classified as ODA, export credits (which are included under "nonconcessional flows" in Hughes' tables), and other official (also included under "nonconcessional flows" in Hughes' tables).

The top bar chart shows the long-run changes since 1960, and the lower chart shows the changes for selected years in the 1980s. (The selection of every second year hides some variation, which is apparent in the raw data.) The two charts show the rapid growth in resource flows to developing countries (at an annual average rate of about 5 percent a year over the 20 years from 1960) due to growth in all categories *except* direct investment and PVA. They also show the stability in those real flows over the 1980s. The charts illustrate points made by Hughes, e.g., the significance of ODA, the rapid growth in private lending over the 1970s, and the fluctuations in private lending in the 1980s. The pie charts (Chart 3) show the changes in shares of inflows due to each source between 1960 and 1984. The significant changes are the drop in the share of official sources, especially ODA, but also nonconcessional funds; and the increase in the share of bank lending, but also the fall in the share of direct investment. In summary, there has been a shift to private sources, away from official sources and from direct investment.

What I found surprising in these charts was the low and declining share of direct investment in resources transferred to DCs. Hughes discusses the optimality of the total flow of resources to the DCs, but does not discuss explicitly and in detail whether the composition of the flow is biased. For a number of reasons, there would be a bias away from direct investment toward debt. The possibility of such bias is important, because of the lack of substitutability between the forms of capital.

For developing countries, direct investment has a number of advantages over debt. It is accompanied by transfers of knowledge or technique, which would otherwise not be available to the capital importer. Hughes says that this information would also be available alongside bank lending or aid flows, but this seems unlikely. For that to happen, the capital and the information, or skill, would have to be separated out and then the original owner of the information asset would be more likely to forgo the quasi-rents on that information and therefore be unwilling to reveal it. Also, a foreign investor shares more of the risk in a project with the host country and its citizens, and therefore places a smaller burden on the country in periods of low commodity prices, etc., contrary to the experience of highly geared countries. Finally, direct investment has more direct effects on trade than debt, because the foreign owners often wish to export the product back to their home country. (Park (1986) tests hypotheses about connections between the intensities of trade, aid, and direct investment in bilateral relationships.)

COMMENT

Chart 3. Shares of Resource Flows to Developing Countries
(1960 and 1984)

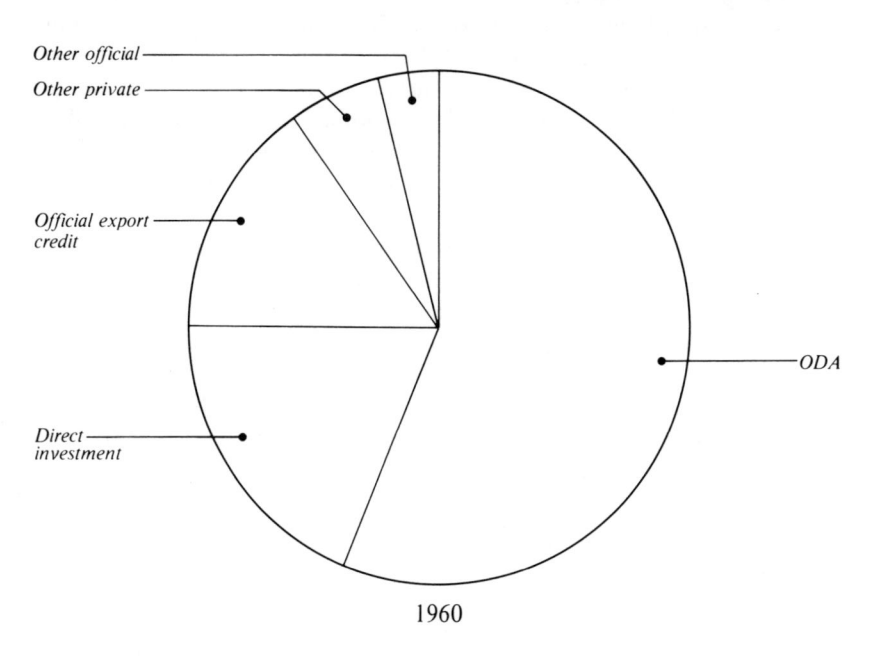

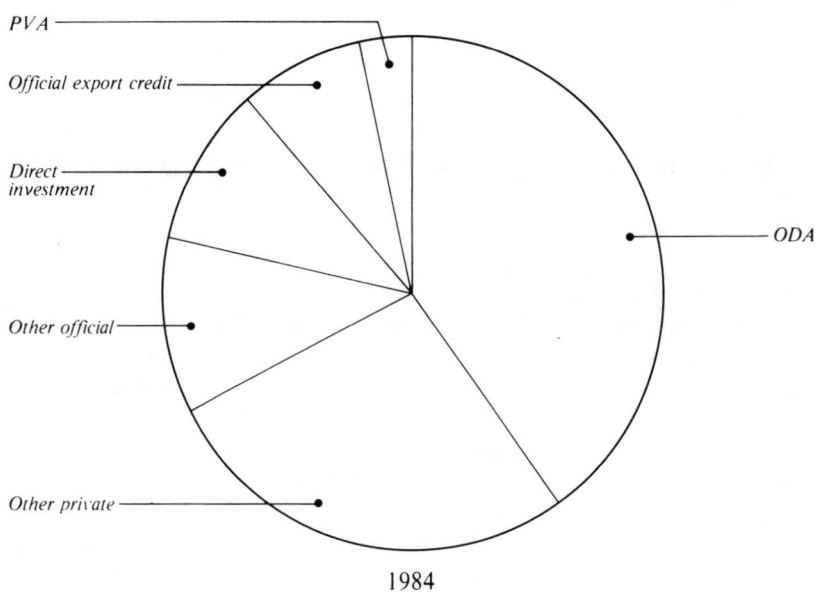

1960

1984

A bias against direct investment could occur because various policies in the host country tend to discriminate against direct investment, for example, rules on local equity. These can often have the effect of putting more risk on local investors (or of dissipating some of the rents from the project in inefficient risk-sharing) and of distributing foreign ownership across more sectors of the economy than originally might have been the case. From the investor's point of view, the main problem associated with direct investment is the risk of being caught with an obsolescing bargain, a problem also referred to by Hughes as the high level of sovereign and country risk.

While direct investment flows are burdened by these imposts, debt receives an implicit subsidy from the guarantees offered, or expected to be offered, by central banks and international agencies. These taxes and subsidies change the relative prices of debt and equity, so that the share of direct investment in total flows ends up being too low. To return to the Hughes theme, foreign capital inflows could contribute even more markedly to growth if this bias were removed. But removal of the bias requires a change in the policy environment.

III. The Policy Environment

Policy advisers and politicians are increasingly aware that biases toward import-substituting industries will hinder growth (see, for example, Ariff and Hill (1986)). Hughes notes that a protectionist trade policy, along with a repressed financial system and inappropriate fiscal policies, will distort the volume and direction of the capital inflow. However, the making of economic policy takes place in a political market, which can produce policy sets radically different from those that will maximize growth, even though the rhetoric of the political leadership is in favor of growth (see Findlay and Garnaut (1986) for a review of the experiences of Association of South East Asian Nations (ASEAN) and Australia). The policymaking challenge is then to shift the policy set toward the growth-maximizing package.

A traditional approach to setting the agenda for policymaking is to use the work on the economics of the second best. However, this approach is excessively conservative. It limits the extent to which policymakers can use the influence of events in markets for substitute goods and services to facilitate across-the-board liberalization. For example, strict application of the rule from the traditional static second-best world would have inhibited the liberalization of Australia's financial sector because it would have restricted the growth of substitute financial assets. This growth put pressure on the banks to argue for liberalization of their regulatory environment (see Harper (1986)). In other words, for long-run growth, it may be worth putting up with an increase in short-run distortion in the allocation of resources. This argument applies to the process of tariff reduction within the import-competing sector. It could also apply at an aggregate level; for example, it could be used to support the deregulation of markets for capital whether or not a distortion in the labor market continues to exist.

With respect to direct foreign investment, the "substitute principle" can also be applied by identifying motives for policies that inhibit the use of such funds. If the motive of local equity rules, for example, is to capture more of the benefits of projects for host countries, this directs attention to the use of more efficient fiscal devices (e.g., resource rent taxes in mineral projects) as a substitute form of intervention. Fiscal instruments are then an important part of the agenda for reform.

It is difficult to define an effective agenda for policy change. More work on the operation of the political market for structural adjustment policy would be useful for that purpose.

References

Ariff, Mohamed, and Hall Hill, 1986, *Export-Oriented Development: The ASEAN Experience* (Sydney: Allen and Unwin, 1986).

Findlay, Christopher C., and Ross Garnaut, eds., *The Political Economy of Manufacturing Protection: Experiences of ASEAN and Australia* (Sydney; Boston: Allen and Unwin, 1986).

Harper, Ian, "Why Financial Deregulation?" Center for Economic Policy Research Discussion Paper No. 132, (Canberra: Center for Economic Policy Research, Australian National University, October 1986).

Pangestu, Mari, "Japanese and Other Foreign Investment in the ASEAN Countries," Australia-Japan Research Center Paper No. 73 (Canberra: Australia-Japan Research Center, Australian National University, July 1980).

Park, Y.I.1, "The Changing Pattern of Country Bias in Australia's and Korea's Trade Relationships" (mimeographed, Adelaide, Australia: University of Adelaide, January 1986).

5

Fiscal and Monetary Policies: Their Role in the Adjustment Process

*Grant H. Spencer and Robin T. Clements**

I. Introduction

While it is true that the economic problems that emerged in the 1970s were initiated by influences beyond the control of individual countries, the countries were not therefore relieved of the necessity to adjust their economies to the new realities. Since the early 1980s most industrial countries have accepted the need to adjust to fundamental changes in the external environment, and several have successfully shifted to a path of monetary restraint. However, there remain significant differences in beliefs concerning the degree to which the fiscal/monetary policy mix can be used to soften the unemployment impact of a firm monetary policy.

One point of view put forward, for example, by Mundell (1976) advocates the simultaneous use of expansionary budgetary policy and contractionary monetary policy to overcome the problem of stagflation. The alternative monetarist viewpoint suggests that any positive impact from a fiscal expansion will be at best short-lived, and that, in the long run, the effect on output will be negligible or even negative, as increased net government expenditure crowds out private investment and/or foreign demand through interest rate and exchange rate pressures.

The objective of this paper is to examine selected country experiences over the 1970s and early 1980s, with a view to finding evidence in support of one or other of these views. Rather than undertaking a detailed econometric analysis of annual data, an attempt is made to identify the main medium- to long-term policy responses simply by comparing averaged variables over three broad subperiods: 1970–73, 1974–78, and 1979–83. Prior to the comparative analysis of the averaged data in Section IV, we look first, in Section II, at the monetary and fiscal stances of some Organization for Economic Cooperation and Develop-

---

*The views expressed in this paper are those of the authors and do not necessarily reflect those of the Reserve Bank of New Zealand.

ment (OECD) countries in order to identify examples of countries that have adopted firm monetary policies combined with various degrees of fiscal restraint. Once the most useful cases have been identified, a discussion of policy and economic developments in each country follows in Section III, with a view to clarifying the impact of the adopted policy mix as well as the nature of other major influences on the selected economies. The final section summarizes the analysis in Section IV and draws some conclusions about the nature of macroeconomic responses to changes in the fiscal/monetary policy mix based on the observed country experiences.

II. Monetary and Fiscal Policy Profiles

Over the 1970s the oil-consuming countries were experiencing high rates of inflation, sluggish growth, and rising unemployment. The superior comparative performance of several countries in this group tends to suggest that those countries reacted differently to the two major supply shocks of 1973/74 and 1979/80. Fiscal and monetary policy reactions were varied both in terms of fundamental direction and in terms of the degree to which they were applied.

The three main alternatives were to (a) adopt a more expansionary stance for both monetary and fiscal policy aimed at offsetting the negative effects on domestic demand and supply of the decline in the terms of trade; (b) maintain a firm monetary policy to restrain the inflationary effect of the oil price increases, while allowing some easing in fiscal policy to support domestic demand; and (c) shift both monetary and fiscal policies in a more restrictive direction, with the object of encouraging fundamental resource movements and a rapid reduction in inflation. In terms of this simple categorization, the most common response to the first oil shock in 1973/74 was to adopt (a) or (b), with the overall effect leading to higher inflation and lower real growth. The responses to the second shock, however, were more a mixture of (b) and (c). The major reason for this shift was an apparent general acceptance among industrial countries that the reduction of inflation should be accorded the highest priority in policy formulation. Action to alleviate the inflationary pressures therefore included a more determined recourse to stricter monetary control, with a tendency, on average, toward larger fiscal deficits contributing to significant increases in real interest rates.

With respect to the stance of monetary policy, various indicators are shown in Table 1 for a range of large and small OECD countries. For most countries the averages do not point to a definitive conclusion with respect to their monetary stance. The United States appears to have maintained a moderately tight stance through the second and third subperiods. Most of the indicators for Japan and the Federal Republic of

Table 1. Monetary Policy Indicators, 1970–73, 1974–78, and 1979–83
(Averages of annual percentages)

	Money[1]			Real Money[2]			Credit[3]			Real Interest[4]		
	1970–73	1974–78	1979–83	1970–73	1974–78	1979–83	1970–73	1974–75	1979–83	1970–73	1974–78	1979–83
United States	12.4	10.9	10.4	6.9	3.3	2.6	12.2	9.4	9.1	0.9	−0.3	3.2
Japan	20.7	12.1	6.8	12.5	3.2	6.7	20.9	10.6	8.9	−0.5	−0.6	6.0
Germany	14.1	7.3	6.6	6.8	2.4	2.4	13.3	8.1	8.4	1.5	2.8	4.4
United Kingdom	19.5	10.6	16.5	10.6	−4.6	4.5	39.8	13.8	21.8	1.5	−2.2	0.2
Canada	15.2	17.8	9.5	8.8	7.1	−0.2	16.6	15.4	12.7	1.9	−0.9	3.0
Denmark	9.9	12.4	14.0	0.9	1.6	4.6	9.7	9.8	9.6	2.3	4.4	8.3
Belgium	13.7	12.2	5.7	7.4	3.1	0.3	13.3	14.0	6.7	1.4	—	6.5
Sweden	10.4	10.6	11.6	3.4	−0.5	2.0	9.2	12.1	12.0	0.5	−1.8	2.5
Australia	14.2	10.8	11.8	6.2	−1.6	1.7	14.6	16.2	13.0	−0.6	−2.6	2.7

Sources: Organization for Economic Cooperation and Development (1984 and 1985a).
[1] Money: M1 plus quasi-money.
[2] Real money: M1 plus quasi-money deflated by GDP implicit price index.
[3] Credit: Credit to the economy.
[4] Real interest: Yield on long-term (five years or more) government bonds divided by the ratio of the GDP implicit price level index to that of the previous year.

Germany are clear evidence of a firming of monetary policy over the latter two subperiods with the growth in monetary aggregates falling and real interest rates rising. While the United Kingdom was able to bring the rate of monetary expansion under control over 1974–78, a move in the opposite direction can be seen for 1979–83. In contrast, Canada appears to have responded to the first oil shock in a relatively expansionary way, but subsequently made considerable progress in tightening the monetary stance over the latter period. Denmark exhibits mixed indicators, with nominal and real money growth becoming progressively more expansionary, while credit growth was falling slightly and real interest rates were increasing significantly. Belgium's record suggests that there was no substantive change in monetary stance in response to the first oil shock, but that there was a clear shift to a tight monetary policy after the second oil shock. The last two countries in Table 1—Sweden and Australia—both show, to differing degrees, symptoms of a loose monetary stance, although some moderation is detectable in the 1979–83 period.

The fiscal policy indicators of Table 2 show that the average fiscal balance for all countries deteriorated between 1970–73 and 1974–78, and with the exception of the United Kingdom, continued to deteriorate through 1979–83. Of the six countries that can be considered to have adopted generally firm monetary policies over one or both of the post-shock periods, Belgium best represents the case of a loose fiscal policy stance throughout the sample period. The other two countries that will be considered in detail are Japan and the Federal Republic of Germany. Both of these countries have maintained firm to moderate fiscal policy stances, with the deficit to gross national product (GNP) ratios probably

Table 2. **Fiscal Policy Indicators: General Government Fiscal Balance**
(As percent of GNP)

	1970–73	1974–78	1979–83
United States	−0.6	−1.5	−1.8
Japan	1.1	−3.1	−4.0
Germany	0.2	−3.1	−3.2
United Kingdom	0.2	−4.1	−3.1
Canada	0.5	−1.5	−3.3
Denmark	4.1	0.1	−5.8
Belgium	−3.1	−4.8	−9.9
Sweden	4.5	2.1	−4.5
Australia	1.8	−0.8	−1.0

Source: Tanzi (1985), p.2.

tending to understate the degree of restraint. The main difference between the policy responses of these two countries, although again not well reflected in the average deficit ratios, is seen in the relative fiscal positions adopted following the oil shocks. Germany's fiscal response to the second shock was considerably less accommodating than that following the first, while Japan's fiscal response to the first shock was less accommodating than that to the second. The comparison between Germany and Japan is also of interest, because both countries have experienced similar average fiscal deficits relative to GNP, while Japan has maintained a significantly higher savings ratio.

III. Review of Historical Developments

The purpose of this section is to present a short characterization for each of the three selected countries of the monetary and fiscal policy record over the sample period, with a view to highlighting interactions with other external developments and the overall consequences for economic performance. The discussion for each country is accompanied by a table containing the economic variables of interest for the period 1970–83.

Japan

In the early years of the 1970s, before the first oil shock, the Japanese monetary authorities gave priority to maintaining a fixed exchange rate in the face of strong upward international pressure on the yen. While this policy was consistent with the domestic objectives of the time, it involved accepting an unusually rapid rate of monetary growth for more than two years. As the Japanese economy entered a strong upswing phase in 1972, the Bank of Japan moved actively to reverse the accommodative monetary stance, but it was not until the floating of the yen in February 1973 that any real scope emerged for directing monetary policy toward domestic objectives. By 1973 the Japanese economy was showing clear signs of becoming severely overheated. Inflation had begun to accelerate, pushing long-term real interest rates into the negative. These negative rates, combined with strong real growth in the economy, resulted in investment rates expanding faster than saving rates and a consequent deterioration in the current account of the balance of payments. The monetary authorities took further steps toward monetary restraint, and inflation appeared to be abating in late 1973, but the first oil price rise markedly aggravated the situation.

Fueled by the impact of a dramatic worsening in the terms of trade of some 22 percent over 1973/74 and, more significantly, by an unprecedented 28.1 percent rise in unit labor costs, inflation spiraled to 24.5 percent in 1974. Monetary policy was tightened further and the rate of money growth on average in 1974 was brought down to 9.5 percent. The cost of the oil shock in terms of the effect on domestic demand conditions and output was severe, with gross domestic product (GDP) growth falling from the high level of 8.8 percent in 1973 to −1.0 percent in 1974. The tight monetary policy, which was maintained into 1975, resulted in a rapid reduction in the rate of inflation in 1975. As the Japanese economy recovered from this anti-inflationary phase, the authorities detected a deficiency in real domestic demand. Fiscal policy measures, which up until then had kept the fiscal balance in surplus, were aimed at sustaining domestic demand. The central bank provided support by easing up somewhat on monetary policy. The fiscal balance deteriorated from a surplus position of 0.4 percent of GNP in 1974 to a deficit of 2.7 percent in 1975, while, at the same time, money growth expanded to 14.5 percent. The expansionary fiscal policy appeared to contribute significantly to the reflation of the economy, with an estimated stimulative impact of demand on the order of 3 percent of GDP.

Throughout the period 1976–78 the overall stance of fiscal policy, and to a lesser extent monetary policy, was designed to support the recovery of domestic demand. Fiscal deficits grew to over 5 percent of GNP, while monetary expansion remained moderate. Despite the concerns about the weakness of domestic demand, real growth during this period was consistently in the range of 5 percent per annum.

Against this background, the Japanese economy responded very differently to the second oil shock in 1979 than it had in 1974/75. A real appreciation of the exchange rate and the strengthening of domestic demand were already eroding the current account surplus, and the real exchange rate was beginning to depreciate. These developments raised concern among the authorities that inflation would be refueled. They moved quickly to keep the situation under control by preventing any acceleration in the growth of the money stock. Although money growth was restrained to 7.8 percent in 1980, the oil price rise, together with more general increases in world commodity prices late in 1979, caused domestic inflation to accelerate to 8.0 percent in 1980. However, maintenance of the firm monetary stance brought inflation down in the following year to 4.9 percent and to 2.7 percent in 1982. Throughout this period, with the impact of the oil shock, some firming in the initial expansionary fiscal position of 1978–80, and a nonaccommodating monetary policy stance, real output continued to grow at around 4 percent per annum. The financing requirements of a still sizable fiscal deficit, in conjunction with low rates of inflation, meant that real rates of interest were held at around 6 percent. Investment rates fell steadily over 1980–83 at a faster rate than saving rates, resulting in a gradual improvement in the current account.

The policy responses to the two oil shocks, although similar in nature, exhibit contrasting approaches and results. To cope with mounting inflationary pressures, demand management policy had already started to firm six months before the first oil shock. However, due to the relatively loose monetary conditions that prevailed in the economy at that time, the impact of the tighter monetary policy was slow and became significant only later in the course of 1974. Fiscal policy, on the other hand, had maintained its firm stance of the earlier period, and the overall demand impact of government transactions in both 1973 and 1974 was negative.

Before the second oil shock, demand management policy had been shifting toward a restrictive stance throughout 1979, and the overall pressure of demand was moderate compared with the earlier experience. The tightening of monetary controls had a relatively rapid effect on credit conditions, with the result that general monetary conditions were probably more stringent than in 1974, even though the deceleration in the growth of the money supply was more moderate. With fiscal policy, the intention was to adopt a firmer stance; however, little improvement in the government's financial position was achieved over 1979/80, and fiscal deficits remained substantially larger than in the 1974/75 period. The overall character of the macroeconomic policy mix would appear to have been relatively easier for the latter period, mainly as a result of the fiscal position.

Federal Republic of Germany

As the export-led upturn developed from the end of 1972, demand management policies in Germany, which had been broadly countercyclical with rising money growth and fiscal deficits in 1971/72, became more restrictive. Both fiscal and monetary disinflationary measures were imposed at an early stage in order to avoid the risk of overheating and a further acceleration of inflation. The effectiveness of monetary policy, which had previously been severely limited, was enhanced by the exchange rate float in May 1971. Over the 1973–75 period, monetary expansion was reduced significantly from the high levels of 1972. The dampening impact of the monetary restraint on domestic demand was felt very quickly. Money growth fell from 14.4 percent in 1973 to 5.2 percent in 1974, which, combined with the trebling of crude oil prices, had a pronounced deflationary impact on demand. Fiscal policy responded quickly, with the fiscal balance moving from a surplus of 1.2 percent of GNP in 1973 to deficits of 1.3 percent and 5.7 percent in 1974 and 1975, respectively. The relaxation of fiscal restraint put further pressure on already positive real interest rates and was also interpreted as a shift away from the price stabilization objectives. The resulting jump in inflationary expectations contributed to a period of high

Table 3. Japan: Selected Economic Indicators, 1970-83

	1970	1971	1972	1973	1974	1975	1976	1977	1978	1979	1980	1981	1982	1983
	(In percent)													
Gross domestic product	9.8	4.6	8.8	8.8	−1.0	2.3	5.3	5.3	5.0	5.1	4.9	4.2	3.1	3.3
Inflation[1]	7.7	6.1	4.5	11.7	24.5	11.8	9.3	8.1	3.8	3.6	8.0	4.9	2.7	1.9
Unemployment	1.1	1.2	1.4	1.3	1.4	1.9	2.0	2.0	2.2	2.1	2.0	2.2	2.4	2.6
Money[2]	16.9	24.3	24.7	16.8	9.5	14.5	13.8	10.7	12.2	11.0	7.8	10.5	7.9	7.6
Real long-term interest rate	−0.1	2.0	1.4	−4.2	−9.4	1.3	2.2	1.6	1.4	4.9	6.2	5.8	6.2	6.7
Relative normalized unit labor costs	101.0	100.0	109.0	118.0	119.0	109.0	107.0	114.0	129.0	112.0	100.0	111.0	101.0	108.0
Terms of trade[3]	1.3	−1.4	6.1	−3.6	−22.4	−7.9	−4.0	2.7	14.8	−15.4	−20.2	2.5	0.8	2.8
Unit labor costs[4]	5.3	9.1	3.8	11.0	28.1	12.6	−2.4	2.4	−1.8	−2.1	−2.0	1.8	−2.8	−2.0
Real unit labor costs[5]	1.8	10.3	2.8	−4.0	1.5	10.3	−7.7	−0.4	−2.6	−7.1	−16.7	0.7	−3.3	−1.2
Fiscal surplus or deficit (−)														
(as a percentage of GNP)	1.9	1.4	0.4	0.5	0.4	−2.7	−3.7	−3.8	−5.5	−4.8	−4.5	−4.0	−3.4	−3.1
(as a percentage of gross private saving)	5.7	4.5	1.2	1.5	1.3	−9.3	−12.1	−12.8	−17.8	−16.4	−15.4	−13.9	−12.1	−11.1
	(percent of GDP)													
Current account balance	1.0	2.5	2.3	—	−1.0	−0.1	0.7	1.6	1.7	−0.9	−1.1	0.5	0.7	1.8
Central government debt	6.5	6.5	7.2	6.8	7.2	10.3	12.7	17.7	22.7	26.4	29.7[6]	31.7[6]	34.4[6]	38.0[6]
Exports	10.8	11.7	10.6	10.0	13.6	12.8	13.6	13.2	11.2	11.7	13.9	15.0	14.9	14.3
Gross private saving	33.5	31.2	32.3	32.5	30.0	29.1	30.7	29.6	30.9	29.2	29.3	28.8	28.0	28.0
Gross private fixed capital formation	31.1	29.2	28.7	30.7	29.6	27.1	26.1	24.9	24.6	25.7	25.7	24.8	24.0	22.9

Sources: Organization for Economic Cooperation and Development (1984, 1985a, and 1985b), and International Monetary Fund (1984).
[1] Annual percentage changes in consumer prices.
[2] M1 plus quasi-money.
[3] Index, base 1980 = 100.
[4] Annual percentage change of unit labor cost in manufacturing.
[5] Unit labor cost less annual percentage change in the manufacturing producer price index.
[6] Estimates.

nominal wage increases. Contrary to perceptions at the time, the Bundesbank did not accommodate the wage increases by an easing of credit conditions. Subsequently, businesses were not able to pass on the cost increases. The resultant severe profit squeeze caused a cut in investment and employment. Despite erratic fluctuations in the value of the deutsche mark, export performance continued to be strong up to the middle of 1974 as demand levels remained relatively buoyant in trading partners and competitor countries.

In 1975 the recession reached its lower turning point, with GDP falling by 1.7 percent. The prolonged period of tight monetary policy had successfully defused the inflationary psychology that had developed in the early 1970s, and consumer price inflation began to fall. The strong fiscal injection of 1975 was clearly an important factor affecting the eventual upswing experienced in 1976. Subsequent action taken to strengthen the financial position of the public sector was based on the assumption that private demand had developed sufficiently to hold aggregate demand at an adequate level. Little progress had been made in eliminating unemployment or the current account surplus, however. As the weakness of aggregate demand became apparent in the course of 1977, the emphasis of fiscal policy shifted back again toward demand support. Also, the monetary authorities moved to accommodate a relatively high demand for liquidity at declining interest rates.

For much of the period 1977–79, fiscal and monetary policies remained stimulatory with the aim of reducing the persistently high level of unemployment. Fiscal measures were somewhat constrained by the objective of gradually reducing the public sector deficit. The authorities subsequently succeeded in reducing the size of the deficit from 5.7 percent of GNP in 1975 to 2.7 percent in 1979. In most respects, economic performance in 1979 was highly satisfactory. Demand, led by business-fixed investment, expanded strongly and unemployment continued to fall. However, the related rapid growth in Germany's imports and the impact of the second oil shock on import prices swung the current external balance into deficit for the first time since the mid-1960s. Fueled by the oil price hike and other commodity price rises, consumer price inflation accelerated in 1979, despite the fact that domestic sources of inflation had been restrained by a firming of monetary policy. A fall in the external value of the deutsche mark in 1980 exacerbated the inflationary environment, and the authorities responded by further restricting money supply growth and gradually raising interest rates. The direction of fiscal policy represented a moderately expansionary stance, in contrast to the strong expansionary stance adopted after the first oil shock.

The relatively easy fiscal policy stance was continued into 1981 in an attempt to stimulate the weak domestic demand situation; however,

Table 4. Federal Republic of Germany: Selected Economic Indicators, 1970-83

	1970	1971	1972	1973	1974	1975	1976	1977	1978	1979	1980	1981	1982	1983
					(In percent)									
Gross domestic product	5.1	3.1	4.2	4.6	0.5	−1.7	5.5	3.1	3.1	4.2	1.8	—	−1.0	1.0
Inflation[1]	3.4	5.3	5.5	6.9	7.0	6.0	4.5	3.7	2.7	4.1	5.5	6.3	5.3	3.3
Unemployment	0.6	0.7	0.9	1.0	2.1	4.0	4.0	3.9	3.7	3.3	3.3	4.6	6.7	8.2
Money[2]	10.5	14.5	17.0	14.4	5.2	−0.1	6.8	11.3	13.1	8.3	8.4	8.5	5.0	2.6
Real long-term interest rate	0.7	0.2	2.4	2.6	3.4	2.3	4.3	2.4	1.4	3.3	3.9	5.9	4.1	4.6
Relative normalized unit labor costs[3]	86.0	90.0	91.0	100.0	102.0	95.0	96.0	101.0	103.0	104.0	100.0	89.0	90.0	89.0
Terms of trade	6.8	2.4	3.1	−2.3	−9.4	6.5	−2.3	−1.0	4.0	−5.4	−6.4	−6.6	3.7	1.7
Unit labor costs[4]	14.3	7.8	4.0	6.4	9.1	6.8	0.6	5.3	5.0	2.4	7.3	5.2	4.1	−1.0
Real unit labor costs[5]	9.3	3.6	1.7	−0.4	−4.2	3.5	−2.9	2.5	4.2	−2.7	0.2	−0.8	−0.7	−2.5
Fiscal surplus or deficit (−) (as a percentage of GNP)	0.2	−0.2	−0.5	1.2	−1.3	−5.7	−3.4	−2.4	−2.5	−2.7	−3.1	−3.8	−3.5	−2.7
(as a percentage of gross private saving)	0.9	−0.9	−2.3	5.9	−6.2	−26.5	−16.3	−12.3	−12.0	−12.9	−15.1	−18.7	−17.1	−12.9
					(percent of GDP)									
Current account balance	0.6	0.4	0.4	1.3	2.7	1.0	0.9	0.8	1.4	−0.8	−1.8	−0.8	0.6	0.7
Central government debt	7.0	6.5	6.7	6.7	7.3	10.6	11.5	12.6	13.8	14.5	15.7	17.7	19.3	20.5
Exports	21.2	21.0	20.9	22.1	26.7	25.0	26.3	26.1	25.5	25.7	27.1	29.9	31.3	30.0
Gross private saving	22.3	21.5	21.7	20.5	20.9	21.5	20.8	19.5	20.8	20.9	20.5	20.3	20.5	21.0
Gross private fixed capital formation	20.9	21.6	21.3	20.1	17.5	16.5	16.7	17.0	17.4	18.3	19.1	18.5	17.7	18.1

Sources: Organization for Economic Cooperation and Development (1984, 1985a, and 1985b), and International Monetary Fund (1984).
[1] Annual percentage changes in consumer prices. [4] Annual percentage change of unit labor cost in manufacturing.
[2] M1 plus quasi-money. [3] Index, base 1980 = 100.
[5] Unit labor cost less annual percentage change in the manufacturing producer price index.

in 1982 and 1983 it underwent a period of consolidation, bringing the deficit down from 3.8 percent of GNP in 1981 to 2.7 percent in 1983. Monetary policy maintained a restrictive stance throughout the 1981–83 period. Even though consumer price inflation was already substantially below that in the OECD area as a whole, it was considerably reduced further to below 5 percent in 1983. The current external account returned to a surplus position in 1982 and the rate of unemployment rose rapidly to its highest postwar level.

In contrast to Japan, which appears to have reacted with a relatively easier macroeconomic policy mix to the latter of the two oil shocks, Germany appeared to respond in the opposite way with a tighter mix for the second oil shock. The non-accommodating stance of monetary policy in the face of the first oil shock was combined with fiscal policy moves that were decidedly expansionary in order to support domestic demand, which had lost much of its earlier momentum. Similar motives of wishing to stimulate domestic demand, while not aggravating inflationary pressures, led to the more moderate fiscal stimulus that followed the second oil shock. Monetary policy was tightened, as in the earlier episode, although the degree of restrictiveness does not appear to have been as severe.

Belgium

Belgium has consistently opted for a hard currency policy, the stability of the Belgian franc's exchange rate against the main trading partners being an important aim of the monetary authorities. Two important characteristics of the Belgian economy have contributed to the significant role of the exchange rate in monetary policy. First, in terms of openness, Belgium's exposed sector, as a percent of GDP, is around three times the OECD average. Second, Belgium has a comprehensive system of wage and salary indexation, both in the private and public sectors, which has tended to accentuate the inflationary impact of terms of trade shocks. These features, in particular, made the Belgian economy vulnerable to the two oil shocks and led the monetary authorities to put the objective of exchange rate stability ahead of internal objectives whenever the Belgian franc came under pressure on the foreign exchange market.

The first oil shock came at a time when the Belgian economy had experienced a period of sustained economic growth associated with moderate rates of inflation and unemployment. Monetary and fiscal policies were flexible and aimed at supporting the level of activity, while attempting to stem the upward pressure on the Belgian franc. The oil price rise resulted in an adverse shift in the terms of trade of around 5 percent in 1974 which, combined with the commodity price boom and the impact of high wage indexation, pushed consumer price inflation up

Table 5. Belgium: Selected Economic Indicators, 1970-83

	1970	1971	1972	1973	1974	1975	1976	1977	1978	1979	1980	1981	1982	1983
	(In percent)													
Gross domestic product	6.4	3.7	5.3	5.9	4.1	−1.5	5.2	0.4	3.0	2.0	3.5	−1.3	1.1	0.4
Inflation[1]	3.9	4.3	5.4	7.0	12.7	12.8	9.2	7.1	4.5	4.5	6.6	7.6	8.7	7.7
Unemployment	1.8	1.8	2.3	2.3	2.4	4.4	5.8	6.6	7.1	7.3	7.7	10.0	11.7	12.9
Money[2]	9.0	13.6	17.5	14.8	11.2	17.1	13.6	9.6	9.3	6.4	2.4	5.5	5.8	8.4
Real long-term interest rate	3.0	1.6	0.8	0.2	−3.4	−3.2	1.4	1.2	4.0	4.9	8.0	8.1	5.9	5.5
Relative normalized unit labor costs[3]	93.0	92.0	96.0	95.0	98.0	100.0	102.0	106.0	104.0	102.0	100.0	95.0	83.0	78.0
Terms of trade	0.9	−3.9	2.7	0.7	−4.7	0.2	−2.2	−0.3	−0.6	1.6	−3.7	−5.0	0.3	−1.2
Unit labor costs[4]	2.5	8.1	4.2	5.1	15.5	16.2	2.4	6.3	1.4	3.5	3.8	5.1	0.9	2.5
Real unit labor costs[5]	3.7	7.0	0.7	1.7	−1.8	9.3	−1.4	3.1	0.6	−0.9	−1.5	−1.5	−6.1	−0.8
Fiscal surplus or deficit (−)														
(as a percentage of GNP)	−2.0	−3.0	−4.0	−3.5	−2.6	−4.7	−5.4	−5.5	−6.0	−7.0	−8.2	−12.1	−11.0	−11.1
(as a percentage of gross private saving)	−8.1	−12.8	−16.4	−14.8	−11.1	−21.2	−23.1	−25.0	−26.9	−32.9	−39.0	−55.5	−52.6	−47.4
	(percent of GDP)													
Current account balance	2.8	2.1	3.6	2.0	0.4	−0.1	0.1	−1.3	−1.4	−2.7	−4.5	−4.5	−3.5	−1.0
Central government debt	48.4	45.8	45.3	42.9	39.2	40.1	40.3	43.3	46.8	50.3	55.9	66.9	78.3	88.6
Exports	51.9	50.6	51.1	55.6	61.3	53.7	57.0	55.6	54.0	59.5	62.9	68.5	73.7	74.4
Gross private saving	24.6	23.5	24.4	23.7	23.5	22.2	23.4	22.0	22.3	21.3	21.0	21.8	20.9	23.4
Gross private fixed capital formation	19.3	19.5	17.4	18.1	19.7	19.3	18.7	18.4	18.5	17.6	17.9	14.9	14.6	13.6

Sources: Organization for Economic Cooperation and Development (1984, 1985a, and 1985b), and International Monetary Fund (1984).
[1] Annual percentage changes in consumer prices.
[2] M1 plus quasi-money.
[3] Index, base 1980 = 100.
[4] Annual percentage change of unit labor cost in manufacturing.
[5] Unit labor cost less annual percentage change in the manufacturing producer price index.

to 12.7 percent for that year. Further high increases in unit labor costs in 1975, and expansionary monetary and fiscal policies in response to a fall in external demand, served to hold inflation at the same high level for the following year.

A strong recovery in both domestic and external demand in 1976 saw a return to positive real GDP growth, although the domestic recovery was supported by a further worsening of the fiscal balance and a continuation of the loose monetary policy. The pronounced extent to which the economy is dependent on foreign trade and the weakness of demand in the major European countries largely explain the depressed activity in 1977. Performance improved through 1978/79, with inflation falling back to 4.5 percent in both years. Public finance continued to have an expansionary effect, with the budget deficit growing in 1978 and 1979, as the Government sought to alleviate the growing problem of unemployment. Monetary policy, which had been expansionary, became progressively more restrictive, interest rates having been raised substantially because of exchange rate pressures.

The impact of the second oil shock had quite different implications for the Belgian economy. Inflationary pressures were less pronounced than for the earlier episode, international commodity prices were more stable, and domestic demand was less buoyant. In addition, more restrictive monetary conditions limited the scope for a resurgence in wage growth. As in most other OECD countries, the economic situation in Belgium deteriorated significantly in 1981. In Belgium's case, however, the economy was already experiencing serious imbalances, so that the results for 1981 were in many respects among the worst recorded in the OECD area.

Interest rates were adjusted upwards on several occasions, but the monetary authorities had little room to maneuver owing to the dual constraint of having to finance the public deficit as well as restricting the decline in the Belgian franc. The real conflict between the objectives of monetary policy came at the domestic level. On the one hand, the monetary authorities did not wish to raise interest rates, the aim being to support domestic activity; at the same time, however, private sector saving needed to be stimulated so that the public sector deficit could be financed. In practice, this conflict was not resolved. Interest rates declined, with the result that household saving was insufficient to meet the borrowing requirements of private enterprises and the public sector. Thus, the authorities had to resort increasingly to financing the budget deficit by monetary means, including borrowing abroad. The latter form of borrowing helped to finance the widening current account deficit as well as preventing excessive pressures in the domestic money and capital markets.

IV. Comparative Analysis

The discussion in this section centers on the effects of changes in policy mixes on economic developments in the selected countries as represented by movements in various (averaged) economic variables and ratios over the three subperiods: 1970–73; 1974–78; and 1979–83.

These movements are depicted in Charts 1 through 5 and quantified in Table 6. The particular combinations of ratios presented and the ordering of the charts are intended to help facilitate the analysis, with each combination representing a cross section of the transmission mechanism illustrated in Diagram 1. The arrows in Diagram 1 represent the main linkages by which changes in the fiscal/monetary policy mix are assumed to affect economic performance.

However, it is well recognized that a range of "other factors" often bear heavily on particular outcomes observed at the various intermediate stages of the transmission mechanism. Some of the more important

Diagram 1. TRANSMISSION CHANNELS

TRANSMISSION CHANNELS

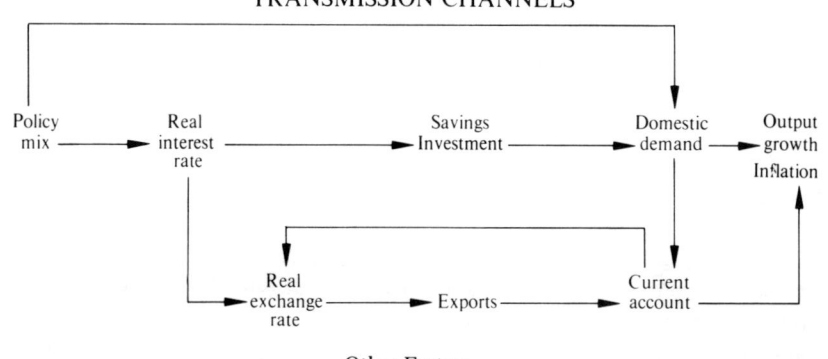

Policy mix → Real interest rate → Savings Investment → Domestic demand → Output growth / Inflation

Real exchange rate → Exports → Current account

Other Factors

Policy mix	Real exchange rate	Savings/investment/	Output growth/
cyclical position	exchange rate regime	exports	inflation
	capital mobility	relative cyclical position	cyclical position
	foreign interest rates	expectations	expectations
		real wages	real wages

Real interest rate
foreign interest rates
cyclical position
public debt
deficit/savings
velocity trends

terms of trade
accelerator effects

Domestic demand/
current account
propensity to import

external factors are listed on the diagram below the system variables that are most likely to be directly influenced by those factors.

Chart 1 summarizes the relative position of fiscal and monetary policy stances (the "policy mix") across the three periods; these are represented by fiscal deficits as a proportion of GNP and annual rates of growth in broad money, respectively.

Chart 1. Fiscal and Monetary Policy Stance: Relative Position

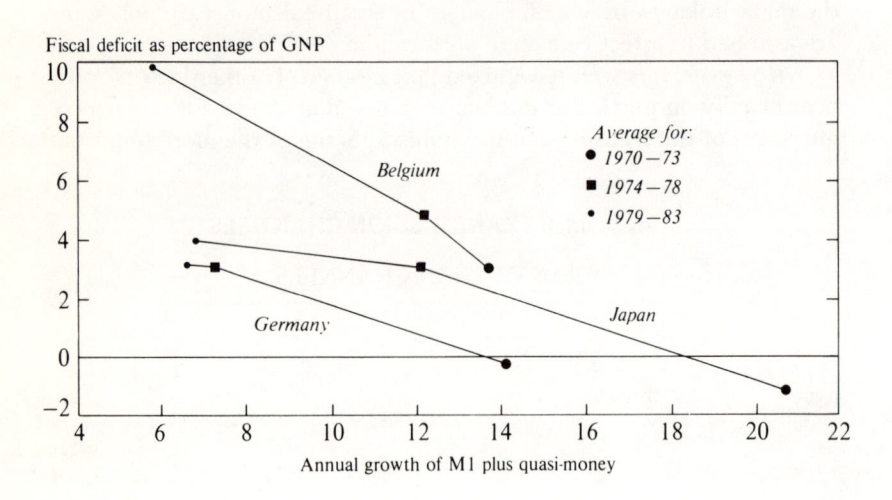

The second chart represents the first stage of the transmission mechanism with plotted movements in the averaged real interest rates and real exchange rates. According to conventional short-run macroeconomic analysis based on the Mundell-Fleming type framework, a policy shift involving an easing of fiscal policy and a tightening of monetary policy should, ceteris paribus, lead to an increase in real interest rates and also cause a real exchange rate appreciation as expected rates of return on foreign currency securities are adjusted upward toward the high domestic currency returns. The relative size of the real interest rate and real exchange rate effects may be expected to be inversely related to the degree of integration between the domestic and foreign capital markets.[1] In principle, real adjustments of this sort may occur under both

---

[1] See, for example, Frenkel and Mussa (1981).

fixed and flexible exchange rates. However, in a fixed exchange rate situation—as for Belgium through much of the sample period and for

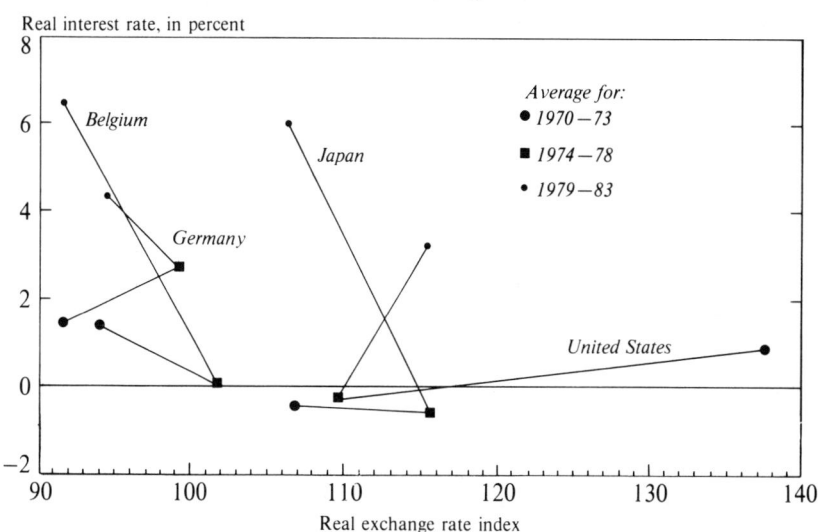

Chart 2. Policy Mix Effects: Movements in Interest and Exchange Rates

Real interest rate, in percent

Average for:
● 1970–73
■ 1974–78
• 1979–83

Real exchange rate index

Germany and Japan in the early years of the sample—the adjustments are likely to be far slower and less concise, as they rely for their effect on movements in domestic relative to foreign price levels as opposed to nominal exchange rate movements.

In the longer term the outcomes may be substantially different. First, to the extent that the change in policy mix is due primarily to a relative tightening of domestic monetary policy, it should have no long-run impact on real interest and exchange rates. Second, the long-run impact of a pure fiscal expansion may well be to lower rather than increase the real exchange rate, as the influence of widening current account deficits (arising from increasing debt service payments) begins to dominate short-run capital account effects.[2] This reversed exchange rate effect may also occur in the shorter term in situations where capital mobility is restricted, or where the current account is particularly sensitive to changes in aggregate domestic demand, or indeed where expectations of long-run outcomes have a strong influence on short-run behavior. A further situation where the exchange rate effect may be reversed

---

[2] As discussed by Rodriguez (1979).

in the short term, as discussed by Sachs and Wyplosz (1984), arises when there is low capital mobility and a high degree of crowding out through a large domestic interest rate effect. In this case, the current account improves rather than worsens and the real exchange rate appreciates in the long run.[3]

The potential differences between the short- and long-run effects of the monetary and fiscal policy components of the overall policy mix mean that it is useful to maintain the conceptual distinction between these components. This is not to say that observed movements in the averaged real interest rates and exchange rates may be interpreted solely as long-run responses to pure fiscal shocks, with real monetary policy effects assumed to be negligible. Indeed, the assessment of underlying fiscal policy responses will be blurred not only by short-term responses to relative shifts in monetary policy stances, but also by other factors, such as shifts in relative cyclical positions, the differential effects of the two oil shocks, and the variable influence of expectations (depending, for example, on policy credibility). Attempts to disentangle contributions from fiscal policy changes will be made here in the context of both the individual country commentaries and historical tables in the previous section and the averaged gross and net savings/investment ratios presented in Charts 3 and 4.

In Chart 3 the vertical axis is the net private savings ratio (total private savings less private investment as a proportion of GNP). An increase in real interest rates arising from a relative easing in the domestic fiscal/monetary policy mix (i.e., an easing of fiscal policy and a tightening of monetary policy) would normally be expected to reduce both private consumption and investment relative to GNP, thus causing an increase in the net private savings ratio. However, if such an increase is insufficient to compensate for the government's dissaving arising out of a higher fiscal deficit, then net national savings may be expected to fall. This will be seen as a worsening in the current account deficit as a proportion of GNP, measured on the horizontal axis.

In order to help identify the transmission channels through which changes in the real interest rates and real exchange rates are affecting the private and national net savings ratios, Chart 4 shows averaged ratios of both gross national investment and total exports of goods and services relative to GNP. In a situation where fiscal expansion reduces gross national savings by crowding out private investment and foreign uses

---

[3] For a survey of the literature on this subject, see Penati (1983).

Chart 3. Policy Mix Effects: Movements in Saving/Investment and Current Account

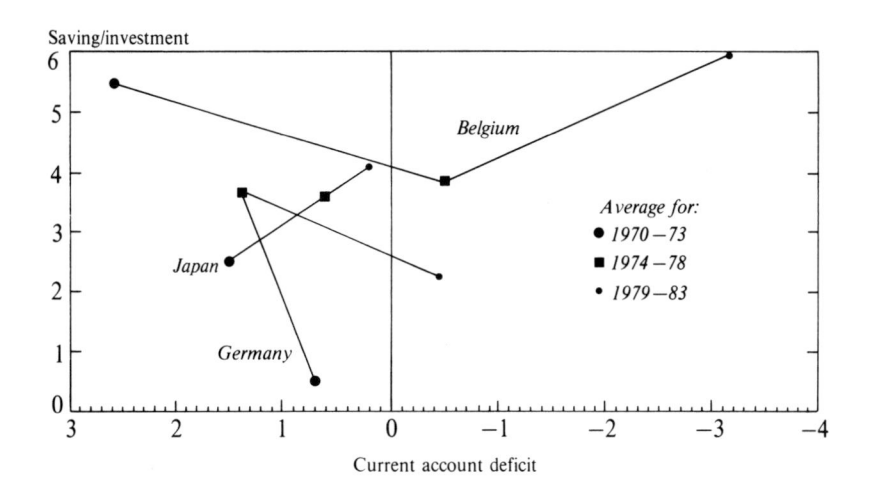

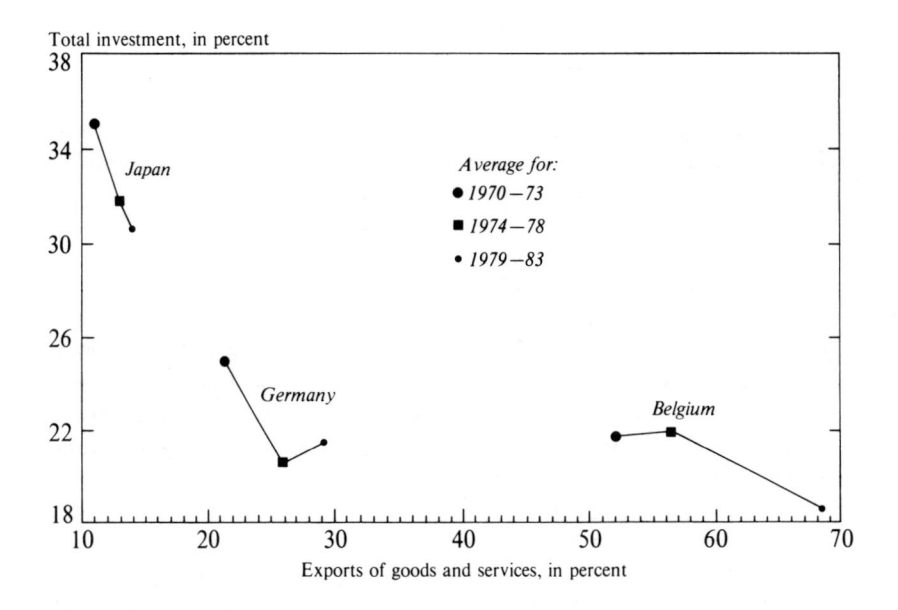

Chart 4. Policy Mix Effects: Movements in Investment and Exports

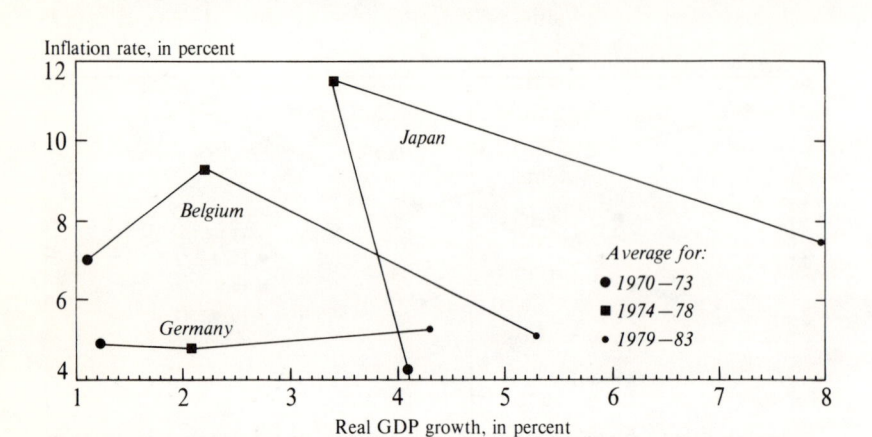

Chart 5. Policy Mix Effects: Movements in Inflation and GDP Growth

of national resources, movements in these ratios may help to indicate the relative significance of real interest rate versus real exchange rate pressures.

Finally, Chart 5 summarizes the relative economic performance of the three countries over the three subperiods as represented by average real GDP growth and inflation rates.

Japan

Considering first the case of Japan, the shift from period 1 to period 2 involves responses to the first oil shock, a tightening of monetary policy relative to the United States, and a significant easing in fiscal policy as represented by the fiscal deficit as a proportion of GNP. The overall effect of this shift on average real interest rates appeared to be negligible, compared to an approximate 1 percent decline in U.S. rates, while the average real exchange rate increased substantially by 8 1/2 percent (Chart 2). Net private savings increased by about 1 percent as private investment dropped off sharply, but an increase in the average fiscal deficit of over 4 percent of GNP caused a decline in total national savings, with the current account position falling to an average balance close to zero.

Given the negligible real interest rate response to the changing fiscal/monetary policy mix, it would be difficult to attribute the sharp falling off in investment to a crowding-out phenomenon. Even though potential interst rate responses may have been dampened by the shift to a lower relative cyclical position in period 2, it seems clear that the investment response was driven mainly by the severe oil price shock and the subsequent supply-side reaction to the general deterioration in Japan's economic outlook.

The alternative possibility of crowding out through a capital-inflow-induced real exchange rate appreciation also seems unlikely in this instance. The increase in the ratio of average exports to GDP in period 2 and the coincidence of the exchange rate appreciation with a significant strengthening in the current account late in the period instead suggest that the real appreciation arose out of the continued underlying strength of Japan's external performance.

Moving from period 2 to period 3, Japan experienced a further deterioration in the net national savings ratio, with a further increase in the fiscal deficit again more than offsetting a small increase in net private savings. In contrast to the first shift, however, this coincided with a real exchange rate depreciation—back to about the average level experienced in period 1—and a large 6½ percentage point increase in the average real interest rate.

In view of the insignificant real interest rate response to the substantial change in the policy mix in period 1, the large interest rate increase in period 2 must presumably be largely attributed to external interest rate pressures arising out of the change in the U.S. policy mix. Furthermore, the relative shifts in policies observed in Chart 1 would seem to suggest that any additional interest rate pressures from domestic sources are more likely to be in response to the firming of monetary policy rather than the easier fiscal stance. If it can thus be inferred that the current account deterioration was not significantly influenced by any fiscal stimulus to domestic demand, then the second oil shock and the associated reduction in external demand is left as the main contributing factor to both the current account and real exchange rate deteriorations. In support of this interpretation, the current account position improved every year following the sharp terms of trade reductions of 1979 and 1980.

If, indeed, in the United States real interest rate pressures are due more to the mix of fiscal/monetary policies in the United States than in Japan, then, in the context of the standard IS/LM-type analysis, the United States would appear to have a steeper IS curve (less interest-elastic demand for money). Alternatively, in the context of a broader portfolio balance model, the demand may be considerably less elastic for U.S. public debt than for Japanese public debt. It is interesting to note that if the size of this elasticity is positively related to the total size of the public debt relative to GDP on the basis of some notion of saturation, then the average ratios shown in Table 6 would suggest that, in period 3,

Table 6. Period Averages: 1970–73, 1974–78, and 1979–83

	United States 1970–73	United States 1974–78	United States 1979–83	Japan 1970–73	Japan 1974–78	Japan 1979–83	Germany 1970–73	Germany 1974–78	Germany 1979–83	Belgium 1970–73	Belgium 1974–78	Belgium 1979–83
				(In percent)								
Gross domestic product	3.5	2.6	1.1	8.0	3.4	4.1	4.3	2.1	1.2	5.3	2.2	1.1
Inflation[1]	4.9	8.0	8.9	7.5	11.5	4.2	5.3	4.8	4.9	5.2	9.3	7.0
Money[2]	12.4	10.9	10.4	20.7	12.1	6.8	14.1	7.3	6.6	13.7	12.2	5.7
Real long-term interest rate	0.9	−0.3	3.2	−0.5	−0.6	6.0	1.5	2.8	4.4	1.4	—	6.5
Relative normalized unit labor costs[3]	138.0	110.0	115.0	107.0	116.0	106.0	92.0	99.0	94.0	94.0	102.0	92.0
Fiscal surplus or deficit (−) (as a percentage of GNP)	−0.5	−1.5	−1.8	1.1	−3.1	−4.0	0.2	−3.1	−3.2	−3.1	−4.8	−9.9
(as a percentage of gross private saving)	−3.1	−7.0	−9.1	3.2	−10.1	−13.8	0.9	−14.7	−15.3	−13.0	−21.5	−45.5
						(percent of GDP)						
Current account balance	—	0.1	−0.2	1.5	0.6	0.2	0.7	1.4	−0.4	2.6	−0.5	−3.2
Central government debt	28.4	28.4	30.7	6.8	14.1	32.0	6.7	11.2	17.5	45.6	41.9	68.0
Exports				10.8	12.9	14.0	21.3	25.9	28.9	52.3	56.4	67.8

| Gross private saving[4] | 2.5 | 3.6 | 4.1 | 0.5 | 3.7 | 2.3 | 5.5 | 3.8 | 6.0 |
| Net national fixed capital formation | 35.1 | 32.0 | 30.7 | 25.2 | 20.7 | 21.6 | 21.9 | 22.1 | 18.8 |

Sources: Organization for Economic Cooperation and Development (1984, 1985a, and 1985b), and International Monetary Fund (1984).
[1] Annual percentage changes in consumer prices.
[2] M1 plus quasi-money.
[3] Index, base 1980 = 100.
[4] Gross private saving, less gross private fixed capital formation.

there was as much fiscal pressure on capital markets in Japan as in the United States. This possibility would not be inconsistent with the small interest rate response to the fiscal expansion in period 2: Japan's average debt to GDP ratio, at 14 percent, was then only half that of the United States.

To the extent that the high real interest rates in period 3 may have been due to this buildup in Japan's public debt, arising through a sustained increase in the size of fiscal deficits through periods 2 and 3, then the further decline in the private investment ratio may, in part, be attributable to crowding out. However, the overall fall in investment in period 3 was not great, and the continued strength of the export sector helped to keep average real GDP growth at a high level (Chart 5).

Compared to the overall relative performance in period 2, where average inflation increased and real growth fell from 8 percent to 4 percent, Japan's relative performance in period 3 was significantly better; the high average real growth rate was maintained while inflation fell sharply. However, the only suggestion of a possible crowding-out effect is in the latter period. The poor performance in period 2 was dominated by the first oil shock of 1973/74, which apparently led to a structural reduction in Japan's investment and savings ratios. The effect of the subsequent decline in the potential growth path was accentuated between periods 1 and 2 by the relatively high cyclical position observed in period 1. The underlying expansionary position of period 1 also added to the difficulty of containing the inflationary impact of the first terms of trade shock. In the third period, there may have been some contribution to the high interest rates from the relatively easy fiscal stance, but the policy mix was, nevertheless, effective in maintaining high real growth, while at the same time countering the effects of the second oil shock and reducing inflation to below 5 percent per annum. It would thus seem difficult to argue that the easier fiscal stance adopted in Japan over periods 2 and 3 contributed to any significant worsening in the country's overall economic performance.

Federal Republic of Germany

Considering the policy shift in Germany between periods 1 and 2, an overall tightening in monetary policy relative to the United States, combined with a significant easing in the fiscal stance, gave rise to a 1 percentage point increase in the average real interest rate and a $7^{1/2}$ percent appreciation in the average real exchange rate. The net private savings ratio increased by over 3 percent, mainly as a result of lower private investment; this was enough to offset the higher fiscal deficit and so effect an improvement in the current account balance.

The improvement in the current account tends to support the hypothesis that the strength of the exchange rate was due more to the relative tightening in monetary policy than to the easier fiscal position. This suggests that, if any crowding out were occurring in period 2, it would be attributable to the higher real interest rate and lower investment ratio. A closer examination of developments in this period, however, does not suggest a significant crowding-out effect. In particular, the investment ratio fell sharply at the start of period 2 in 1974, whereas the fiscal deficits did not increase substantially until 1975 when the authorities were attempting to support domestic demand during a period of significant negative real growth. This suggests that the major falling-off in investment was due mainly to the oil shock of 1973/74, its flow-on effects to external demand, and the tight monetary conditions applying in 1974/75. Certainly, the other measures of fiscal pressure presented in the tables, and in particular the ratio of public debt to GDP, do not indicate any large effect on financial markets from the easier fiscal stance; the higher fiscal deficits claimed an average of over 14 percent of private savings during period 2, but the ratio of public debt to GDP, at about 11 percent, remained very low compared to other OECD countries.

Moving from period 2 to period 3, the monetary/fiscal policy mix in Germany did not change substantially. There was some further monetary policy tightening, but this was clearly less severe than in the United States, and real interest rates on average increased by only 1½ percent, compared to 4 percent in the United States. The net result was a significant worsening in the current account and a real exchange rate depreciation. While external demand was generally weak through most of this period, the depreciation contributed to some improvement in the export to GDP ratio.

Real growth declined further to just 1 percent, on average, in period 3, but, with a significant decline in net private savings and increases in both the investment and export ratios, there is no clear suggestion here of a crowding-out effect. In terms of the claim of the fiscal deficit on the flow of private savings, this ratio did not increase substantially in period 3. Furthermore, in contrast to Japan, where the further fiscal expansions led to a significant increase in the public debt ratio in period 3, the debt ratio in Germany remained at a relatively low level. It would thus seem more appropriate to explain the lower growth performance mainly in terms of the weakness in external demand, as financial policy mixes were tightened more in some of Germany's major trading partners than at home.

The observed responses could even suggest some element of crowding *in* with respect to traded goods production. This would follow if the relatively easy fiscal stance contributed to the lower current balance through its overall positive impact on domestic absorption, thus further lowering the exchange rate and giving added support to export demand.

Belgium

The shift in Belgium's policy mix from period 1 to period 2, as characterized in Chart 1, involved a moderate tightening of monetary policy and an increase in the average fiscal deficit from 3 percent to nearly 5 percent of GNP. Real interest rates fell on average by about 1½ percent, compared to an increase of about 1½ percent in Germany. However, despite the high degree of integration between the two economies, Belgium's real exchange rate appreciated by some 8½ percent. Given that Belgium continued to adopt a managed exchange rate policy through this period, the real exchange rate appreciation cannot be viewed as a response to either a capital- or trade-based improvement in the balance of payments. Rather, it should be seen as resulting from the combined effects of a relatively high inflation rate and an inflexible nominal exchange rate.

The effects of this real appreciation, combined with the relatively easy fiscal/monetary stance, were a fall in the average net private savings ratio arising from increased consumption rather than investment, and a much larger fall in the average current account balance. With the export ratio holding up despite the real appreciation (Chart 4), the current account deterioration was mainly due to a relative expansion in private and public consumption. The ability of Belgium to continue to attract foreign savings under relatively low real interest rates and the strengthening real exchange rate were clearly dependent on transfers from the European Community and/or the Government's willingness to guarantee borrowings on foreign capital markets.

The movement between periods 2 and 3 provides a good opportunity for indentifying a possible crowding-out effect. Between the periods 2 and 3, monetary policy was tightened more sharply than in most other countries and, at the same time, fiscal policy was eased substantially. The large increase in real interest rates of 6½ percent may be broadly attributed to a combination of three main factors: the domestic monetary tightening relative to the rest of the world, the crowding-out effect of U.S. fiscal policy, and the domestic fiscal/monetary policy mix. Whatever the size of the relative contributions, the overall effect of the interest rate increase was to push net private savings above the period 1 level, based largely on a significant decline in the investment to GDP ratio. However, this increase was wholly offset by the large increase in the public sector deficit, while the current account deficit rose on average by nearly 3 percent of GDP.

A deteriorating current account balance can signify the presence of a crowding-out effect if the deterioration is at least partly due to the relative price effects of a real exchange rate being pushed higher by capital flowing into high-interest domestic securities. In the Belgian situation, however, the real exchange rate was significantly weaker and the export ratio considerably larger, indicating that the current account deficit was due primarily to an excess of domestic absorption, which, in turn, put downward pressure on the real exchange rate. Thus, there is a possibility, as in the case of Germany, that the strong fiscal expansion may have, to some extent, crowded in export demand.

There is little doubt that private investment was to some extent crowded out through the contribution of the fiscal expansion to the large increase in the real interest rate. Unfortunately, it is not possible to identify how much of the interest rate increase was due to domestic fiscal policy pressures and how much to the effects of domestic monetary policy and the higher external interest rates. As in the case of Japan, however, a large increase in the average debt to GDP ratio makes it difficult to discount the potential influence of domestic fiscal policy.

The particular combination of effects observed here, although in contrast to the standard short-run analysis (and the apparent U.S. experience), has been discussed in the literature more in the context of long-run responses to fiscal shocks. As mentioned earlier, such outcomes may also be expected to occur more rapidly in situations where factors such as a low degree of capital mobility or a high propensity to import out of domestic expenditure allow current account developments to dominate the exchange market in the short term. It is certainly true that Belgium exhibits characteristics that would tend to emphasize the role of the current account. First, under the various European exchange rate arrangements, local and European authorities have continued to have a dominant influence on the capital account of the balance of payments. Second, the Belgian economy is a very open one; consequently, relatively small proportionate shifts in domestic demand can show up as large changes in the current account balance.

In terms of the overall influence on real growth, the net effect of the domestic fiscal expansion, like the contribution to the higher interest rate level, must remain uncertain. Nevertheless, the significant fall in GDP growth from an average of 2 percent per annum in period 2 to 1 percent in period 3 does not suggest that the export crowding-in effect was particularly dominant, even though the export ratio did increase on average by more than 11 percentage points. The relatively small decline in the investment ratio over the same period suggests that care must be taken when interpreting the relative export and investment ratio movements in Chart 4; the presence of any accelerator effects causes the investment to GDP ratio to understate the extent of any investment crowding out.

V. Summary and Conclusions

From the above analysis, it is clearly not possible to make any general statements about whether an easier fiscal stance is likely to improve or worsen economic performance during a period of monetary restraint. Over the historical period considered, the variable effect of other important factors, across time and between countries, tended to dominate actual economic performance, thus making the assessment of pure fiscal effects an extremely hazardous business. More specifically, relative changes in macroeconomic performance over the period were heavily influenced by differing responses to domestic programs of monetary restraint, supply shocks in the form of the 1973/74 and 1979/80 oil price increases, external interest rate effects arising out of the domestic U.S. fiscal/monetary policy mix, and the changing cyclical position of world demand.

In addition, the relationships between policy mixes and economic performance were strongly affected by changing expectation effects. This means that, while a particular country may seem to have retained a degree of independence between fiscal and monetary policies, it is certainly not possible to view this result as general to other countries with differing past experiences and, hence, differing expectation patterns. Indeed, similar caution is called for when analyzing responses to policy changes in individual countries over a period of time during which expectation effects may have been modified substantially in the light of past experiences.

All of the above influences had a significant bearing on observed real interest rate and real exchange rate responses to changes in the fiscal/monetary policy mix, thus complicating the identification of fiscal effects, which are expected to work through these channels. It is, nevertheless, possible to draw certain conclusions from the above analysis about the types of channels that have been most active in the transmission of both fiscal and other domestic and external shocks. It is also of interest to review the conditions that seem to have been conducive to particular crowding-in and crowding-out effects in the countries considered, and to compare these experiences with predicted outcomes from theoretical models.

With respect to the transmission channels, it is useful to consider the impact of the observed relative shifts in real interest and exchange rates arising from both policy and external influences. As would be expected, it was found that interest rate effects on the net private savings ratio generally occurred through declines in the investment ratio rather than increases in the private savings ratio. The overall responses in investment relative to GDP did not seem particularly large when one considers that the significant declines in investment observed in Germany and Japan in the early 1970s were mainly attributable to the first oil shock and the subsequent impact on world demand conditions. However, as mentioned earlier, the presence of accelerator effects may cause the investment to GDP ratios to understate the true interest rate impact on investment and real growth.

In general, increases in net private savings that have accompanied fiscal expansions—through interest rate effects as well as from unrelated sources such as supply shocks—have been outweighed by the reduced saving of the government sector, resulting in a net deterioration in the current account balance. The exception was the case of Germany between periods 1 and 2, when investment fell so sharply that the current account improved.

While the easier fiscal policy stances tended to be associated with larger current account deficits, these seemed more likely to involve reductions rather than increases in the real exchange rate, as would be expected from the simple Mundell-Fleming model. In those cases where significant shifts in relative real interest rates across countries were associated with consistent exchange rate movements—e.g., in Germany in periods 2 and 3—the movements in the current account balance were also in a direction consistent with the Mundell-Fleming framework, thus suggesting that the dominant influence at work was the relative tightness of domestic monetary policy rather than the influence of fiscal policy. Alternatively, in the earlier periods in Japan and Belgium, where real exchange rate appreciations were associated with current account deteriorations, the particular prevailing circumstances (including low interest rate effects) did not suggest fiscal policy developments as a significant factor.

The evidence would thus indicate that changes in fiscal policy as well as relative monetary policy stances have influenced the balance of payments more through changes in absorption and the current account rather than indirectly through the capital account. This evidence also helps to throw light on the relative strength of the various pressures on interest rates. In particular, the negative exchange rate and current account effects associated with the large interest rate increases in Japan and Belgium in period 3 tend to imply that easier fiscal policies were a significant additional pressure on interest rates over and above external and domestic monetary policy influences. It may be noted further that, if these are indeed valid conclusions, then the apparent weakness of the observed interest rate responses in period 2 suggests that the fiscal deficit is not a very consistent indicator of fiscal policy pressures on financial markets. The evidence is, however, consistent with the view that interest rate pressures from fiscal shocks are significantly affected by the size of the existing public debt. The ratio of public debt to GDP averaged over period 3 was particularly high in Belgium and, in Japan, was over twice the average observed in period 2.

In the context of the theoretical models of fiscal policy transmission, the predominance of current account influences on the exchange rate may be seen to confirm with the long-run outcome in a Mundell-Fleming model extended to include a government budget constraint; in this model, the current account influence must eventually come to dominate the capital account as debt servicing continues to magnify the initial trade imbalance. Alternatively, the result is also consistent with short-run outcomes in various models that assume a relatively low degree of substitution between domestic and foreign financial assets, or forward-looking rational behavior with mobile capital, or a high propensity to import out of consumption. Given the medium-term nature of the present analysis, it would perhaps be more appropriate to adopt the former long-run interpretation of the observed outcomes. However, there is little doubt that Belgium has specific characteristics conducive to a strong current account effect in the short term, and the same might be true for Japan and Germany.

The overall picture, then, is one in which any medium-term crowding-out effects have tended to work through domestic interest rates and private investment demand rather than through the real exchange rate and foreign demand. Indeed, as discussed earlier, in Belgium, in particular, the tendency for fiscal expansion to depreciate the real exchange rate through pressures on the current account may well crowd *in* export demand. This general pattern of responses is certainly consistent with other recent evidence that international capital markets may not be as closely linked as the size of short-term capital flows would suggest.[4] This means that expected real rates of return on real capital (and long-term financial assets) may vary significantly

---

[4] For evidence on this matter see, for example, Feldstein (1983), and Penati and Dooley (1983).

between countries even in the long term and that the level of real investment in each country tends to be constrained by the available domestic savings.

While the evidence points to some potentially significant investment crowding-out effects in the medium term, which may at times have been counteracted by a crowding in of exports, there is no clear indication of the net impact of the fiscal expansion observed in the three countries considered. However, in the cases of Germany and Japan it seems unlikely that the fiscal expansions contributed to a significant worsening of overall economic performance. In the case of Belgium, in the early 1980s a significant net crowding-out effect appears more likely, even though there was, apparently at the same time, a substantial crowding in of exports.

References

Feldstein, Martin, "Domestic Savings and International Capital Movements in the Long Run and the Short Run (White Plains, New York)," *European Economic Review*, Vol. 21, (1983), pp. 129–51.

Frenkel, Jacob A., and Michael L. Mussa, "Monetary and Fiscal Policies in an Open Economy," *American Economic Review, Papers and Proceedings* (Nashville, Tennessee), Vol. 71 (May 1981), pp. 253–58.

International Monetary Fund, *International Financial Statistics Yearbook*, Vol. VIII (Washington: International Monetary Fund, 1984).

Mundell, Robert A., "Comments [International Capital Markets]," *Economic Integration: Worldwide, Regional, Sectoral: Proceedings of the Fourth Congress of the International Economic Association held in Budapest, Hungary*, ed. Fritz Machlup (London: Macmillan, 1976).

Organization for Economic Cooperation and Development, *OECD Economic Outlook Historical Statistics: 1960–1982* (Paris: OECD, 1984).

―――, (1985a), *OECD Economic Outlook Historical Statistics: 1960–1983* (Paris: OECD).

―――, (1985b), *National Accounts, 1971–1983*, Vol. II (Paris: OECD).

Penati, Alessandro, "Expansionary Fiscal Policy and the Exchange Rate: A Review," *Staff Papers*, International Monetary Fund (Washington), Vol. 30, (September 1983), pp. 542–69.

―――, and Michael Dooley, "Current Account Imbalances and Capital Formation in Industrial Countries, 1949–81," *Staff Papers*, International Monetary Fund (Washington), Vol. 31 (March 1984), pp. 1–24.

Rodriguez, Carlos Alfredo, "Short and Long Run Effects of Monetary and Fiscal Policies Under Flexible Exchange Rates and Perfect Capital Mobility," *American Economic Review* (Nashville, Tennessee), Vol. 69 (March 1979), pp. 176–82.

Sachs, Jeffrey and Charles Wyplosz, "Real Exchange Rate Effects of Fiscal Policy," National Bureau of Economic Research, Working Paper Series No. 1255 (Cambridge, Massachusetts: National Bureau of Economic Research, January 1984).

Tanzi, Vito, "The Deficit Experience in Industrial Countries " (unpublished, International Monetary Fund, February 11, 1985).

Comment

*Christopher Higgins**

I. Introduction

Spencer and Clements address the question of whether an easier fiscal stance is likely to improve or worsen economic performance during a period of monetary restraint. Their conclusion, based on comparative analyses of three economies—Japan, the Federal Republic of Germany, and Belgium—over the period since 1970, is that definitive general statements are not possible: the varying influence of other forces tended to dominate "pure fiscal effects."

It is difficult to dispute this conclusion. Indeed, I would argue that Spencer and Clements' treatment of "other forces" is incomplete—in particular, the changing climate of expectations and the partly associated conditions for wage determination. Consideration of such influences might well strengthen their agnostic conclusion.

On the other hand, however, there is probably more to be said about the conditions in which policymakers could be more definitively advised that a relatively firmer fiscal stance is likely to improve economic performance. Spencer and Clements provide a number of pertinent illustrations, but they do not develop that line of reasoning in a systematic fashion.

The more detailed comments which follow essentially develop these two points. The first is basically methodological: to what extent is their framework of analysis incomplete? The second attempts to say something more in response to their central question, or at least to indicate what considerations seem to have led policymakers over the past decade or so to combine fiscal restraint with monetary restraint in pursuit of improved economic performance.

---

*The views are those of the author and do not necessarily reflect those of the Australian Treasury.

II. The Framework of Analysis

Spencer and Clements proceed by comparing key variables averaged over three subperiods: 1970–73, 1974–78, and 1979–83. Comparisons are across periods and across the selected countries.

The strength of this approach clearly depends on the selection and definition of the key variables—how successfully they represent the phenomena to be investigated. Since some influences are necessarily omitted, the authors are obliged from time to time to bring additional variables into the description and analysis; the skill with which this is done will obviously condition the success of the approach. There is also the question of the suitability of the three subperiods chosen.

First, a comment on those time periods. It is commonplace in macroeconomic studies covering the last 15 years or so to use the two major oil price increases of 1973 and 1979 as historical points of departure. These events represented major changes in variables, normally treated as exogenous to the macroeconomic system. They were not, however, the only forces with which macroeconomic policy was grappling during the 1970s. Thus, explanations of poor performance—the stagflationary decade—run well beyond tracing the consequences, including policy reactions, of the two oil shocks. To illustrate, one needs only to refer to the buildup of inflation in the late 1960s and early 1970s—mentioned in the paper—and the generalized move toward floating exchange rates after 1972, both forces at work before the first oil shock.

The dating scheme used by Spencer and Clements thus tends to exclude from their sphere of attention developments which should rightly have been there. I would not maintain, however, that this is a major defect in the paper.

On the selection and definition of variables, two points are warranted. Spencer and Clements use the ratio of general government fiscal deficit to gross national product (GNP) as the sole indicator of fiscal policy. There are considerable conceptual and practical difficulties in breaking aggregate deficits down into components that reflect, on the one hand, passive reaction to developments in the economy, and discretionary (i.e., conscious policy) action, on the other. Nonetheless, this distinction seems quantitatively very important.

The Organization for Economic Cooperation and Development (OECD) regularly publishes estimates of *changes* in actual budget balances broken down into "change in built-in stabilizers" and "change in structural balance." (The latter is also available on an "inflation-adjusted basis" for recent years.) Some OECD estimates are set out in the following table. It can be argued, quite apart from the cyclical/structural distinction, that changes in budget balances provide a better fiscal indicator than the levels employed by Spencer and Clements.

Table 1. Fiscal Policy Indicators—General Government Fiscal Balances
(In percent of GNP[1])

	1970–73	1974–78	1979–83
United States			
Actual	1.5	−0.5	−4.0
Structural	−0.1	0.8	−0.8
Japan			
Actual	−1.4	−6.0	2.0
Structural	−1.6	−5.4	2.2
Germany			
Actual	1.0	−3.7	−0.1
Structural	1.0	−1.7	1.7
Belgium			
Actual	...	...	−6.2
Structural			−3.4

Sources: Organization for Economic Cooperation and Development (1983, 1984, and 1985).
Note: The absolute levels of fiscal deficits in these OECD sources correspond closely to the figures shown in Table 2, p. 157.
[1] Cumulative change over period shown.

From these measures of changes in fiscal positions, it can be seen that only in the case of Japan is the distinction between actual and structural deficits small. In some instances the differences are large, and occasionally the measures are of opposite sign.

The other main comment I have on the selection and definition of variables is less precise. It concerns, essentially, the role of factor shares in the history of the 1970s. In many countries, including the three selected for detailed analysis by Spencer and Clements, the inflationary problem of the 1970s was not just that of the rate of change of the absolute price level, there was also a relative factor price problem of macroeconomic significance.

Some of these major shifts in factor shares arose from domestic wage push (e.g., Australia in the early 1970s), while others arose from the concatenation of the oil price shocks with domestic indexation systems and a world moving into recession. To spell that out a little more precisely, after the first oil shock, especially in many of the open European economies, external price increases were built into domestic wages, which could not be passed on in higher selling prices due to the international downturn.

The aggregate loss of real income implied by the deterioration in the terms of trade induced by the rise in oil prices came about one way or another in all countries; but the different ways in which different economies reacted strongly influenced both the final magnitude of that loss and the extent of overall price inflation associated with it.

Thus, after the first oil shock, money wages were relatively sticky in the United States, and a considerable part of the initial real income loss fell on the household sector. However, the counterpart of this was that inflation did not ratchet up once the initial oil price pulse passed through, and profitability was reasonably well maintained. Employment fared better. The foundations for medium-term performance were not severely eroded.

In the other polar case—of which Belgium is an example—the factor share distortion severely damaged traded goods sectors, and a stable growth path could not be resumed without a restoration of profitability. This was the dominant origin of the "real wage problem," which came to loom so large in the European debate in the late 1970s. Such debate has been particularly important in Germany and Belgium.

In this wages-reaction dimension, there were also differences between the two oil shocks for the same country. Japan is a very clear case in point; after the second oil shock, wages bore more of the initial terms of trade loss than after the first (see Table 3, p. 161). Both Germany and Belgium show the same sort of relativity.

Spencer and Clements largely omit the wages-reaction dimension in their analysis. They provide some historical data in their tables and there are some quite appropriate references for Germany (p. 162) and for Belgium (p. 164); and they list it among "other factors" in their diagram (p. 167). I would argue, however, that even for economies without highly centralized wage determination, agent response has been sufficiently independent of monetary and fiscal policy settings to require its separate treatment as a quasi-exogenous factor (albeit not closely policy controlled). Such a wages-climate factor deserves inclusion in the formal framework along with monetary and fiscal policy settings. This, I contend, is a serious limitation.

III. Other Considerations Influencing Policymakers

The profit squeeze and induced decline in the Belgian traded goods sector was protracted. Partly as a result of this poor economic performance (other forces were at work as well), social security dependency burdens increased. Budget deficits climbed and with them government interest bills, creating consequent budgetary lock-in. Social security taxes (on wage bills) raised in the face of expanded payments tended further to reduce the demand for labor, external competitiveness, and profitability.

This sequence of events had the first oil shock as an important trigger. In the Netherlands, with substantial gas resources and, hence, an initial immunity to a negative terms of trade shock, the problem of the size of the "dependent" sector also developed. This came to be known in the literature as the "Dutch Disease": expansion of social provisions based on growth in natural resource revenues, which created sustainability problems when the resource revenue declined.

In many economies, the expansion in social spending sectors arose more generally from the progressive buildup of entitlements during the golden growth decades of the 1950s and 1960s. The poorer performance of the 1970s revealed that the welfare state had created "overload" on the economy. Similar concerns arose in respect of government involvement beyond the social spending sectors, running the whole gamut of regulation, taxation, and subsidization captured in the term "Eurosclerosis." Much has been written on these issues.[1] The relevant point to be made about the Spencer and Clements analysis is that its traditional short-term stabilization focus leaves such considerations largely out of account.

In the late 1970s and 1980s much of the motivation for attempts to constrain public expenditures and to reduce fiscal deficits arose from this medium-term concern with public sector overload.

In Germany this drive has been termed medium-term budget consolidation, and it has been a very weighty objective conditioning the use of fiscal policy for short-term stabilization in that country over the past several years. Germany also provides an illustration of another factor that has influenced policymakers' attitudes on the use of expansionary fiscal policy, which Spencer and Clements do not discuss. Widespread disappointment with the pace of recovery from the 1974/75 recession provided the backdrop for plans for concerted expansionary action, which began to be formulated in 1977. The process culminated in the coordinated decisions of the Bonn Summit of 1978. The key political bargain was domestic demand stimulus in Japan and Germany in return for decontrol of domestic oil prices in the United States.

Interpretation of the wisdom of the concerted recovery plan conceived in Bonn is a controversial area. The onset of the second oil price hike and policy responses to it make disentangling the history very difficult. It is clear, however, that the effects of those measures were still in a reasonably dense portion of their lag distribution when it was already difficult to appreciate how they could have been adopted—such was the rapidity of the change in the climate of opinion, nowhere more noticeably than in Germany. There, and elsewhere, there was a marked change in belief about the extent to which fiscal expansion could con-

---

[1] A useful survey is provided in Saunders and Klau (1985).

tribute to sustained growth in the light of the overall experience of the 1970s.

German expositions have stressed the role of expectations and attitudes. The strength and pervasiveness of expectations in the 1970s constitute one important reason why it has been observed that fiscal and monetary policy, while representing more than one instrument, represent significantly less than two. In a program of medium-term inflation control and restoration of conditions for sustained growth, fiscal policy cannot be allowed to give rise to expectations/attitudes that would negate the intentions of the monetary stance (and vice versa).

Partly for these expectational reasons, but also because of the more mechanical direct linkages between public sector borrowing and money creation in the United Kingdom (and similar systems), the medium-term financial strategy adopted there also reflects the less-than-two-instruments proposition.

The United States experience under the present administration can also be illuminated by the expectations perspective. More benign inflationary expectations and other attitudes, in part conditioned by supply responsiveness, were such that a program of fiscal expansion and monetary restraint did produce a period of strong noninflationary growth. More recently, for reasons of the kind captured in the Spencer and Clements framework, very large imbalances on external account have emerged.

There is at least one more consideration that has rightly borne heavily on fiscal decisionmaking in the late 1970s and 1980s. I refer to the stock dimension of public borrowing: the growth in public debt stemming from an unusual string of large budget deficits. The need to focus on this stock dimension emerged not so much because the buildup was large and rapid, but because it was accompanied, especially in the early 1980s, by nominal interest rates substantially and persistently above nominal growth rates. This raised important issues of sustainability.

For many policymakers—Japan being a clear example among the countries treated by Spencer and Clements—the problems of debt buildup and sustainability provided necessarily strong impetus to fiscal consolidation efforts in the 1980s. In their tables Spencer and Clements systematically track a measure very relevant to the flow dimension of this issue (fiscal deficit to gross private saving), but they pay only scattered infrequent attention to the portfolio aspects.

To conclude, Spencer and Clements have provided a rather sophisticated and informative comparative short-run macroeconomic analysis based on the "Mundell-Fleming type framework." I find little to disagree with among the detailed remarks in Section IV. However, I have sought to argue that it is an incomplete analysis. Thus, for example, if we look at Chart 1 (p. 168), we can be struck as much by the similarity between the countries (all show negatively sloped policy lines and all have the three time periods in the same spatial relativity) as we are by the differences between countries, or between time periods for individual countries. Clearly, there were broad decade-long forces at work, which the framework tends to miss.

Without suggesting that in all instances the perceptions of policymakers were correct, I have argued that there were important factors, largely neglected by Spencer and Clements, which conditioned fiscal policymaking, especially but not only, in the post-1979 period. These included: growth of government (welfare state "overload" and "Eurosclerosis"); entrenched inflationary expectations/attitudes (fiscal policy cannot be independent of monetary policy); sustainability of swollen stocks of public debts; and partly reflecting all of that, some doctrinal disenchantment with fiscal fine-tuning.

References

Organization for Economic Cooperation and Development, "Public Sector Deficits: Problems and Policy Implications," *OECD Economic Outlook Occasional Studies* (Paris: OECD, June 1983), pp. 13–44.

____, *OECD Economic Outlook*, No. 35 (Paris: OECD, July 1984).

____, *OECD Economic Outlook*, No. 37 (Paris: OECD, December 1985).

Saunders, Peter, and Friedrich Klau, "The Role of the Public Sector: Causes and Consequences of the Growth of Government," *OECD Economic Studies* (Paris: OECD, 1985).

6
The Role of Exchange Rate and Other Pricing Policies in the Adjustment Process

Peter Wickham

I. Introduction

The external environment faced by policymakers in both the smaller developed economies and in oil-importing developing countries during the 1980s has been difficult. The increase in the price of crude oil and refined petroleum products of 1979/80 was followed closely by prolonged recession in the major industrialized countries, accompanied this time, in contrast to the situation after the first oil price shock, by tight monetary policies, which resulted in declining inflation and high real interest rates. The recession led to a marked weakening in the major industrialized countries' import demand for manufactures and to a substantial decline in primary product prices. The reduction in world trade associated with the recession also served to increase protectionist tendencies in the major industrialized countries, particularly against some agricultural commodities, such as meat and dairy products, and certain labor-intensive manufactured goods, like textiles. And in some cases, protectionist policies had repercussions outside the markets of immediate concern to the policymakers. A notable example is the high support price provided under the Common Agricultural Policy to sugar beet growers in the European Economic Community (EEC), leading in a period of reduced internal demand to the "dumping" of excess supplies in the world market. Such actions contributed to low prices for sugar in the "free" market and adversely affected the export earnings of non-EEC sugar producers. And although ACP[1] sugar exporters, for example, do have access under quota to the EEC market at favorable prices, they nevertheless must often still sell significant amounts outside the protected EEC and U.S. markets.

---

[1] African, Caribbean, and Pacific States that are signatories with the EEC to the Lomé Convention.

While the discussion above concentrates on external factors influencing trade account performance, external payments positions of debtor countries were significantly affected by high real interest rates and the reduced availability of credit in international financial markets. In addition, the high real interest rates influenced in varying degrees the behavior of both short-term capital flows and interest rates on domestic financial instruments.

These external developments have not been conducive to attaining stable growth rates with low inflation and have made the task of economic management more difficult for policymakers. The changes in the external environment and the attendant pressures on payments positions have in a number of instances heightened concerns about lack of effective coordination among exchange rate, monetary, and fiscal policies. At the same time, the need to re-establish a viable current account often has to be considered in light of a lack of diversity in the structure of trade and the difficulty of quickly transferring or channeling more resources into the tradable goods sectors. This aspect of the adjustment process is often of particular importance, although not exclusively so, to the smaller developing countries. Increased attention has therefore been focused on past policy-induced barriers or disincentives to appropriate resource allocation. Often among these are trade policies (tariffs, import quotas) and the pricing of foreign exchange and money.

It is against such a background that this paper seeks to comment on the role to be played in the process of adjustment by exchange rate and other pricing policies. The outline of the paper is as follows. Section II discusses the nature of the different types of shocks that countries face and whether policy changes are necessary to facilitate adjustment. Section III examines both the role of exchange rate policies when there is a need for adjustment and the consequences either of not recognizing or not accepting that exchange rate policy should be changed. The section also considers the problems and difficulties of altering the "real" exchange rate, while Section IV considers the closely related issue of the choice of exchange rate regime. Section V examines reforms in financial and goods markets and issues related to policy coordination. To illustrate some of the points being made, reference is made in these two latter sections to recent experience and policy response in New Zealand.

II. Types of Shocks and the Need for Adjustment

It is often useful in thinking about external account imbalances to try to make distinctions between types of disturbances that impinge upon an economy. It is common, for example, to distinguish between real and monetary (or financial) shocks, shocks of internal and external origin, and between transitory shocks and more lasting changes in the economic environment (which are referred to somewhat anomalously as "permanent shocks"). A bad harvest, which reduces output available for export or requires import of food grains for domestic consumption, can be classified as a real transitory shock of internal origin. The increase in the real price of crude oil that occurred in 1973/74 is an example of a more durable external real shock. The high real interest rates that have prevailed since the start of the present decade might be similarly regarded. A one-period surge in a country's money supply due to domestic credit expansion can be considered as a transitory internal monetary shock, while a sustained expansion to finance budgetary deficits, for example, may be viewed as a more lasting monetary disturbance. It should be noted, however, that not all external balance difficulties manifest themselves in a deterioration in the current account; net capital inflows may change, either temporarily or because of more lasting developments affecting creditworthiness, savings rates, or the productivity of capital investment.

The notion of transitory disturbances has encouraged theoretical work in open economy macroeconomics using a stochastic framework (see, for example, Frenkel and Aizenman (1982)). The emphasis in these studies is clearly on the issues relating to short-run stabilization policies and the properties of particular policy reaction functions. An example of one prescription offered on the basis of such analyses is that purely transitory real disturbances that affect the current account should not occasion exchange rate changes under a pegged rate regime. Foreign reserves and/or official borrowing should be used to accommodate the current account deficit and cushion domestic expenditures. The usual application of the prescription is to small developing countries whose export earnings are heavily dependent on a limited range of commodities subject to price cycles of considerable amplitude. However, with limits on foreign borrowing and on the use of official reserves under a pegged exchange rate arrangement (or on the behavior of private net capital inflows under a float), some real or monetary developments require or will engender a more substantive adjustment in an economy's aggregate demand-supply balance.

In practice, of course, it is often very difficult for agents (including policymakers) in the economy to distinguish the source of the shock and to decide whether a shock is transitory, cyclical, or more permanent. Furthermore, real and monetary shocks may occur together or follow closely upon one another. For example, the second round of oil price increases was accompanied by a significant tightening of monetary policies in the major industrialized countries, which resulted in high real interest rates and a downturn in these countries' average trend rate of inflation. Another example was the upward phase of the price cycle for certain primary commodities in the mid-1970s, which boosted the export earnings of a number of developing countries producing such commodities. As is well known, such developments often present the authorities with difficult stabilization problems due to the problems of sterilizing the impact on the domestic money supply. However, government tax revenues also increased owing to their sensitivity to developments in the trade accounts, and this factor, combined with the favorable initial development in foreign reserves, encouraged some governments to overexpand the scope and substance of their expenditure programs. The difficulty of adjusting government expenditures and the need to finance budget deficits in the subsequent down-phase of the cycle resulted in continued expansion in domestic credit, which was accompanied by domestic inflationary pressures and foreign payments difficulties.[2] In these cases, the cyclical nature of the shock was mistaken for a favorable permanent development with unfortunate consequences.

Current account imbalances resulting from various types of shocks are mirrored in differences between aggregate expenditure and domestic output. If the imbalance must be reconciled, a decrease in aggregate domestic demand, an increase in domestic supply, or a combination of both must take place. This is, of course, well understood, and the role of various policies, including that of exchange rate policy, in achieving the reconciliation has been widely discussed in various forums and in the literature (see, for example, Khan and Knight (1981) and the references therein). Nevertheless, the role of exchange rate policy remains controversial, particularly so in many developing countries. Often, exchange rate policy is seen principally as a relatively short term balance of payments correcting device and as a means of dealing with surges in the domestic rate of inflation. This view is probably linked to the main role that was traditionally assigned to nominal exchange rate adjustments in stabilizing the economies of the well-developed and diversified industrialized countries. Within this paradigm, considerable scope is assumed to exist for substitution in demand and supply to take place in the short term in response to exchange rate changes.

For countries with less diversified economic structures, however, the appropriateness of the paradigm has been called into question and has provoked considerable debate. There has been much discussion, for example, about whether a devaluation, which has both an expenditure-dampening and expenditure-switching effect, will or will not be con-

---

[2] Even where fiscal policies do not follow this pattern, windfall gains and monetary expansion can often spill over quite quickly into the labor market, so that in the upward phase of the cycle nominal (and real) wages rise. With downward stickiness in money wages and other prices, monetary contraction in the downward phase of the cycle could have a significant impact on output and employment. This puts pressure on the monetary authorities to attempt sterilization.

tractionary in terms of domestic output for such economies in the short run. (See, for example, Krugman and Taylor (1978), and Gylfason and Schmid (1983).) A common weakness of these analyses is that they tend to ignore the fact that the need for "adjustment" is in many cases made evident by an incipient or actual balance of payments crisis, that is, evidence that the current account deficit is indeed unsustainable and that relative prices are out of alignment. In an immediate sense, the response must be to tackle the inconsistency in real income claims and to implement measures aimed at stabilizing (in a noncyclical sense) the situation. This involves reducing the current level of aggregate domestic expenditure relative to output. Such a reduction (in which an exchange rate change may play a part) brings with it the possibility that in the short run output may fall in comparison with the level attained in the run-up to the crisis, although such a comparison may well be moot.

The focus then must shift to policy options or combinations that, together with available financing, can reduce the welfare costs in a transition period during which resource reallocation takes place in the economy. For example, the need to transfer resources from one sector to another may be hampered by distorted price signals stemming from previous government intervention policies (including exchange rate policy). Policy reforms aimed at providing the appropriate relative price signals and at removing other distortions in the economy may be required in order to reduce the real costs over time of the adjustment process. The focus on the efficiency or otherwise of exchange rate policy as an instrument of short-run stabilization has frequently tended to obscure the role of exchange rate and other pricing policies in inducing allocative and structural changes (desirable or undesirable) in the economy over the longer term. In what follows, therefore, emphasis will be given to the implications of price signals provided to agents in the economy and which are sustained over time by the exchange rate and associated policies adopted by the authorities.

III. Real Exchange Rates and the Adjustment Process

A needed point of reference for the discussion that follows is some notion of what constitutes an appropriate alignment of the exchange rate. Under the Bretton Woods system, adjustment to a par value was deemed justifiable if a country's exchange rate could be considered or shown to be in "fundamental disequilibrium." Williamson (1983) has suggested that the criterion of fundamental disequilibrium for an exchange rate change under the Bretton Woods system can be inverted to help establish the desired reference point. To use Williamson's terminology, the "fundamental equilibrium exchange rate" or FEER is that level of the real effective exchange rate (here defined as the nominal effective exchange rate adjusted for differences in price performance at home and abroad) consistent with both internal balance and medium-term or cyclically adjusted external balance.[3] Although the use of FEERs by Williamson was directed toward the issue of target zones for the major industrialized countries whose currencies are floating, he also noted that the idea of a FEER is still widely used in analyzing exchange rate policies of countries maintaining a pegged exchange rate arrangement.

Abstracting for the moment from the practical difficulties of determining the equilibrium real exchange rate (either by the authorities or by market participants), the discussion of various types of shocks can be reintroduced. A so-called nontransitory shock in this policy framework may be regarded as one that causes a sustained departure of the real exchange rate from its fundamental equilibrium value or as one that changes the equilibrium value itself. Examples of these are, respectively, the pursuit over time of domestic policies that lead to worsening inflationary performance and real effective appreciation under a pegged exchange rate arrangement, and an exogenous change in the terms of trade that can be regarded as being secular and that requires a real effective depreciation for external balance adjustment.

The pursuit of over-expansionary monetary and fiscal policies, for example, will lead at a pegged exchange rate to reserve losses and inflationary pressures. If the trading system remains relatively open in terms of tariff or quota incidence, the prices of nontradable goods and services (including wages) are more affected by excess demand pressures than the prices of tradable goods. Even where exports or import substitutes are differentiated products, for which the "law of one price" does not hold in the short to medium term, substitution possibilities and the pressures of arbitrage in goods markets will constrain the inflation in tradable goods prices.

Real effective appreciation is thus likely to be closely linked to a rise in the price of nontradable goods relative to tradable goods. This relative price is often referred to as the real exchange rate. The change in relative prices, that is, appreciation of the real exchange rate so defined, alters relative profitability in the tradable goods sectors, thus adversely affecting current account performance, even where reserve losses and the reduction in the money supply are acting to help restore equilibrium in the external accounts. In some economies the deterioration may occur

---

[3] Allowance is made for "underlying" capital flows, the stance of commercial policies, and the the need to abstain from the imposition or intensification of damaging trade restrictions. The internal balance criterion usually refers to unemployment levels. So-called stop-go episodes in the United Kingdom during the 1960s are often cited as examples of the incompatibility of the real exchange rate with the internal balance criterion.

quite quickly in response to changes in relative price signals (including price/cost relationships). This may be the case for countries with a diversified trade structure and where manufactures play a dominant role in trade performance.

It is often claimed, however, that in countries with less diversified trade structures and where primary products are the dominant source of export earnings, trade volumes are likely to respond only modestly in the short run to changes in relative prices. Indeed, there is empirical evidence to support this claim, although it is insufficient to justify complete short-run "elasticity pessimism" (Goldstein and Khan (1984)). Thus, even abstracting from the difficulties of obtaining changes in the real exchange rate, it is clear that the structure of production and trade is important in determining the role of real exchange rate movements in short-run external adjustment. Nevertheless, the important allocative role of changes in relative prices cannot be neglected. If inappropriate price signals are maintained over time, disinvestment can occur and resources can be transferred out of the tradable goods sectors to other sectors or uses. There have been notable cases in Africa, for example, of agricultural disinvestment and reductions in export earnings due in major part to real exchange rate overvaluation and the steady erosion over time of producer price incentives. Such a process might be termed structural maladjustment. By the same token, the need to transfer resources or to channel new investment to the tradable goods sectors in response to a secular adverse change in the external terms of trade requires the correct prices and incentives, even if the full response is likely to be spread out over a medium-term period and requires the implementation of other supportive measures.

Failure to direct exchange rate policies toward correcting or realigning the relative prices means that the burden for such an adjustment will fall on downward movements in domestic prices and costs. If real appreciation has occurred at a pegged rate, this would call not only for changes in domestic financial policies to stem current account deterioration but further tightening in order to achieve the requisite disinflation. If nominal prices (including wages) tend to be sticky downwards, the stringency in demand management policies needed to achieve the adjustment in the real exchange rate may well involve recession and unemployment significantly in excess of what could be expected under an alternative adjustment strategy.

Another avenue other than the exchange rate through which prices can be altered directly is to introduce changes in the structure of tariffs and export subsidies. If a fall in export prices is the source of a deterioration in the current account, an export subsidy could be used to reestablish profitability and domestic relative price relationships. Similarly, an import tariff/export subsidy package could aim to raise the relative prices of tradable goods following a period of internal inflation during which real appreciation has occurred, although as with devaluation this presupposes restoration of discipline over domestic demand management policies. However, because such measures are frequently introduced in an ad hoc fashion or in response to pressures from specific industries, achieving neutrality in effective protection or subsidization between different activities is often difficult to ensure. Differences in sectoral or industrial incidence can lead to serious inefficiency in resource use and to structural weaknesses. In addition, extensive use of export or production subsidies can place a growing burden on the government budget. This, in turn, makes the conduct of fiscal and monetary policies more difficult, particularly in those cases where the need for adjustment stems from policy error.

Policy actions undertaken by the authorities are often aimed not at attempting to change the real exchange rate and at ensuring the consistency of real income claims but at containing the external payments situation and suppressing other symptoms of imbalance in the economy. If the country has access to international capital markets, extensive foreign borrowing may be undertaken in an attempt to sustain the levels of private and public consumption rather than to finance capital formation. Alternatively, rather than accepting the consequences of a decline in foreign assets on the money supply at a pegged exchange rate, trade restrictions and exchange controls may be introduced or intensified to narrow the current account deficit and to lessen other demands of bank and nonbank residents on the foreign exchange resources of (or under the control of) the central bank. Many developed and developing countries have regulations prohibiting or strictly controlling portfolio investment abroad. Furthermore, other capital account transactions, such as those involving direct investment, private sector term borrowing, and trade credits, are frequently subject to regulation. Access to the official foreign exchange market for current account transactions is also often closely controlled in developing countries: import licensing schemes, regulations concerning service payments and private transfers, and surrender requirements on export proceeds are not uncommon. With the administrative machinery for the controls regime in place, attempts to tighten the system in response to pressure on foreign reserves are frequently tempting to the monetary authorities.

The enforcement of a tight system of exchange controls also allows the establishment of a wedge between the domestic money and financial markets and those in the rest of the world. The controls serve to prevent or limit flows of private saving abroad and interest rate arbitrage in financial assets by the private sector (both bank and nonbank). Frequently, the system of controls is closely linked to extensive regulation of the domestic financial system. A central element is typically the imposition of controls on interest rates and the subjection of financial intermediaries to various reserve and liquidity ratios beyond those that might be recommended for prudential reasons. The recourse to such regulation usually stems from inadequate control of fiscal policy and the desire to ease the placement and decrease the servicing cost of public debt. Even in the absence of current account pressures, repressed yields on domestic financial instruments and the resulting interest differential between foreign and domestic financial markets provide incentives for the acquisition of foreign financial assets; hence, the need to try to enforce the capital and exchange controls regime to prevent the private sector from exchanging its domestic financial assets for the foreign currency assets of the central bank.

But the domestic regulatory framework is also likely to have an adverse effect on the efficiency and development of the financial system. Both the brokerage function of intermediaries (i.e., bringing together ultimate lenders and borrowers at minimum resource cost) and the maturity transformation function (which enhances the liquidity of the nonbank private sector) can be compromised. Constraints on the deposit rates (particularly on time deposits) that can be offered by regulated intermediaries and the excess demand for loans at the interest rate ceilings encourage disintermediation or less efficient forms of intermediation. The existence of curb markets is symptomatic of this development in a number of developing countries, where so-called policies of financial repression and relatively strict exchange controls are in effect. The different market-clearing mechanisms employed, that is, by quantity rationing in the regulated market versus rationing by price in the unregulated market, distort the flow of funds in the economy and lead to inefficient use of resources.

The dependence on and the efficacy of control systems differ considerably between countries attempting to postpone or avoid exchange rate action and other corrections to the policies being pursued. In many countries, the authorities' attempts at containing the external balance pressures are sooner or later undermined by evasion of capital and exchange controls leading to rising speculation in the official foreign exchange market (i.e., a full-blown foreign exchange crisis). In other cases, the trade and payments regime may be made sufficiently repressive and effective that the non-official sector's response takes the form of increased goods smuggling and the growth of unofficial markets for foreign exchange. In several developing countries that have permitted the latter type of situation to develop in recent years, the resulting severe resource misallocation and economic dislocation has reduced both realized real output and growth prospects.[4] However, even where the

---

[4] A notable example is Ghana, where real GDP declined almost continuously in the period 1973–83.

regime of controls is less repressive, the distortions that build up in the goods and financial markets in the period before a crisis in the foreign exchange market can be very costly and disruptive.

It must, of course, be recognized that using exchange rate policy in an attempt to achieve real effective exchange rate adjustment may be very difficult. There is certainly the extreme view that nominal exchange rate changes will be almost totally ineffective in this regard. A devaluation would quickly lead to an offsetting increase in domestic prices and costs, bringing the economy back to the original situation. There can be little doubt that in the inflationary environment of the 1970s and 1980s, the tendency for offsetting to occur has increased, and it can be argued that this tendency may well be stronger and quicker for small specialized economies with relatively open trading regimes. An additional factor that will increase the extent of the offset is the presence of wage-indexing schemes with cost of living adjustments explicitly or implicitly included in labor contracts. In such circumstances, the scope for changes in exchange rate policy to bring about a realignment in relative prices and costs would appear very limited. Nevertheless, the need for some kind of policy response cannot be ignored. It may well be necessary for the authorities and labor to enter into socially and politically difficult negotiations to achieve modifications to the wage-indexation schemes. Failure to do so will mean that a greater burden of the unpleasant necessity for change will be placed on tight monetary policies. Having to bring about adjustment in this fashion increases the likelihood that the process will be associated with decreased output and high levels of unemployment. Nevertheless, if real factor prices are inflexible downwards, external balance will be realized only at high continuing domestic cost.

IV. Achieving Appropriate Real Alignment

The previous section stressed the costs involved in failing to direct policies to achieving and maintaining a realistic exchange rate. An important question is the extent to which permitting or opting for some degree of nominal exchange rate flexibility can contribute to this objective. Conceptually, two issues can be distinguished: first, there is the response to existing disequilibria; and, second, there is the question of whether in the future greater flexibility in the exchange rate would permit smoother adjustment to changing economic circumstances. The latter question itself raises a number of closely connected issues concerning the choice of exchange rate regime, the trade and exchange control system, and the conduct of monetary and fiscal policies.

A necessary condition for the maintenance of an unchanging exchange rate peg over time is the acceptance by the authorities of constraints on the conduct of domestic economic policies—in particular, monetary policy—which influence domestic price performance relative to that being experienced abroad. The country, in effect, undertakes to keep its inflation rate (at least in terms of the medium-term trend) in line with that of the standard to which it is pegged. It also means that even if such a commitment serves to prevent internal inflation, which otherwise could lead to a sustained real appreciation, the burden for achieving a real depreciation over time falls on a tightening of domestic policies sufficient to produce a fall in nominal prices and costs (including wages). However, exchange rate pegs are not immutable: except perhaps in the case of a genuine common currency area, there is always the possibility of parity changes. The case for parity adjustments is the familiar one of achieving the required relative price and cost change more directly and at lower cost in terms of output losses and increases in unemployment than would be the case if reliance was placed solely on tight demand management policies.

Both theoretical considerations and the lessons of the past indicate that the so-called adjustable peg arrangement can be maintained over time only if devaluations are relatively rare events. Otherwise, the economy (even if exchange and capital controls are fairly strict) will be subject to recurrent disruptions to the trade accounts (and hence, to output and employment) and to seriously debilitating speculative episodes.[5] In countries where inflation rates historically have been very high and variable and where the prospects for disinflation (at least to a rate of inflation more nearly comparable to that being experienced in the major industrialized countries) without "shock" treatment are remote, this probable outcome has been recognized by the authorities. They have accordingly adopted a form of crawling peg regime based on depreciating the nominal exchange rate in line with the difference between domestic and foreign inflation. Experience with such exchange rate regimes has been greatest in Latin America, where ongoing inflation rates in the high two-digit or even three-digit range have not been uncommon.

While similarly chronic rates of high inflation have been outside the experience of countries in the Asian and South Pacific regions, high rates of domestic monetary expansion have resulted in episodes of moderate to high inflation. Dealing with these episodes presents policymakers with difficult problems of policy coordination. This is particularly so in an environment in which inflation rates in the major industrialized countries have themselves been variable, and intercountry disparities, marked at times.[6] A crawling peg based on the inflation differential (in

---

[5] This clearly rules out discrete devaluations in any anticyclical role.

[6] This has been the case in the 1980s during which time the key industrialized countries have succeeded in bringing down their rates of inflation to fairly low levels.

effect, a real exchange rate rule) does seem to provide a means of dealing with some of the worse consequences of differences in inflationary trends. However, strict adherence to such a policy rule is not without its dangers. Several writers (McKinnon (1981), Niehans (1984), and Adams and Gros (1986)) have questioned whether the inflationary process will be stable if the monetary authorities persist in following real exchange rate rules.

With the prospects for disinflation to the norm established by the major industrialized countries seemingly not as remote as for countries with histories of chronic inflation, the key issues for policymakers are how to deal with real appreciation when it has emerged and the attitude and approach toward disinflation. It may well take considerable time to re-establish a policy commitment toward lowering the domestic rate of inflation. This would seem to be a reasonable description of the rationale behind New Zealand's crawling peg between 1979 and 1982. Clearly, instituting a crawling peg based on the inflation differential that has emerged would only make sense if the initial real appreciation were first reversed. It should be emphasized here that although relative purchasing power parity indicators may be very useful in determining the extent of the needed correction, it is usually necessary to supplement information from such indicators with additional judgmental analysis. This is the case, for example, if the emergence of balance of payments difficulties prompted a reassessment of commercial policies and a determination to liberalize trade. The important policy issue is whether reversal of the real appreciation should be attempted in one step through a large discrete devaluation, or whether it would be better to make some initial adjustment in the exchange rate, to be followed by a number of further small adjustments.

The "shock" approach to disinflation is usually considered to have distinct merits in very high inflation countries (e.g., Argentina, Brazil, Israel), but for countries with more moderate rates of inflation, the decision on "gradualism versus shock" is less clear cut. Much depends on the special characteristics or circumstances of the particular country being considered, but it is often felt that the costs of disinflation can be more equitably shared and the strains on the social fabric reduced if a gradualist approach is adopted. While the rate of inflation is being reduced by credit, fiscal, and incomes policies, it will be necessary to continue the depreciation of the nominal exchange rate.

While crawling peg regimes may be required in response to ongoing domestic inflation and/or during the period of disinflation, changes in other circumstances or conditions may, as previously suggested, call for real depreciation or appreciation. An important issue is the extent to which some form of crawl or active exchange rate management can be used in conjunction with changes in other policies to deal with such developments. Unfortunately, there are no simple objective indicators that can be relied upon to reflect the changing economic conditions. This means in effect that the authorities must enter into a series of judgments based on various sources of information to determine if and by how much the equilibrium real exchange rate has changed. Certain indicators of pressure in the foreign exchange market can be utilized, such as reserve losses departing from previous experience of seasonal and cyclical patterns. Terms of trade developments can be monitored and cyclically adjusted. Wage rate, employment, and output trends in various sectors can be followed, as can developments overseas in financial and goods markets.

Nevertheless, the equilibrium real rate can undoubtedly be very difficult to measure. Concepts such as the "cyclically adjusted" current account and underlying capital flows must be given empirical counterparts; various scenarios for the external environment as well as policy scenarios at home and abroad have to be specified. Misgivings about the accuracy that can be expected from such judgmental analysis certainly have some validity, but the analysis can at least provide the basis for giving warning of a serious misalignment of the real exchange rate. If so, policies can be formulated (including, if necessary, negotiating access to external financing) to achieve the new target at lower cost than would be the case if adjustment were delayed and a crisis situation allowed to develop. The case for a crawling peg rather than a one-step devaluation under an "adjustable" peg regime would then seem to rest on two considerations: first, that a sizable discrete devaluation may require a greater degree of confidence in the initial prognosis; and second, that there may be a case for gradualism rather than shock, as discussed earlier.

Empirical evidence reviewed by Khan and Knight (1983) on the balance of payments problems faced by non-oil developing countries in the 1970s supports the hypothesis that both the external environment (indicated by low growth in the major industrial countries, a secular shift in the terms of trade, and an increase in foreign real interest rates) and domestic factors (fiscal deficits, real appreciation) were important in explaining deteriorations in current account positions. The persistence of external balance difficulties and the fact that many adjustment programs were implemented from positions of near or actual balance of payments crisis suggest that a number of countries would have been better served by taking adjustment measures (including exchange rate action) at an earlier stage.

Because of the difficulties and complexities inherent in the judgmental approach, the question arises of whether, in looking to the future, greater reliance should not be placed on market forces in the foreign exchange market to help bring about requisite real exchange rate adjustments in response to changes in underlying economic conditions.

This was certainly one of the conclusions of the New Zealand authorities when, following the foreign exchange crisis and discrete devaluation of July 1984, they elected in March 1985 to change the exchange rate regime from an administered arrangement to a floating regime, with the stated intention of refraining from direct intervention in the foreign exchange market.[7]

V. Removal of Distortions and Aspects of Policy Coordination

The decision to adopt a floating rate regime in New Zealand was in part the result of a more general assessment that greater reliance should be placed on market forces and the resultant price signals to determine the allocation of resources rather than government intervention policies. This conclusion was reflected in the financial sector by decisions to abandon interest rate controls and credit guidelines, to remove mandatory reserve requirements, and to permit wider portfolio selection by the removal of remaining controls on capital movements. With respect to the traded goods sectors, the intention was announced of further reducing the reliance placed on subsidies, quotas, and tariff protection. Additional reforms were introduced in other areas where it was considered that regulation or other government intervention policies were giving rise to an inefficient use of resources. One such problem area targeted was the pricing policies of public enterprises. Although it is clear that the removal of major policy-induced distortions influences aggregate demand, these initiatives were directed at enhancing the supply side of the economy.

There has been growing awareness in developing countries, also, that removal of distortions in order to promote more efficient resource use is desirable. Where, for example, extensive reliance has been placed on quantitative restrictions, the first steps in a program of reform would be to replace the quotas by tariff protection to be followed over time by rationalization and then reduction of the tariff structure. Another area where reforms are often required is agricultural pricing policies. For example, the desire to increase yields may be attempted by introducing subsidies on fertilizer, which, however, by altering relative input prices can result in wasteful usage. Or, prices for particular agricultural commodities may be controlled for social reasons, acting as an incentive to increased domestic consumption and as a disincentive to production and exports.

---

[7] It should be emphasized here that the reference is to the type of regime to be operated in the future starting from a position of equilibrium. There were clearly other factors behind the decision to float, including considerations relating to other major policy reforms and the control over the money supply.

In financial markets, the control of interest rates and the system of financial regulation can inhibit competition and the efficiency and growth of the financial intermediaries. Detailed regulation of the rate structure for deposits and loans, for example, suggests that any competition between intermediaries will be of a nonprice variety and will act to retard efficiency in and inhibit entry into the sector. There is, however, the concern that relying on market-determined rates to clear financial markets could give rise to serious imperfections because of the degree of concentration in the sector. The small scale of the domestic financial market and scale economies in banking may mean that the market structure is monopolistic or oligopolistic, a particular concern in some very small island economies. In such a situation, freeing interest rates from controls would lead to much higher loan rates and widened spreads.

In an inflationary environment, controls on deposit rates can result in highly negative real interest rates on financial savings for considerable periods of time. Such a development can depress flows into the financial intermediaries, as the nonbank private sector hoards real goods or otherwise attempts to adjust to the high opportunity cost of holding domestic financial assets.[8] As real credit availability is restricted, real investment is similarly affected.

Apart from efficiency and resource allocation aspects, the implications of controls on interest rates cannot be divorced from the degree to which domestic financial markets are or can be isolated from foreign markets by exchange and capital controls and other factors.[9] If exchange controls are fairly strict, the extent to which domestic residents hold foreign currency assets (or foreign residents hold domestic currency assets) and thus engage in interest rate arbitrage will be limited. At the other extreme, under a fixed exchange rate and the absence of exchange and capital controls, interest rate parity conditions would tend to be met. Failure to meet these conditions is often referred to as the abrogation of capital mobility, although it is clear that even countries with extensive exchange and capital controls can still mobilize resources from abroad through foreign currency bond issues, Euro-currency loans, and aid flows. Some degree of independence for the determination of domestic interest rates will exist either through a market-determined rate or some form of interest rate controls.

How long interest rate controls can be sustained depends on how consistent the authorities' monetary policy is with the exchange rate policy adopted, given that the exchange control system allows some addi-

---

[8] See, for example, Lanyi and Saracoglu (1983).

[9] The need for and effectiveness of controls vary between countries. The degree of financial development is clearly an important factor, as is the monetary history of the country concerned.

tional degree of latitude. In New Zealand strains on the system became increasingly evident in the late 1970s and early 1980s because of lack of sufficient coordination and consistency between domestic credit, fiscal, and exchange rate policies in the face of continuing difficult external conditions. Both the closed economy constraint—if one controls the price of money one cannot control its quantity—and the open economy constraint—if one fixes the exchange rate one can control credit but not the money supply—proved too much for the controls regime.

The size of the imbalances that had arisen in New Zealand in terms of the fiscal and current account deficits meant that the process of adjustment and the re-establishment of monetary control would inevitably be very difficult. The need in the postdevaluation period to restrict the rate of domestic credit expansion, coupled with the large fiscal deficit, required the removal of interest rate controls. As has occurred elsewhere following a devaluation and the freeing of interest rates, control of domestic liquidity was made difficult due to capital reflows and inflows, the latter also being made easier by relaxation of capital controls applied to foreign borrowing both by financial intermediaries and by the nonbank corporate sector. Remaining exchange and capital controls were lifted at the end of 1984. Other elements of the financial reform, such as the removal of reserve ratios and other portfolio restrictions, dismantled remaining barriers to financial integration. In this environment and the continuing uncertainty surrounding economic conditions and policies, the move to a floating rate in March 1985 was not surprising. The period between the devaluation in the face of a crisis in the foreign exchange market and the decision to float, and subsequent developments in New Zealand, have shown how difficult the dynamic path of adjustment is following a needed major change in the conduct of monetary and fiscal policies.

While the resource allocation and monetary control arguments may be used to support financial reforms in smaller developing countries, the extent to which it is desirable for them to fully open up their financial markets remains debatable. Given their lower level of economic development, most would be expected to be capital importers, with resources from abroad supplementing domestic savings in financing both private and public capital formation. But this does not require that all capital and exchange controls be removed, giving complete freedom to domestic residents to hold foreign currency assets in their portfolios. For this reason, many developing countries continue to employ regulations and controls governing capital account transactions.

Nevertheless, as the trading and domestic financial system becomes broader and more developed over time, links to conditions in external financial markets are likely to become closer. For example, a reasonable degree of freedom for nonbank residents to engage in current account transactions and negotiate trade financing arrangements will increase the influence of interest rate factors on the timing of receipts and payments. Such factors also influence the development and depth of the foreign exchange markets.[10] Greater responsibility could devolve onto the financial intermediaries in the payments clearing process, allowing the central bank to consider operating a band around a parity and encouraging the development of an active forward market. Central bank intervention policies would then be determined by such factors as the size of public sector capital inflows, which influences the role of the central bank as a residual supplier of foreign exchange, and the insulating role that can be played by official reserves and foreign borrowing in response to cyclical disturbances to export earnings.

References

Adams, Charles, and Daniel Gros, "Some Illustrative Examples of the Consequences of Real Exchange Rate Rules for Inflation" (unpublished, International Monetary Fund, January 24, 1986).

Frenkel, Jacob, and Joshua Aizenman, "Aspects of the Optimal Management of Exchange Rates," in *The International Monetary System: Choices for the Future*, ed. by Michael B. Connoly (New York: Praeger, 1982), pp. 19–48.

Goldstein, Morris, and Mohsin Khan, "Income and Price Effects in Foreign Trade," in *Handbook of International Economics*, Vol. 2, ed. by Ronald W. Jones and Peter B. Kenen (Amsterdam: North-Holland, 1984), pp. 1041–1105.

Gylfason, Thorvaldur, and Michael Schmid, "Do Devaluations Cause Stagflation," *Canadian Journal of Economics* (Toronto), Vol. XVI (November 1983), pp. 641–54.

Khan, Mohsin, and Malcolm D. Knight, "Stabilization Programs in Developing Countries: A Formal Framework," *Staff Papers*, International Monetary Fund (Washington), Vol. 28 (March 1981), pp. 1–53.

———, "Determinants of Current Account Balances of Non-Oil Developing Countries in the 1970s: An Empirical Analysis," *Staff Papers*, International Monetary Fund (Washington), Vol. 30 (December 1983), pp. 811–42.

Krugman, Paul, and Lance Taylor, "Contractionary Effects of Devaluation," *Journal of International Economics* (Amsterdam), Vol. 8 (August 1978), pp. 445–56.

Lanyi, A., and R. Saracoglu, "The Importance of Interest Rates in Developing Countries," *Finance & Development*, International Monetary Fund–World Bank (Washington), Vol. 20 (June 1983), pp. 20–23.

McKinnon, R., "Monetary Control and the Crawling Peg," in *Exchange Rate Rules*, ed. by John Williamson (New York: St. Martins, 1981), pp. 38–49.

Niehans, Jurg, *International Monetary Economics* (Baltimore: Johns Hopkins University Press, 1984).

---

[10] See Wickham (1985).

Wickham, Peter, "The Choice of Exchange Rate Regime in Developing Countries," *Staff Papers*, International Monetary Fund (Washington), Vol. 32 (June 1985), pp. 248–88.

Williamson, John, "The Exchange Rate System," *Policy Analyses in International Economics*, No. 5 (Washington: Institute for International Economics, 1983).

Comment

David G. Mayes[*]

I. Introduction

The essence of Peter Wickham's paper is that countries tend to go through contortions in order to avoid using the real exchange rate to eliminate unsustainable deficits on the current account of the balance of payments. He argues that the measures commonly used tend to distort the economy and not only impede structural development, but also do not contribute effectively to solving the underlying balance of payments problem.

The basic contentions of his paper are undoubtedly correct. Distortions to the economic system, which prevent the bringing of the external sector into structural balance, impede the development of the economy, in particular, creating increasing foreign indebtedness. This, in turn, adds to the payments difficulties and increases the extent of the structural change eventually required to bring the system back to balance. The distortions should therefore be removed. In these comments I want to make two additions to his remarks and introduce some caveats to explain why it is that many countries have persistently not followed his advice. In practical circumstances more factors are involved and second-best policies may, in fact, be the only viable possibility.

II. Two Additions

The New Zealand Example

Wickham has posited as his paradigm for an assessment of the adjustment problems facing countries a country with relatively undiversified exports under fixed (but adjustable) or crawling peg exchange rates. This paradigm, however, does not reflect either the experience of New Zealand and Australia, both of which are included in the definition of the South Pacific used here. Although the paper does discuss some facets of the New Zealand experience, it does not go into any detail, and Australia is not discussed at all. Both countries have independently floating exchange rates, which would be responsive to a different set of

---

[*] The views expressed here are the author's and do not necessarily reflect those of NEDO.

options from those appropriate to Wickham's paradigm. Furthermore, not only does New Zealand have a freely floating exchange rate, but the striking feature of its export pattern is the rapid rate of diversification, both in terms of products and destinations, as is shown in Tables 1 and 2. This diversification and shift from the position of Wickham's country model were achieved by an economy subject to most of the distortions he cites. It is, therefore, possible to achieve substantial measures of structural adjustment, despite the existence of distortions.

Makeup of the South Pacific

Not surprisingly, International Monetary Fund (IMF) discussions on the South Pacific focus only on member countries, while nonmembers are excluded from consideration. These other countries are, however, a diverse group, and though they may have some similarities, considerable individual analysis is warranted.

Of the other South Pacific countries that the IMF identifies in addition to Australia and New Zealand, Tonga is pegged to the Australian dollar, Vanuatu to the SDR,[1] and Fiji, Papua New Guinea, and Solomon Islands to other baskets of currencies; Western Samoa has a man-

Table 1. New Zealand: Composition of Exports
(In percent)

	Year Ended June	
	1964	1984[1]
Dairy products	22.8	13.7
Meat and by-products	30.5	21.2
Wool	36.7	10.6
Horticultural products	1.8	3.8
Fish	0.1	1.8
Forest products	3.0	5.0
Iron ore and aluminum	—	4.7
Other commodities (mainly manufactures)	3.6	18.1
Tourism (excluding fares)	1.5	5.5
Hydrocarbon import substitution[2]	—	15.6
Total	**100.0**	**100.0**

Source: New Zealand, Department of Statistics.
[1] 1984 estimated by New Zealand Institute of Economic Research, based on provisional data.
[2] Equals savings in imports by use of domestic oil and natural gas supplies.

---

[1] See note on p. 239.

Table 2. New Zealand: Destination of Exports

	1964		1984	
	(In millions of NZ dollars)	(In percent)	(In millions of NZ dollars)	(In percent)
United Kingdom	342.4	47	886.6	11
EEC (excluding United Kingdom)	138.3	19	805.5	9
United States and Canada	119.5	17	1,248.6	15
Australia	36.4	5	1,247.2	15
Japan	32.3	4	1,310.5	16
Asia/Pacific (excluding Australia and Japan)			1,465.0	17
Middle East	59.5	8	630.2	7
Other			807.2	10
Total	**728.4**	**100**	**8,400.6**	**100**

Source: New Zealand, Department of Statistics.

aged float.[2] In its classification of countries, the IMF labels Australia and New Zealand as industrial; Fiji, Papua New Guinea, and Solomon Islands as primary product exporters; and Vanuatu and Western Samoa as service and remittance countries. This last distinction is important, as the chief distortions affecting the balance of payments may originate in the country from which the remittances come.

One must therefore be cautious about treating these countries as a single group. Some parts of the South Pacific with fixed exchange rates have particular adjustment problems because they are not independent territories. Structural adjustment in countries such as Fiji, where a substantial proportion of the labor force is involved in manufacturing, may mean something quite different in a country like Papua New Guinea whose strength lies in its mineral resources.

III. Some Caveats

Why Are Distortions Employed?

In some sense, imposing distortions such as trade controls or subsidies can be seen as a soft option. They appear to obviate the need for some unpleasant and politically difficult actions. When attempts are made to remove these distortions, it may be beyond the capabilities of a demo-

---

[2] International Monetary Fund, *International Financial Statistics* (Washington: International Monetary Fund, January 1986).

cratic government to remove some of them. It is unrealistic to expect governments to act in a way that would result in their own demise. The well-worn saying, "politics is the art of the possible," is still apt.

A second obstacle to removing distortions is that they have usually been introduced for various purposes, some of which will aid the process of structural adjustment, some of which will hinder it. It is often difficult to assess clearly, either ex-ante or ex-post, which category a particular distortion should fall into.

If we take the New Zealand example, some of the "Think Big" projects were introduced to achieve a change in the structure of production and the balance of payments. The projects were engineered by the public sector because their sheer size would have made them very difficult to implement through the open market in the private sector. Even in the United Kingdom and France, it has taken many years of maneuvering to obtain private sector backing for the Channel Tunnel.

Problems of Small Countries

The economic system in a small country is inevitably distorted. A single deal can alter the nature of the balance of payments for many years. Many markets will be so thin that they cannot operate effectively and need to be administered, possibly by linking them to some larger market as in the case of exchange rates or through "smoothing" operations.

This "small country problem" applies certainly to countries as large as New Zealand, where the re-equipment of Air New Zealand or the arrival of a single oil rig can have a very noticeable effect; but the problem is, of course, much more acute in the smaller nations of the South Pacific.

A major problem for such countries is, thus, simply one of stabilization. Enormous fluctuations in receipts are possible, both within years and during years. It is very difficult to tell if a particular shock is, ex-ante, temporary, or permanent, especially in many primary product markets, where a climatic disaster elsewhere can affect the market within a few days. In the simplest cases, stabilization boards have been used. Although their success rates have been low for the economy as a whole, such stabilization can occur through the exchange rate system.

Major projects once started need to be seen through—in most cases—because, although the relative prices expected at their conception may not materialize, the alternative may be even worse and a partial repayment of the capital loss may be better than nothing.

In a sense, this need to see projects through is a very trivial point to make about lumpiness, particularly in physical capital. Many balance of payments distortions are introduced not merely to protect employment in particular industries, but also to protect extant or contracted capital projects.

Process of Change

One dimension missing from Wickham's analysis is growth and, indeed, dynamics. He quite rightly looks at the longer term, but countries get into distorted circumstances because of the rapidity of change required and the equal rapidity with which a distortion can build up. The appropriate real exchange rate will depend on the achievable rate of growth. We are all aware of the difficulties a sudden fall in the rate brings. Countries may feel that they have a choice—adjusting to that lower rate of growth or taking measures to re-instate it. If these measures are successful, then they will themselves offset the interim costs of maintaining or even exacerbating the balance of payments problem.

Also important is the problem of whether the economy can react to a change in the exchange rate in a manner that will right the problem. If both import and export prices are fixed in foreign currency, an exchange rate change may have little effect on behavior. Real allocations will require direct intervention. Such views have certainly been expressed in New Zealand.

What Is the Long-Term Equilibrium Exchange Rate?

It is not clear to me that one can assume what the long-run equilibrium real rate of exchange will be, especially if it is difficult to distinguish long-run from short-run shocks. One solution to this problem is to have a freely operating economy that will tend to move to the equilibrium level, whatever it is. However, there is not necessarily a single outcome. Any action taken may influence the equilibrium. For example, if a country were to set as a target a desired ratio of monetary and fiscal deficits to gross domestic product (GDP), the cyclical evolution of the economy would affect the outcome. Such a policy, which was applied, for instance, in the United Kingdom, contributed to a higher real exchange rate in the short run and to a massive scrapping of capacity in manufacturing and, hence, to a different longer-run path than would have otherwise occurred had the original capacity been retained. This policy does not have a predetermined result. If growth falls short of the implicit target, the economy is driven down further by a reduction in the deficit to meet the ratio target, or it is further stimulated if growth turns out to be greater, particularly as fiscal drag automatically provides more revenue and less expenditure.

Means of Achieving Change

If the change in the current balance is relatively short lived under fixed but adjustable rates, it is probably unwise to introduce a radical change in government policy. The tendency is for the government to try to adjust the imbalance through internal policies, allowing deflation to make the real income adjustment. However, if prices prove unresponsive, or the cost in terms of unemployment is unacceptably high, other more specific means may need to be employed—by, for example, leading the market (one of the small-country problems referred to earlier).

On rare occasions, country authorities have opted for a steep devaluation as a means to get around this dilemma. However, in cases where prices are largely fixed abroad and opportunities for restructuring exports are therefore limited, it is unlikely that this approach will have much success. Another option—the crawling peg—may also prove ineffective in bringing about a real adjustment.

In some cases a government may legitimately conclude that its foreign exchange difficulties are not internally induced and that the balance should be restored, not through painful adjustment on its part, but by some compensation from the external agents who caused the problem. An example of such an externally administered act might be the imposition by a major purchaser of a trade barrier; such a barrier was imposed by the European Communities through the Common Agricultural Policy on New Zealand.

In so far as it not possible to solve the problem of external imbalance through relative price change, balance must be achieved through deflation or reflation of the domestic economy. In these circumstances, the balance of payments will still act as a constraint even under floating exchange rates.

Wickham says that "policy actions undertaken by the authorities are often aimed not at changing the real exchange rate, but at containing the external payments situation . . . " (p. 199). I suggest that the authorities could frequently have both aims in mind. Something must be done in the short run if reserves are not to run out while the chosen measures are bringing about long-term change.

Overseas borrowing for investment in hydrocarbon substitution or energy saving is a case in point. The borrowing both assists the investment and offsets the deficit. The requirement in the long run is, of course, that the return on the investment generates enough foreign exchange to pay back the loan or, at any rate, stabilize interest payments on it. Exchange controls can, in a similar way, redirect funds.

If, in alternate circumstances, the short-run real gain from a nominal exchange rate change is quickly eroded, say, by wage inflation, it is easy to see why a government might intervene to control flows and enable the structural change to take place before the effect of the stimulus dissipates. Only when the change is permanently avoided does progressive deflation occur. Otherwise, there will be a period of slack during which the resources are being transferred (expenditure switching also requires expenditure reduction) but, subsequently, recovery resumes. It would be gratifying to think that that is a fair characterization of the New Zealand economy and that despite the current recession, we have now made the transition to a rising trend through structural adjustment.

Floating Exchange Rates

My last point concerns flexible exchange rates, which are, unfortunately, only lightly touched on in the paper. The game is much more complicated than might be thought, as floating rates effectively eliminate one policy instrument. Floating rates can also behave perversely. Devaluation and deflation undertaken to achieve a switch in expenditure under an adjustable peg might end up being accompanied by a rising exchange rate. Indeed, a rise in the exchange rate can be the most important transmission mechanism for reducing inflation and, hence, changing the real exchange rate in the longer run. In a fixed case, real rates can be changed by changing the exchange rate or the price level. In a floating case, the two are unfortunately interlinked through the actions of fiscal and monetary policy.

7

Long-Term Structural Adjustment Policies

Stanley Please

I. Introduction

"Adjustment policies," "structural adjustment policies," "long-term structural adjustment policies," "development policies," and so on, and so on. Economists have many neat conceptual categories for undertaking their analyses.

For policymakers, life is less simple. Policy has to be a unified package of measures; it cannot be limited to the simple aggregation of policy measures formulated under each of the above, and other, conceptual categories. Long-term development programs are paper exercises unless they are integrated into programs designed to handle the immediate balance of payments situation. Policy analysis becomes largely irrelevant unless the interface of macro with sectoral issues is covered; unless the short- and long-run effects of policies are fully integrated; and unless concerns over balance of payments viability, growth objectives, alleviation of poverty, provision of basic needs, and other dimensions of economic development are addressed by the analysis. It is within this unified approach to policymaking that it seems most useful to discuss the subject of this paper—long-term structural adjustment policies.

The need for adjustment policies arises when the present program of policies is not sustainable from the point of view of a country's balance of payments. This nonsustainability might arise from external or internal sources. It could arise from a deterioration in the external global economic environment facing the country, which is expected to be of a medium- or longer-term nature—adverse movements in its external terms of trade, market access problems for its exports, high levels of real interest rates, and the limited availability of commercial and concessionary capital flows. Or, it could arise from shortcomings in domestic policies that are leading to, or have already resulted in, levels of demand for foreign exchange to meet import needs and debt-servicing obligations that are unsustainable given the country's ability to earn or obtain foreign exchange.

In practice, the need for adjustment is likely to arise for a combination of external and internal reasons, with the balance between them varying from one country to another and from one period to another. Nevertheless, whatever this balance of causation might be, ultimately it is countries facing an unsustainable balance of payments situation that have to adjust their economies. This process can be accomplished explicitly and rationally by adjusting policies and programs to the new situation or, alternatively, adjustment comes about by default, as the economy adjusts itself, but at a high cost because inappropriate policies have remained unaltered.

The ultimate burden of adjustment has to fall on those countries in balance of payments difficulty, and while the implications of this burden for long-term structural adjustment policies will be the focus of this paper, it should be put on record that this burden can be grossly unfair. It seems particularly unfair if the countries are poor, have maintained reasonable levels of domestic economic management, and have been forced to adjust primarily because of an unexpected and large deterioration in the world economic conditions that they face. This comment has particular relevance to East Asian developing countries whose record of economic management has—with some exceptions—been markedly above international norms. At times, these countries have had to "run in order to stand still" when confronted with deteriorating export markets and high interest rates.

It is, therefore, important to emphasize the responsibility of those countries that are, first, rich and, second, primarily responsible—deliberately or otherwise—for the deterioration in the external economic conditions confronting East Asian developing countries. Adjustments should, in these circumstances, be a burden on both creditors and debtors alike. It is also important to emphasize the role of the International Monetary Fund (IMF) and the World Bank in this situation for providing both intellectual and policymaking leadership at the global level. The two Bretton Woods institutions might not have any operational leverage over developed country policies, but they have a duty to point out the adverse consequences of these policies to the rest of the world, and particularly for developing countries. Ultimately, however, if the industrialized countries of the world stubbornly refuse to accept their responsibility for adjustment, even when admonished to do so by the IMF and the World Bank, then the burden inevitably falls on the poorer countries.

II. Anticipating Adjustment

In circumstances in which adjustment to an adverse change in the global economy is essential, countries should confront the options that face them and prepare their policies accordingly, rather than let the economy drift and adjust itself through inflation and other inefficient developments. Moreover, it is better that the adjustment policies be introduced as quickly as possible, so that the costs of not adjusting can be minimized. The need to adjust can frequently be anticipated, and, thus, these costs can be avoided altogether. This is partly true of the widespread debt crisis that was triggered by the Mexican problem in August 1982. Of course, higher than anticipated real interest rates on debt incurred at variable rates, world deflation with its consequences of low commodity prices and protectionism, high oil prices for oil importers after the 1979 oil-price hike, stagnation of flows of concessionary assistance, and the pendulum-like behavior of commercial lenders have all aggravated the debt problem. However, most of the countries that are now confronting a debt problem—most obviously in Latin America and Africa, but also some in Asia—failed to take the required adjustment measures when they were incurring their debts in the 1970s. Moreover, these measures were *clearly* known to be necessary if the consequent debt servicing problem was to be met.

The word "clearly" in the previous sentence is deliberately emphasized. For instance, any examination of World Bank economic reports for the 1970s and early 1980s will show that the urgency of the situation had been correctly assessed. For country after country in the developing world, these World Bank reports concluded that the debt service burden then being accumulated could not be serviced consistently with the maintenance of economic growth, unless adjustment measures were taken to increase export earnings and to reduce the import intensity of gross domestic product (GDP) growth—especially for energy (oil), food (particularly in Africa), and manufacturing industry. Devaluation was a critically important component of these recommended measures.

Events since 1982 have demonstrated that most governments did too little and did it too late to head off a debt-servicing crisis, which, in any case, became even more severe than could reasonably have been anticipated, as a consequence of the deterioration in global economic conditions.

Lest it be thought that the World Bank—or the IMF—can, as a consequence, consider itself blameless for the present debt crisis, it should be emphasized that neither institution acted on the clear evidence that adjustment measures (including devaluation) were required in the 1970s to ensure that the growing debt service burden could be met consistently with economic growth. Some of these failures are recorded elsewhere.[1] Briefly, they amount to a failure on the part of the World

---

[1] See Please (1984), pp. 59–80.

Bank to make the policy reforms required for adjustment and economic growth the focus of its lending operations. The Bank continued to believe, until it was too late, that policy dialogue backed by project lending was all it needed to do, all it could do, or was all it should do. As described later in this paper, structural adjustment lending and other forms of policy-based lending were not introduced by the World Bank until 1980, and then only on a limited scale.

The IMF, for its part during the 1970s and early 1980s, was not, in general, making resources available to countries incurring debt. IMF resources were not required when commercial funds were readily available. However, the IMF failed to encourage the World Bank to take the need for policy reform more seriously in the countries which were getting deeper and deeper into debt. On the contrary, and very specifically at that time, the IMF deliberately frustrated World Bank attempts to induce countries to devalue as an essential part of the package of measures required to enable them to meet their longer-term debt service and growth needs. The immediate balance of payments situation of these countries was healthy and, therefore, the IMF saw no need at that time to anticipate the future balance of payments situation and the required policy response.

III. IMF Adjustment Program

Given (1) the widespread failure of developing countries in the 1970s and early 1980s to anticipate the debt service responsibility implicit in the recycling of Organization of Petroleum Exporting Countries (OPEC) surpluses; and (2) the worse-than-could-have-been-anticipated global economic conditions confronting these countries when the debt crisis broke, all they could do was to introduce, or be encouraged to introduce, an emergency, IMF-style adjustment program as a condition for mobilizing additional external support. This additional support was forthcoming through debt rescheduling, net new commercial bank lending, as well as through the use of IMF resources. In the short run, these emergency programs, of necessity, had to emphasize restrictive domestic demand management. The consequent loss of output and the ensuing cutbacks in consumption, in development expenditure, in social programs, and others, have been the real costs of adjustment. The failure to anticipate the need for adjustment made the costs inevitable. The structure of an economy cannot be changed overnight.

But in the midst of the widespread criticism of these restrictive measures, and particularly of their impact on socioeconomic programs (education, health, and others)—about which more will be said later—sight tends to be lost of those other elements of Fund-supported programs that are aimed at the medium- and longer-term structural adjustment of the economy.

The basic issue is the level of activity—production, employment, and so on—at which an economy can operate without stimulating imports or reducing the stimulus to exports to a combined degree that makes the balance of payments unmanageable, given the likely availability of foreign capital inflows. Devaluation has been a near-universal component of IMF programs. At a minimum, the avoidance of an overvalued exchange rate in real effective terms is a central condition for achieving the objective of maximizing production consistent with balance of payments viability. For some countries (e.g., countries in sub-Saharan Africa), a devaluation of much greater magnitude is necessary than would be required simply to maintain historical parity. A major devaluation is required as a necessary condition for countering the colonial legacy of high labor costs and for correcting the bias against the agricultural sector in these countries. This sector is critical both for enabling African countries to regain their competitive advantage in many primary product markets and for reducing the import-intensity of their economies (particularly in meeting their consumption of food and fuel). More generally, devaluation is a necessary condition in most developing countries for increasing the rate of growth without placing an ever-increasing strain on the balance of payments. Devaluation is, unfortunately, usually seen as a contractionary measure rather than as a means of permitting economic expansion.

In this sense, IMF-sponsored programs have always contained components that are essential to structural adjustment. Avoiding an overvalued currency and thereby seeking to exercise a country's comparative advantage through an appropriate exchange rate policy might not be a sufficient condition for structural adjustment, but it is certainly a necessary condition.

Moreover, IMF programs in recent years have gone beyond emphasizing exchange rate adjustment as a necessary condition for structural adjustment. IMF programs have also begun to address some of the other incentive and institutional barriers to improving the balance of payments situation at any given level of economic activity. The most obvious examples of these have been measures to ensure that the increasing price of oil in the early 1980s was passed on to consumers; measures to improve domestic prices to agricultural export producers where these were clearly impeding exports; and most recently, measures necessary to bring pressure to bear on governments to improve the efficiency of agricultural input and output marketing.

Conceptually, these components of IMF adjustment programs are designed to enhance the responsiveness of the economy to the need to improve the balance of payments, given its existing production capacity.

In addition, they also create the correct signals for generating appropriate changes in the production structure of the economy in the medium to longer term.

However, programs of policy and institutional change that are required in order to bring about the long-term structural adjustment of an economy must be more extensive and much deeper than those covered by IMF-supported programs. These longer-term structural adjustment programs comprise, in effect, a series of sector programs buttressed by appropriate public expenditure programs.

IV. Long-Term Structural Adjustment Programs

The longer-term programs must start with the need to regain the rates of growth of economic activity in developing countries that prevailed during the three postwar decades up to 1980. In retrospect, however, these rates of growth can be seen to have been achieved in global economic conditions that were far more favorable than seem likely over the next few decades—for growth of world trade, for growth of concessionary and nonconcessionary external financing, for commodity prices, and for levels of indebtedness and real interest rates. Returning to a high growth path in the future will, therefore, require that sectoral policies be put in place that will, in general, improve the efficiency with which each sector uses resources, but will more specifically also reduce the rate of growth of these sectors' import requirements and increase their contribution to exports. While exchange rate policy and other components of IMF programs are necessary parts of these programs, more detailed sectoral programs are also required.

For instance, in the case of industry, the process of widening and deepening manufacturing activity—in order to increase consumption levels and employment, while ensuring that import requirements do not move too rapidly ahead of export earnings—requires a range of measures beyond devaluation and import liberalization. The level and structure of effective protection through tariffs, investment incentives, and other measures have to be modified. Typically, countries—in Asia as elsewhere in the developing world—have provided protection to consumer goods industries. This has been done for the very "sensible" reason of import-substitution for manufactured goods in which they are likely to have a comparative advantage at early stages of industrialization—for example, textiles, shoes, furniture, and food processing.

Unfortunately, this encouragement has been provided in ways that have resulted in inadequate incentives being given to exporters, to firms supplying machinery and other inputs required by import-substitution industries, and to labor-intensive as against capital-intensive technologies. For instance, investment incentives have typically included exemption of import duties on imported machinery, which implies, of course, zero protection for domestic production of these goods. Yet, firms supplying these goods should be in the vanguard of the deepening of the industrial sector and, more generally, of the economy. They should also provide increased employment opportunities, particularly for skilled workers. Moreover, the development of such firms must be encouraged as part of the longer-term process of balance of payments management.

Avoiding discrimination against exports is also important if the benefits of international comparative advantage are to be reaped. Revising patterns of incentives implied in existing tariff structures, investment incentive legislation, and domestic tax systems is, however, complex and politically controversial. Vested interests in the existing structure obviously exist. Reform of industrial incentives is, therefore, beyond the scope of IMF-type programs. It has to be introduced in a phased and systematic manner over several years.

Moreover, reform of the industrial incentive structure has to be buttressed by other measures if it is to have the impact intended. Many of these measures are of an institutional nature: e.g., developing appropriate industrial research and training centers; and establishing financial and marketing institutions required to support the development of production capacity. It is at this point that structural adjustment merges into the broader needs of longer-term economic development.

In effect, industrial policy must embody three sets of measures. In the first set are measures that relate to industrial activity and its import requirements and export competitiveness in the short run when capacity is fixed. The second set of measures relates to industrial activity in the medium run when capacity can be varied, but when the basic development constraints of technology, skilled manpower, and financial and other institutions are fixed. The third set includes measures that address these basic constraints.

The same phased and multidimensional approach is required in other sectors such as agriculture and energy. For countries at an early stage of development, agricultural policy is of particular importance. In fact, with a few exceptions like Singapore and the territory of Hong Kong, a prosperous agricultural sector is typically a necessary condition for developing a prosperous industrial sector and, therefore, a rapid rate of economic growth in general. Agriculture provides both inputs for industry and a major source of demand for its output of consumer goods and of agricultural goods and equipment. The worldwide concern over the declining per capita incomes and poor prospects of the sub-Saharan African countries primarily derives from the poor performance of the agricultural sectors of most of these countries. While this poor record has been aggravated by weather and other natural factors, by a rapidly rising population, and by adverse international economic conditions, the primary cause has been a pervasive set of policies unfavorable to agriculture.

As in the case of the industrial sector, the reform of agricultural policies has to cover, first, those measures that will have an immediate impact on production or at the next harvest. These measures include, primarily, improvements in price incentives and in the marketing and input supply system. Second, policy reform must cover those on-farm and off-farm investment measures that increase output and its marketability in the medium run—e.g., improved rural roads and water supply. And, third, measures are needed whose payoff could come in the longer run, such as improved agricultural research and long gestation investment in, say, the development of an irrigation system.

V. Long-Term Structural Adjustment and Development Planning

Is the above approach to longer-term issues of structural adjustment any different from development planning as we have witnessed it in developing countries over the past several decades? To the extent that it does not focus on the level and sectoral composition of investments that are required to achieve certain macro objectives, the answer to this question is probably "no." This is not to suggest, however, that formulation and implementation of appropriate public investment policies, which have been the major focus of development planning, should not continue to be a central part of long-term structural adjustment programs.

What is new in the above approach—or, at least, emphasized much more strongly than in most development plans—is the importance of pricing policies for achieving long-term structural adjustment and development objectives. As has been said by others: "Getting prices right might not be the end of development, but getting them hopelessly wrong certainly is."

This could mean that considerable emphasis should be placed on market prices, but it could also mean some official control of market prices is necessary. For instance, in many people's judgment, energy supply is a long-term problem, which should be reflected in user prices for oil and other energy sources, both to discourage energy-intensive technologies and patterns of consumption (e.g., gas-guzzling automobiles) and to stimulate the development of nonconventional sources of energy. It has therefore been viewed as good policy to keep the fall in the price of oil that has occurred over the past two years from being reflected in consumer prices. Similarly, government intervention in agricultural and industrial price determination could be seen as highly desirable for achieving longer-term sectoral and macro objectives. Providing price supports to agricultural producers in times of excess production due to good harvest conditions and providing infant industry support to manufacturing industry are only two of the most obvious and widely accepted examples of such government interventions. There is for most economists—but not for all—a world of difference between the belief in the importance of prices for guiding the decisions of consumers and producers and the belief in the "magic of the market place."

Development planning must, therefore, move more rapidly beyond public investment planning to embody policy analysis for achieving longer-term objectives. This is most obviously essential for providing the correct pricing signals to private consumers and private producers, be they farmers, artisans, or corporations. It is also necessary for improving the efficiency of public sector investment and other economic decisions. In the case of both private and public sector decision makers, the bridge between what they decide to do at the micro level and what needs to be done at the macro level to achieve governmental long-term objectives must be more firmly established through market prices. No government, however authoritarian, can determine by fiat what individuals do day by day. A government might try to do so, but, except in limited instances, it could never adequately monitor compliance or implement sanctions.

The long-term objectives of governments must find more effective expression both in public expenditure policy and in pricing policy. Otherwise, these objectives are likely to remain merely political rhetoric. It is, for instance, of little use for a government to declare that increased off-farm employment is a major objective of its long-term economic program when its industrial policies actively discourage such activities. Yet, in country after country, this is the case. Industrial incentives typically favor large- and medium-scale, capital-intensive projects over labor-intensive projects in the small-scale and informal sectors of the economy. The International Labour Organisation (ILO) has persistently emphasized in its employment studies the efficiency of the informal sector in achieving not only employment objectives but others as well, such as reductions in the import intensity of production, avoidance of the demonstration effect of Western standards of consumption, and improvements in income distribution. Yet, government fiscal and other policies typically impede the development of this sector.

VI. "Structural Adjustment with a Human Face"[2]

It is now a commonplace to assert that economic development must be interpreted as encompassing more than gross national product (GNP)

---

[2] Jolly (1985).

growth. While growth might be a necessary condition for alleviating poverty and providing for the basic needs of the population, experience clearly shows that growth alone is not sufficient. Likewise, longer-term structural adjustment programs, which are directed at reviving economic growth while achieving balance of payments viability, must also concern themselves with the objectives advocated by the development community in the 1970s of alleviating poverty and providing basic needs. Human resource development programs in education, health, and nutrition are essential if the population at large is to enjoy the benefits of economic growth. Similarly, adequate provision of water supply, sewerage, housing, and other services is essential for meeting the basic needs of any society that claims to be developing. These objectives must be put back on the agenda with increased emphasis for national and international action.

One of the most widespread allegations against the IMF is that the adjustment programs it has supported have undermined the implementation of programs to alleviate poverty and meet basic needs. Budgetary constraint has been seen to have fallen particularly heavily on these services, for instance, on nutrition and other programs concentrating on the needs of children, as confirmed by the United Nations Children's Fund (UNICEF).

The allegations against the IMF are easy enough to rebut. In the short run, adjustment, as has already been emphasized, can only be achieved through the reduction of domestic resource absorption. It is likely that a part of this reduction will have to be achieved through a reduction in government expenditure. But many other components of government expenditure can be cut other than programs focused on poverty and basic needs—most obviously defense, administrative outlays, including civil servants' salaries, and white elephant projects. As everyone knows—but most choose to ignore—the decision to cut social expenditure arises not from any IMF preference for such cuts, but from the unwillingness of governments to reduce other items of expenditure. The IMF is a favorite scapegoat for governments, politicians, and others.

Whatever might be the limitations on the options facing a government in a short-run financial emergency situation, longer-run adjustment programs are certainly less constrained. Moreover, the continuing and prospective tightness of the resource situation not only creates the need but should also provide the stimulus for the adoption of more appropriate programs, that is, efficient but low-cost and replicable social programs, which provide the only realistic means to address poverty and basic needs comprehensively.

The required technical-institutional-financial elements of these programs are well known: site-and-service or slum upgrading programs for housing; low-cost technical options for water supply and sewerage;

health and education facilities that are not limited to Western standards for an urban elite, but address the needs of low-income rural and urban families and employ paraprofessional staff wherever possible; and food and other subsidy programs that are more clearly focused on the needs of the poor. In formulating policies for financing basic services, the authorities must recognize that the greatest burden the poor have to bear is the inadequate provision of these services, due to the impossible budgetary constraint imposed by excessive subsidization and excessive design standards. Appropriate standards and a willingness of governments to charge for services are the way to help poor people. Subsidies, which the poor cannot afford, hurt rather than help.

VII. Policy Conditionality for Long-Term Structural Adjustment

The process of converting long-term structural adjustment objectives of economic growth, poverty alleviation, and the provision of basic needs, in the context of a viable balance of payments, into a package of policy measures needs to be more disciplined. In project analysis, this discipline has been provided by the so-called project cycle. This cycle comprises a series of analytical and decision-making steps beginning with project identification, moving through project preparation and appraisal to project implementation, and concluding with ex-post project evaluation.

A comparable analytical framework is needed to impart greater discipline to policy analysis for long-term structural adjustment and development. This framework may be referred to as the "policy cycle."[3]

Briefly, the policy cycle can be seen as comprising seven steps:

1. Formulation of structural adjustment and development objectives.

2. Diagnosis of the policy constraints on the achievement of the objectives.

3. Formulation of alternative policy change packages that could relieve these constraints.

4. Agreement within government on a politically acceptable policy reform package, including its broad time phasing.

5. Formulation of the detailed measures reflecting the politically acceptable program of policy change, i.e., program development.

6. Implementation and monitoring of policy reform measures, including feedback that can be applied to the formulation of subsequent stages of policy reform.

---

[3] For an elaboration of this concept, see Please (1985).

7. Evaluation of the impact of policy changes on the achievement of objectives and lessons for the future.

This conceptual framework is useful for determining the sources of weakness in policymaking. For example, the weakness could originate in the technical staff's ability to analyze the problems and to formulate policy options; or in the institutional arrangements for implementing policy changes; or in the political system's willingness to take the hard decisions that policy reform requires.

While the simple distinction between governments that are technically unable to formulate and implement long-term structural adjustment programs and those that are politically unwilling to do so is useful, it is too simple. For instance, the political unwillingness to take hard decisions on policy issues can be lessened by the formulation of alternative policy options—maybe not first-best solutions, but preferable to existing policies. Moreover, governments are frequently not so much in unified opposition to the necessary policy measures that comprise a long-term structural adjustment program, as fragmented and weak in their handling of these issues. Unless there is a powerful senior minister with political clout in charge of all aspects of economic policy, policy issues tend to fall between the stools of junior ministers and other agency heads. For instance, in many countries, the responsibility for industrial policy tends to be divided among ministers of planning, finance, and industry, as well as involving other policymaking bodies such as the central bank, the tariff commission, the industrial financing institutions, and so on.

External agencies such as the IMF and the World Bank, as well as bilateral donors and the United Nations Development Program, can provide technical assistance to help strengthen the capacity of a government to undertake policy analysis and to implement policy measures. This assistance should be provided in a manner that helps a country to develop its own capacity to undertake the analytical work. Analysis and implementation, moreover, should be conceived not only as the in-house capacity of government, but also as a contribution that can be made by national research institutes, universities, and consultants. Governments too frequently tend to look outside their own country for technical assistance rather than to their own citizens and national institutions.

As a means of helping to combat political weakness, external agencies can also make their lending conditional on the necessary measures being taken. The IMF has been the leading agency in imposing policy conditionality as part of its financial operations. In recent years this conditionality has extended beyond the monetary aggregates, which represent the legal trigger mechanism for the use of IMF resources, to cover preconditions relating to domestic oil prices, producer prices for export crops, and even such institutional matters as the framework of agricultural marketing systems.

Many of these sectoral and institutional activities require constant monitoring and development that are outside the sphere of IMF operations and the expertise of its staff. As a consequence, in recent years the World Bank has moved increasingly from project lending into policy-based lending. This transition began in 1980 with the introduction of structural adjustment lending, and has been extended into sector operations. The policy-based operations are intended to lend greater urgency and emphasis to policy reform than is possible with project lending. While it is possible to make the commitment and disbursement of project funding conditional on agreed changes in policies, in practice this link is often very weak. This is because the primary focus of such lending is on the implementation of each project. If a project is proceeding according to plan, it becomes difficult to hold back World Bank financing because a government fails to change policies in an agreed manner. It is not impossible to hold back funds when the financing of a particular project is undertaken both as part of a comprehensive lending program to a country and as part of a sequence of project loans to a particular sector.

Even with limited efficacy, policy-based lending gives the World Bank a chance to focus more sharply on longer-term policy issues and to foster a disciplined approach to policy reform. These operations are structured to allow for sufficient time for planning and implementation of a policy reform package. A program of action is agreed on, which will be carried out over, say, a five-year period; disbursement of World Bank funding is then made dependent on the implementation of the agreed-upon program.

This movement of the World Bank into policy-based lending has not always been welcomed. Although developed country governments have generally approved the close collaboration between the IMF and the World Bank buttressed by the Bank's own project operations and dialogue on economic policy issues, developing countries have not welcomed the new policy focus of World Bank operations. Typical reactions are that "one IMF is enough," without having the World Bank intruding into policymaking.

But need the World Bank be intrusive? What is required is that governments recognize more clearly what policy changes are necessary if their own long-term structural adjustment and development objectives of growth, poverty alleviation, and the provision of basic needs are to be achieved. In the more constrained balance of payments situation that most developing countries now face, attaining these objectives will require greater urgency in changing policies. Public expenditure on social services will need to be adjusted more rapidly and more closely targeted on the poor; public investment projects will need to be screened more carefully in order to eliminate white elephants and to give priority to those projects that will generate an adequate economic and social rate of return; incentive structures including pricing, taxation, and subsidy policies will need to be modified more expeditiously in order to enable sectoral production, employment, and other objectives to be achieved consistently with their contribution to macro-internal and external financial balance.

Through policy-based lending, the World Bank should be able to impart greater discipline to the process of policy reform. The emphasis should be on monitoring the process of policy analysis and reform rather than monitoring the detailed outcome of this process. In fact, it is unlikely that policy reform can be sustained over several years unless the process is internalized within a country. For, while some reform measures can be forced on governments, particularly if they are relatively "uncomplicated," such as an across-the-board devaluation, these are not likely to be accepted year after year. It is also difficult to force reforms from outside, especially if they are complex and involve a country's national institution—for example, reforms involving financial policy, financial institutions, agricultural producer incentives, marketing systems, or state economic enterprises.

As a development financial institution, the World Bank is uniquely placed and staffed to monitor the implementation by a government of its own long-term structural adjustment and development objectives. In doing so, the World Bank would be complementing the role of the IMF. But, to repeat the point made earlier in this paper, government policy has to be a unified package of measures embodying those which have an impact in the short run, in the medium run, and in the long run. Hence, the need for the World Bank and the IMF, in undertaking their complementary roles, to work in close collaboration. On the one hand, it makes little sense for the World Bank, in the interests of long-term structural adjustment, to insist that a government maintain and increase socioeconomic expenditures, even when the current macrofinancial balance is weak. On the other hand, it makes as little sense for the IMF to insist on large cuts in such expenditures as part of a program dealing with the problem of macrobalance, when it is clear that these cuts would undermine the long-term structural adjustment necessary to achieve balance of payments viability within a framework of economic growth.

Closer collaboration between the IMF and the World Bank has, in fact, developed over the past few years. If growth momentum is to be given greater emphasis in the context of continuing action to handle the debt crisis, this collaboration must become even closer.

References

Jolly, Richard, Barbara Ward Memorial Lecture (Rome, 1985).

Please, Stanley, *The Hobbled Giant: Essays on the World Bank* (Boulder, Colorado: Westview Press, 1984).

―――, "From Project Cycle to Policy Cycle," paper presented at International Symposium on the Effectiveness of Rural Development (the Netherlands, October 1985).

Comment

Te'o I.J. Fairbairn

Professor Please's paper addresses a vital issue facing developing countries, namely, the need to devise long-term structural adjustment policies to achieve a balance of payments viability within a framework of economic growth. The recent period has shown how vulnerable developing countries are to global economic recessions, as dramatically illustrated by debt-servicing problems and balance of payments crises. This vulnerability, in the absence of appropriate and timely domestic countermeasures, has often led to the introduction of draconian emergency measures—the outcome of which has invariably been a loss of production, employment, and economic growth. Forced to seek assistance from international sources such as the International Monetary Fund (IMF), many developing countries have had to surrender a degree of autonomy over the management of their economies—a state of affairs that has not always been free of significant political repercussions.

The paper, which is admirably concise, succeeds in highlighting the importance of long-term structural policies to achieve ongoing growth, free of chronic balance of payments problems. It embraces major policy issues: the need to anticipate adjustment measures, the need for growth-oriented sector policies, the role of development planning, concern for basic needs and other social justice issues, and the role of the IMF and the World Bank.

In general, one is in agreement with the overall theme of the paper, that is, the need for long-term structural adjustment policies based on a unified approach. Certainly, developing countries need to take this message much more to heart than they have done in the past.

Nevertheless, I feel that the paper glosses over several issues that need to be clarified, and the following remarks will be addressed to those issues. In some areas, more specific suggestions are called for, especially on ways to achieve a particular objective and on mechanisms for applying them. The paper also seems to underestimate the difficulty of achieving certain kinds of policy reforms, particularly in areas still heavily influenced by sociocultural factors. Also, the importance accorded to the IMF and the World Bank and their respective abilities to create preconditions for economic growth through conditional lending seems exaggerated. These and related points are amplified below.

The paper quite rightly argues in favor of a unified approach to policymaking. Such an approach is based on an integration of macro and sectoral issues, short- and long-term effects of policies, and economic growth objectives that take into account alleviation of poverty, provision of basic needs, and related dimensions. As the paper states: "Policy has to be a unified package of measures . . . . Long-term development programs are paper exercises unless they are integrated into programs designed to handle the balance of payments situation" (p. 217).

However, the actual implementation of a unified approach is never straightforward. All too often local planning and administrative capabilities fall far short of what is required, while a common obstacle is the existing planning and budgetary system. The two functions are often handled by separate agencies, with long-term planning being the responsibility of one ministry or agency and budgeting that of another. The gulf between such bodies may be wide, thereby offering no real scope for meaningful integration between short- and long-term planning. The institutional requirements for successful implementation of a unified approach need to be tackled.

The paper gives much attention to devaluation as a structural adjustment tool. One accepts devaluation as an essential part of a package of measures aimed at correcting balance of payments disequilibrium and maximizing production based on comparative advantage. As is well known, the IMF has applied devaluation consistently in attempts to resolve the balance of payments problems of client countries and to foster economic growth. However, devaluation may not be effective in certain circumstances and can itself create problems in other directions. All too often, devaluation seems to have been applied as a matter of blind faith.

There are many reasons why devaluation may not succeed in boosting export production. The anticipated favorable effects of devaluation, for example, may be frustrated by low price elasticity of supply. Especially in agriculture, a poor response on the production side may be due to (1) institutional rigidities, for example, the operation of traditional forms of land tenure systems that inhibit factor mobility and, in turn, efficient factor allocation; and (2) the proportionate rise in the cost of imported inputs consequent on devaluation, which, in an open economy, has the effect of blunting production incentives.

Among many developing countries, poor supply response can be explained by a lack of any real export potential stemming from paucity of land-based resources such as arable land. This situation is not uncommon among many Pacific island countries.

Poor export response to devaluation, if coupled with low price elasticity for imports can, at least in the short term, lead to a deterioration in the balance of payments. Furthermore, depending on the extent of the devaluation and the openness of the economy, the inflationary effects of the now higher-cost imports can be quickly transmitted domestically, thus paving the way for a wage-price spiral. In the absence of effective countermeasures, this can present serious problems in terms of inflation, wage justice, and resource allocation, which are not easily controlled.

In small open economies, the maintenance of a hard currency policy may be the preferred option. This policy may make little difference to the balance of payments and it can be a useful device for countering imported inflation. In recent years, Papua New Guinea has adopted a hard kina policy as a means of avoiding excessive imported inflation, and such a policy appears to have been somewhat successful. As Castle (1980, p. 135) has argued, in such cases ". . . it may well be that maintaining a strong exchange rate is the preferable policy . . . ."

However, where subsistence sectors are still sizable, devaluation may stimulate subsistence food production (as distinct from normal import substitution). This can provide relief for the balance of payments by reducing food imports. A swing to greater subsistence food consumption has recently been observed in Western Samoa, following a series of devaluations. Here, currency devaluation has induced a process of import displacement, as opposed to import substitution of the traditional kind.

On the role of the IMF, the paper tends to be somewhat uncritical. A common criticism leveled at the IMF is its propensity to promote policy measures, including devaluation and stringent fiscal measures aimed at curbing the level of domestic activity, without sufficiently taking into account the special features of the local economy. The criticism is often well based and reflects a lack of local knowledge and experience on the part of IMF staff. Given these shortcomings, it becomes all the more important that the IMF's new emphasis on policy-based lending be exercised with extreme care. How far can one go in applying the principles of conditionality to IMF lending?

The paper does point to several difficult, politically sensitive areas where outside interference may be unwelcome and open to rejection. These areas may be the very ones that are so critical for achieving long-term growth. Examples are current policies on government ownership of economic enterprises and property rights systems that are based on tradition. The ability of the IMF or any other outside body to promote meaningful institutional reforms may be severely restricted. A clear idea of the limits of conditionality is essential.

The advantages of taking anticipatory action in response to adverse changes in the world economy are discussed early in the paper. This action demands both good forecasting capabilities and a willingness to initiate appropriate countermeasures. These requirements, as the paper correctly points out, cannot be taken for granted in developing countries. Certainly, powerful constraints have to be overcome, including a lack of local technical capability to undertake forward planning and a failure to grasp the significance of the problem at the political level. I agree that the IMF and other international and regional aid agencies can play a major part in helping to promote appropriate policies and in building up local planning and forecasting skills.

The paper emphasizes the importance of pricing policies for achieving long-term structural adjustment and growth objectives. Such policies have traditionally been overlooked in development planning, although recent evidence suggests that this lack is being remedied. The latter trend reflects the increasing interest in fostering the growth of the private sector as opposed to the public sector.

In many, if not most, developing countries, much scope undoubtedly exists for corrective action to eliminate major distortions in the price system and for intervention for purposes of fostering long-term growth. But in practice the achievement of a "proper" pricing system may be frustrated by obstacles that are not easily surmountable. For example, there may be a continuing distrust of the free market in situations where government intervention through price control has been substantial, pervasive, and longstanding. At the same time, many local economies have not developed to the point where prices can be used effectively as a signaling device. The reason may be as simple as a lack of control over tariffs and exchange rates due to the existence of special political and economic relations with a metropolitan country.

A central question relates to the kind of policy approaches necessary to achieve economic growth with balance of payments viability. This problem has been the subject of recent analysis. Garnaut (1980) has argued that where an economy is subject to considerable external instability, as is true of the small Pacific island economies, deliberate action can be taken to influence the level of domestic activity. The setting of government expenditure on a "steady growth" path consistent with a sustainable level of domestic expenditure is suggested as a possible means.

Where subsistence sectors are still strong, a recent paper (Fairbairn and Kakazu (1985)) shows that balance of payments equilibrium can, in principle, be achieved by encouraging greater food consumption through subsistence production. Several possible growth paths are identified, based on different export-subsistence production ratios, with each path associated in turn with varying balance of payments conditions. A unique growth path is shown to exist where exports and imports are in a state of balance. This growth path is associated with greater self-reliance and a smaller export sector than is technically possible.

In discussing the value of the so-called policy cycle for achieving a measure of discipline in policy analysis, Professor Please's paper draws attention to the many sources of weakness confronting developing countries. These include fragmented planning and policymaking systems, lack of political backing, and weak technical capabilities. On the last, the point is well taken that external agencies can play a vital part in building up local capabilities. However, these agencies have not always been responsive, and a lot more could be done to develop appropriate training and experience-building schemes.

References

Castle, Leslie V., "The Economic Context," in *South Pacific Agriculture Choices and Constraints: South Pacific Agricultural Survey 1979,* ed. by Ralph Gerard Ward and Andrew Proctor (Manila: Asian Development Bank, 1980), pp. 107–36.

Fairbairn, Te'o I.J., and Hiroshi Kakazu, "Trade and Diversification in Small Island Economies with Particular Emphasis on the South Pacific," *Singapore Economic Review* (Singapore), Vol. 30 (October 1985), pp. 17–55.

Garnaut, Ross, "Economic Instability in Small Countries: Macro-Economic Responses," in *The Island States of the Pacific and Indian Oceans: Anatomy of Development,* Development Studies Center, Monograph No. 23, ed. by R.T. Shand (Canberra: Australian National University, 1980), pp. 313–31.

8

Some Aspects of Economic Adjustment in Small Island Economies

Bruce J. Smith

I. Introduction

Over the years, various scholars have agreed that smallness brings particular economic problems, and that islands also face unique challenges. One of the earliest attempts to identify the special problems and, possibly, advantages of small countries, was undertaken by the International Economic Association in 1957 at its Lisbon Conference on the economic consequences of the size of nations.[1] The studies undertaken in connection with this conference and several subsequent studies[2] done in the 1960s were concerned with "small" countries, which, by current standards, would certainly be considered mid-sized.[3] Indeed, many of the results of these investigations of smallness, which at times did not reveal unique problems or patterns of development for small countries, can probably be discounted because of definitional differences and problems.

For my part, I have devised, quite arbitrarily, a definition of the qualifying characteristics of small economies. The small island economies that will be treated in this paper are the independent South Pacific island states. In this category, I include Papua New Guinea, a country which, although noticeably larger than the others, has an economy that is definitely "island" in character, and which faces economic problems that are similar to those facing several other countries in the South Pacific. In what follows, I will be drawing mainly on the experience of four of these countries: Papua New Guinea, Fiji, Solomon Islands, and Western Samoa; but many of the issues are also relevant for the other

---

[1] Robinson (1960).

[2] E.g., Lloyd (1968).

[3] Small countries included Australia, Sweden, Switzerland, and even Canada. Kuznets (1960), in his contribution to the Lisbon Conference, which is a benchmark study cited by a number of later researchers, considered countries with populations of less than about 10 million to be small.

countries in the region, including Vanuatu and Tonga. Specifically excluded from the group are the very small island states and territories, which, it seems, face more acute problems and with which, I confess, we in the International Monetary Fund (IMF) are not familiar.

II. The IMF and the South Pacific Islands

The IMF's involvement with the island countries of the Pacific dates back to the early 1970s. Fiji was the first of the island states to become a Fund member in May 1971. Subsequently, Western Samoa, Papua New Guinea, Solomon Islands, Vanuatu, and Tonga have become Fund members.

Since the first consultation with Fiji in July 1972, the Fund has developed a normal range of contacts with these countries, generally built around annual (or in some cases 18 monthly) consultations which are called for under the Fund's Articles of Agreement. Perhaps more important, the Fund has provided a large amount of technical assistance, in some instances by studies conducted by Fund staff members, and also through the services of experts in the fiscal and central banking areas. Fund-financed experts are presently stationed in all of the island countries (with the exception of Tonga), and in some countries there are several experts. Perhaps the major contribution Fund technical assistance has made in the region is in the establishment and staffing at a senior level of central banking institutions in Papua New Guinea, Fiji, Solomon Islands, Western Samoa, and Vanuatu.

Interestingly, the Pacific island countries have not been major users of Fund resources. With the notable exceptions of Western Samoa, which has had six stand-by arrangements with the Fund since 1975, and Solomon Islands with two stand-by arrangements in 1981–83, the other countries of the region have not borrowed from the Fund to support adjustment programs. However, most countries have made purchases under the compensatory financing facility to finance temporary export shortfalls. The limited use of the Fund's resources reflects in some cases the smallness of the quotas of these countries relative to their financing needs and, in most cases, their ample access to alternative sources of financing from commercial markets. The minimal use of Fund financing in no way implies that the Fund has not been closely involved with economic adjustment efforts in the region.

III. Characteristics of Pacific Island Economies

The Pacific island countries are diverse, in terms of population, size, and topography. While they do not constitute a group of economies that face a unique set of economic problems, they do share elements of economic structure and face many of the same problems when it comes to economic adjustment.

Governments in the South Pacific islands are generally working, participatory democracies of rather conservative political persuasion. For political and social reasons, the approach to economic policymaking is also generally conservative, with an aversion to bold new initiatives or sharp changes in direction. While these are all developing countries, with per capita incomes ranging from around a moderately low SDR 600 in Solomon Islands and Western Samoa up to a middle-income level of around SDR 1,750 in Fiji, they do not suffer from overt poverty.[4] Large and productive subsistence output ensures an acceptable availability of the essentials for life to practically all. Especially in the countries of Melanesia, subsistence village society and modern monetized economies exist side by side, and their interaction creates special problems for economic management. Although varying in form from country to country, the Pacific island states all face formidable structural impediments to growth which render the supply side of their economies relatively unresponsive to policy changes when compared with most other countries.

As much as these common features can be the source of problems, it is two other characteristics—the reliance on foreign trade and transfers, and inflexibilities and imbalances in labor markets—that create particular and, to a degree, unique difficulties for economic management. Right from the start, it has been recognized that small economies (at least economies as small as those considered here) are required to rely more heavily on foreign trade than larger nations. This is because they are likely to be endowed with a narrower range of resources than larger countries, which encourages concentration in a few traded goods industries, and because foreign trade is the only means by which small countries can benefit from the efficiency gains that scale production can allow in even a few product lines. The South Pacific island countries are indeed heavily reliant on foreign trade, with aggregate trade in goods and services as a proportion of gross domestic product (GDP) ranging from a low of about 70 percent in Western Samoa to around 100 percent in Fiji and Papua New Guinea. Heavy reliance on foreign trade has other dimensions. Many island states are reliant on one or only a small number of export commodities and on a small number of export markets. Some are also reliant on one or two predominant suppliers of imports. These characteristics make these countries particularly vulnerable to external shocks and cycles.

---

[4] The SDR is a fiduciary reserve asset created by the International Monetary Fund and used as a unit of count. In the first week of September 1987, its approximate value was SDR1 = US$1.30.

The South Pacific islands are also, and probably uniquely so, heavily reliant on foreign aid. Per capita aid flows to these countries are among the highest in the world.[5] While in theory this adds to their vulnerability to changes in the aid climate, in practice it has not so far been a pressing problem. Papua New Guinea is having to adjust to a gradual reduction in Australian assistance, especially for budgetary support, and to cope with fluctuations in the international value of aid caused by large changes in the value of the Australian dollar. Solomon Islands and, more recently, Vanuatu have also been forced to adjust to a reduction in direct budgetary assistance from former colonial authorities following political independence. However, the Pacific island countries have to a large extent been sheltered from the effects of aid fatigue and cutbacks that have generally affected the developing world. Fortunately, foreign assistance remains relatively plentiful and assured in this region, especially for development projects. The main constraint on the amount of aid is, in most cases, the lack of viable, documented, and prepared development projects that warrant funding from the aid that is available.

The imbalances and inflexibilities in labor markets that are a feature in some countries of the region have their origins in the dual nature of the economies common in Melanesia, poor growth records relative to mostly rich resource endowments due partly to structural impediments, and industrial relations and wage-setting arrangements that have been imported chiefly from the larger countries in the region, particularly Australia. In countries where subsistence sectors are large, a major part of the labor force is likely to be not gainfully employed on a full-time basis, and there is a large reservoir of unskilled labor in the villages from which the formal economy can draw. Many rural workers would welcome the opportunity to enter the wage economy. This is not only because cash wage-earning potential often exceeds that from part-time cash cropping, but also because of the social attraction that the formal sector and urban life hold. While the supply of unskilled labor greatly exceeds the number of job opportunities, skilled labor is in short supply as education and training infrastructure are undeveloped. Skill shortages, historical (and in some cases, present) reliance on skilled workers and managers from expatriate sources, strong unionization, and centralized wage-fixing machinery have worked to establish and maintain a general level of wages that is high in relation to underlying productivity.

In general, it must be recognized that wage aspirations in most Pacific island economies are unrealistically high, being influenced more by the "essential needs" of the wage earner, in some cases set in terms of expatriate standards, than the economic return on employing labor that

---

[5] Statistical details of aid flows to the South Pacific are given in the Report of the Committee to Review the Australian Overseas Aid Program, the so-called Jackson Report.

applies in these economies. High wages inhibit business investment needed to create job opportunities and promote labor-saving production techniques, while at the same time enhancing the attractiveness of wage labor to those in village society. As a result, employment has grown only slowly and urban unemployment has tended to rise. In Papua New Guinea, and to a lesser extent in Fiji, urban unemployment has been a factor leading to increasing strain on basic law and order.

IV. Some Problems of Economic Adjustment

Vulnerability to External Cycles

Because of their heavy reliance on foreign transactions, the South Pacific islands are extremely vulnerable to foreign sector-induced fluctuations in income and levels of activity. In all the island states, fluctuations derive principally from variations in the terms of trade, which are wide because of the concentration of exports in a narrow range of agricultural and mineral exports. The data in Table 1 do suggest that exports in the Pacific island economies are subject to especially wide fluctuations. In some cases, an additional source of instability is introduced by the lumpiness of major development works and mineral projects, which

Table 1. Variability in Exports in Selected Countries, 1960–84[1]

Pacific island countries	
Papua New Guinea	0.39
Fiji	0.23
Western Samoa	0.28
Solomon Islands	0.26
Vanuatu	0.28
Tonga	0.25
Kiribati	0.34
Selected industrial countries	
Australia	0.15
New Zealand	0.15
United States	0.16
Japan	0.14
United Kingdom	0.17
Selected developing countries	
Malaysia	0.20
Philippines	0.20
Thailand	0.21
Sri Lanka	0.13
World exports	0.19

[1] Defined as the standard deviation of exports around a fitted log trend.

undergo an inevitable cycle of construction, peak production, depletion, and closure. Those countries that are heavily reliant on a single major aid donor can experience fluctuations induced by swings in the exchange rate for the currency in which aid is denominated, while those reliant on wage-earner remittances are vulnerable in this way also, as well as to changing employment conditions in host countries.

In the upswing of the cycle, incomes rise. In the typical case of an improvement in the terms of trade, the increase is in exporters' incomes, and where export taxes and royalties or other direct state ties to the export sector are significant (as in the case of mineral exporters), government revenues also rise directly. The initial impact on spending is often weak, and the savings rate, especially for private savings, tends to rise. Private consumption patterns may be influenced by perceived permanent incomes, and export producers may often desire to rebuild financial assets during the early stage of the upswing. In the public sector, there is also normally a lag in the response of general spending decisions to improved revenues. Thus, taking account of the pegged exchange rate regimes followed throughout the region, the immediate effect is likely to be a disproportionate improvement in the external current account, an accumulation of foreign reserves, and a surge in monetary growth.

The lag in the impact on real economic activity is variable and difficult to predict, depending, among other factors, on the depth of the earlier recession, the perceived durability of the recovery, and the public's unsatisfied desire to hold financial assets. Nevertheless, the magnitude of the expansionary impetus is typically so large that, sooner or later, real spending increases. Most often, private consumption spending is the first component to pick up momentum, with investment and public spending being somewhat slower to respond. Often, also, spending only gains this momentum after the upswing in the terms of trade has ended, and the cycle has turned downward.

In the island economies, which are highly open, imports absorb a large part of the rise in spending, providing the domestic economy with an effective "safety valve" from the effects of a possibly rapid buildup in demand pressures. Nevertheless, the fluctuations are typically so large that, even after an import surge, there is a strong residual rise in demand for domestically produced goods and services. The openness of the economies prevents any substantial direct spillover in inflation in traded goods prices. Nevertheless, rising demand tends eventually to be translated into business costs and prices, working mainly through imperfections in the labor market. Spotty shortages of labor coming at a time of buoyant external and domestic demand are often translated into less-than-firm resistance to wage increases. Labor shortages in key occupations can lead to wage concessions that spread more generally. By whatever mechanism, there are numerous examples of unreasonable wage increases becoming entrenched during boom times, which create problems when conditions are lean.

A broadly similar pattern of developments is typical during the subsequent downturn in the cycle. The fall in incomes associated with a deterioration in the terms of trade is translated only slowly into reduced domestic demand. Private savings rates tend to fall as individuals and businesses maintain constant spending levels because financial balances are high, and often also because of delayed perception as to the depth and durability of the downturn. Government spending levels tend to be inflexible downward. Especially in countries where export earnings have a direct impact on government revenues, the budget deficit is likely to widen sharply. Equally important in some cases, commodity marketing boards or other authorities that set producer prices for exports are often slow to reduce prices paid to growers to reflect falling world price levels. A sustained level of aggregate demand, coupled with weak export receipts, results in a deterioration in the external current account. However, if the government chooses to finance the rising budget deficit by borrowing abroad (as is often the case), international reserve levels may be maintained. In other circumstances, external pressures may become severe and necessitate policies of adjustment.

In time, the drop in incomes will be reflected in domestic demand. As on the upside, the largest part of the cutback will be reflected in import levels as consumption and investment spending weaken. However, demand for domestically produced goods and services is also affected. Most of the impact of reduced demand on domestic industry is reflected in lower output levels. There may be some downward pressure on prices in traded goods industries if the terms of trade weakness is associated with a more generalized world recession, but domestic costs are unlikely to decline significantly. In particular, wage rates, which tend to be inflexible on the downside in most countries, are particularly inflexible in many Pacific island economies (especially in the public sector). As a result, unemployment is likely to rise.

All this is fairly commonplace. Most economies are, after all, subject to the same basic forces during the international economic cycle. What sets the island economies apart is the magnitude of these fluctuations, and, because of this, the extent of the economic disruption that they create. While swings in import demand absorb an unusually large part of the external shocks, the sheer size of the external fluctuations is such that the residual impacts on domestic activity tend to be severe.

The adverse economic effects of such fluctuations are many, but three seem particularly important. First, while total investment tends to be more variable, it is also, in the aggregate, likely to be reduced as a result of economic fluctuations. The uncertainty associated with swings in activity tends to be discouraging, and even in nontraded goods industries, aggregate returns on investment tend to be reduced as a result of fluctuations. Second, fluctuations tend to encourage budgetary problems. The surge in revenue that comes on the upswing promotes a liberal approach to government spending decisions. Ample revenues encourage acceptance of marginal spending proposals, which in other circumstances would be rejected, promoting waste and inefficiency in government programs. Moreover, unsustainable expenditure growth is difficult to trim back later, especially if it comes in the form of an expanded wages bill. When cuts are made, they tend to fall disproportionately on public investment, which may also involve a cutback in externally aided projects. In a number of instances, there has been a tendency for secular increases in deficits, and for excessive reliance on external public borrowing. Third, because wages are considerably more flexible upward than they are downward in the Pacific island states, wide economic fluctuations are likely, over time, to encourage an increase in wages toward a level that can be accommodated at cyclical peaks, but is excessive at all other phases of the cycle.

The adaptation of policies to the changing economic circumstances associated with cyclical forces is the central task of economic management in the Pacific island states. Some, such as Papua New Guinea, have developed a fairly elaborate strategy to counter the impact of cyclical forces on the domestic economy, while others, such as Solomon Islands, are more inclined to accept the impact of external cycles on the domestic economy and focus primarily on countering their adverse impact over the long term. In either case, the essential tools of management are the same: fiscal policy, monetary policy, and wages and exchange rate policies. These are the essential core policies around which comprehensive programs can be built and are the ones I propose to concentrate on here. They are by no means the only policy content of workable adjustment programs, nor are they likely to be sufficient on their own in any case. But these other policies are outside the scope of this paper, as are the many structural and institutional aspects of policies bearing mainly on the supply side, which are unique to each case but common in principle and vital in all. These include issues related to development and export diversification, financial market development and deepening, issues in taxation, and trade and protection policies.

Role of Demand-Management Policies

Demand-management policies provide a means of moderating the impact of external fluctuations on the domestic economy, but they also play a much more fundamental role in adjustment strategies. This is because demand shifts tend to be the major cause of external difficulties in island economies. Certainly, misaligned price levels can also cause external problems of a structural nature and amplify those of cyclical origin. However, in large part, the periodic external difficulties experienced by island economies in association with the international trade cycle are primarily the product of shifts in the balance between domestic demand and supplies. As noted earlier, the supply side of the Pacific island economies is particularly unresponsive in the short and medium term. Let me hasten to add that this does not mean that supply policies, including policies affecting prices, do not have a place in adjustment programs in the island states. However, the importance of demand imbalances is such that demand-management policies have the major role to play in economic management and adjustment.

Fiscal Policy

Public finances are typically the source of much instability in the Pacific island states, both because of the size of government operations relative to the economy as a whole (which partly reflects heavy reliance on foreign aid) and the substantial involvement of the public sector (defined broadly to include marketing boards and public enterprises) in the export sector. The aim of fiscal policy in adjustment programs in broad terms must be to set limits to demand through government spending and financial deficits that are consistent with external viability.

The first requirement in establishing such a fiscal policy is to come to a realistic assessment of future economic prospects. The scope for future growth and public spending increases depends critically on the future flow of external receipts. The response of policymakers in an economy experiencing a deterioration in the terms of trade should be entirely different depending on whether the weakness turns into a medium-term slide in the terms of trade, a temporary downturn in a normal cycle, or an aberration from a strengthening trend in the terms of trade over the medium term. The first scenario would normally require the immediate introduction of fiscal adjustment policies; the second may justify maintaining a steady stance of fiscal policy, allowing the built-in fiscal stabilizers to operate; while in the third case, a more aggressive fiscal policy, possibly involving an increase in spending levels, would be justified.

Fiscal policy must, therefore, be made in a medium-term context, with a wary eye to the future. A wary eye is warranted because the costs of overreaching in the event that circumstances turn more adverse than expected are likely to outweigh those of shooting for growth below the peak rate. Also, it must be borne in mind that in democratic countries, it is tempting to postpone the hard decisions associated with a tight fiscal stance if there is even a chance that events will turn out satisfactorily.

The assessment of the future foreign exchange earning prospects sets an outer limit for fiscal policy. Public spending must be constrained within an amount that limits the growth of domestic demand, import demand, in line with the expected foreign exchange earnings and an acceptable change in international reserves, and a viable accumulation of external debt. This projection does not demand perfect foresight. Adjustments to the direction of policy will be needed in the normal course to take account of unforeseen developments. Of course, the sharper the foresight of policymakers the more effective policies will be in overcoming externally induced fluctuations. But, regardless of the authorities' ability to see the future, a fiscal policy conducted within this framework and limits is essential to adjustment in the island economies. The following examples, drawn from experience during the last international recession, serve to illustrate the different ways in which fiscal policies have been operated in support of adjustment in different countries.

During the late 1970s, Western Samoa attempted to invigorate a lagging economy by undertaking an ambitious program to develop infrastructure and industry. Government and public enterprise spending was raised sharply. Domestic demand and activity levels did increase as desired, and for a time the external position was able to accommodate the expansion because of an improvement in the terms of trade. However, budgetary and external deficits expanded, monetary growth accelerated, and external indebtedness increased.

The situation became unsustainable when, after peaking in 1979, the terms of trade fell precipitously during 1980–82. The fall in the terms of trade, which reached a cumulative 45 percent during this period, had a direct adverse effect on the external accounts, but its indirect effects, operating largely through public finances, were one major factor contributing to an acute imbalance in the economy. This came about through the powerful effects of an automatic fiscal stabilizer, which in other circumstances would be expected to play a useful role in evening out the effect of external stocks on the domestic economy. However, in this case (which is fairly typical for the island economies), the economy was badly positioned when the downturn occurred, and adjustment, rather than countercyclical action, was necessary. Government revenues fell sharply with the downturn in export incomes, while spending had gained considerable momentum, in part because of the spillover of gathering inflation on wage costs. Thus, despite strong efforts to cut spending—and, indeed, investment outlays were curtailed noticeably—the budget deficit rose to 17 percent of GDP in 1981, and financing by the domestic banking system rose abruptly to about 10 percent of GDP in 1981 and 1982 from about 4 percent previously. At the same time, financial losses of the public enterprises also rose sharply, doubling to about 6 percent of GDP in 1981. Largely as a result of the burgeoning public sector financing requirement, domestic credit expanded at an average rate of 40 percent in 1980–82. The growth in liquidity averaged over 20 percent, and inflation was also around 20 percent. Despite continued official external borrowing, external commitments could not be financed, and sizable payments arrears accumulated during 1980–82.

The comprehensive adjustment program adopted by the Western Samoan authorities in 1983 to address these problems, which was supported by a stand-by arrangement with the Fund, sought to achieve external adjustment through fiscal strengthening, cautious monetary policy, and flexible exchange rate management. Arguably, the most crucial element of the program was fiscal policy. The program called for a cut in the budget deficit in 1983 to 6 percent of GDP, 10 percentage points lower than in the previous year, with deficit financing by the banking system being reduced from 10 percent to 1 percent of GDP. In fact, an even larger adjustment was achieved, and the budget deficit was cut to only 2 percent of GDP in 1983. The adjustment came in part from a major discretionary tax increase (amounting to as much as 4 percent of GDP). However, revenue enhancement was matched by expenditure restraint, most importantly by close containment of the government wages bill and the reduction of domestically financed development spending by a quarter (and substantially more in real terms). Also, disbursements of foreign assistance increased substantially, so that the government was able to reduce its net indebtedness to the domestic banking system. Improvements in the government budget were complemented by a strengthening of the financial position of the public enterprises, which were also able to reduce their net indebtedness to the banking system in 1983.

The strength of the fiscal adjustment implemented by the Western Samoan authorities in 1983 was the foundation of their success in overcoming severe difficulties. Of course, other elements of the program also played an important role, and fiscal adjustment had to be maintained. In 1984 the authorities introduced further new tax measures equivalent to 1.7 percent of GDP and, despite less stringent expenditure constraint, including a large increase in domestically financed development spending, the deficit was maintained at 2 percent of GDP and net indebtedness with the banking system was again reduced. These fiscal efforts were instrumental in reducing inflation and, together with an upturn in the terms of trade, generated a strong turnaround in the balance of payments. The Western Samoan experience illustrates that, just as external imbalances can be relatively large in the island countries, these countries also have the ability to make and absorb unusually large domestic financial adjustments that would probably be impossible in larger countries.[6]

---

[6] The Jackson Committee (1984) noted that, for small islands, "smallness means that modest economic changes would be sufficient to solve some of the balance of payments, income and other problems" (p. 175). While this perceived advantage of being small was seen in a developmental context, it may also have some validity in economic adjustment.

Fiji faced broadly similar problems during the early 1980s. With a 25 percent downturn in the terms of trade beginning in 1980, fiscal deficits expanded rapidly. Current spending continued to rise strongly, as wage levels were indexed to inflation and the share of wages in GDP rose. Capital spending also increased strongly, and the overall budget deficit more than doubled to 6.5 percent of GDP during 1980–82. The financial position of the public enterprises also weakened sharply (partly because of the recession and low sugar prices). However, the extent of the imbalance was smaller than in the case of Western Samoa, and although domestic demand grew at an unsustainable rate, monetary growth remained moderate and inflation followed rates abroad. Nevertheless, the impact on the balance of payments was substantial, and the authorities adopted expenditure-restraining measures—especially in 1983 when capital spending could be cut back. Despite these steps and an upturn in the terms of trade in 1983, the budget deficit remained at about 3 percent of GDP in 1984. Although the authorities did not undertake substantial new tax measures, revenues held up during the recession. The problem remained on the expenditure side, especially current spending which rose from 18 percent of GDP in 1980 to 25 percent in 1984. Although part of the increase reflected higher interest payments, much of the increase reflected persistent increases in the government's wage bill, owing not only to indexation, but to substantial merit and seniority increases. Thus, partly with the aim of fiscal adjustment, the government introduced a wage freeze in November 1984 to last until the end of 1985. As a result, the persistent increase in the current expenditure ratio has been arrested, and despite a recovery in capital spending, the overall budget deficit is likely to be reduced somewhat in 1985.

In many respects, Papua New Guinea has the most clearly articulated medium-term approach to fiscal policy in the region. This is partly because of the particular vulnerability of its government budget to external shocks arising from the importance of mineral revenues. In Papua New Guinea it is understood that fiscal policy is the principal instrument for ensuring external viability, and budgetary policy is directed toward this objective. Annual government budgets are prepared within a rolling five-year perspective, and real government spending is constrained to a level that is projected to be sustainable over the medium term. The broad idea is that expenditures should not rise to absorb a temporary boost in revenues during a cyclical boom and that, similarly, expenditure levels should be sustained during a temporary downturn, financed if necessary by a larger deficit and external borrowing.

This is a realistic approach to fiscal management in an island economy, combining elements of countercyclical and adjustment policies in a logical balance. By and large, this strategy has served Papua New Guinea well. Nevertheless, its implementation has not always been easy, as the experience during the 1980s illustrates. The commodity price boom of 1979 was followed by a substantial increase in government spending in the 1980 budget. However, even as expenditures were hiked, the external environment became less favorable. The terms of trade turned downward in what would amount to a 30 percent decline over the next three years, and future export prospects became clouded by a significant downward revision to the estimated ore reserves at the huge mine operated by Bougainville Copper Ltd. The authorities did not immediately recognize the severity of the worsening external outlook, and again in the 1981 budget expenditures rose strongly. However, revenues declined in 1981, and the budget deficit rose to 6 percent of GDP from 1 percent of GDP in 1980.

By 1982 the authorities recognized that budgetary policy was supporting a level of domestic demand that was unsustainable, as the external current account deficit had widened to over 20 percent of GDP in 1981. Real government spending on goods and services (the main indicator of policy monitored by the authorities) was budgeted to decline by 3 percent in 1982. Also, new revenue measures to yield over 1 percent of GDP were introduced. Even with these measures, the budget deficit was expected to widen further as a result of the severe compression of incomes and government revenues. Subsequent to the budget's preparation, external pressures intensified and the revenue outlook worsened. Therefore, in midyear, the authorities courageously tightened the fiscal belt a notch further, when expenditures were reduced by a further 1.3 percent of GDP. However, even with sizable underspending, the shortfall in revenues was so severe that the budget deficit remained at 6 percent of GDP in 1982.

The policy of budgetary adjustment was sustained in 1983 and 1984. In 1983 the government retrenched about 10 percent of the civil service in an effort to trim the size of the government to a viable level. In both 1983 and 1984, the process of fiscal consolidation was aided by unintentional underspending on capital works as a result of project implementation difficulties. Also, the terms of trade recovered, and revenues recovered strongly. By 1984, with the budget deficit reduced to only 1 percent of GDP, the process of fiscal adjustment to the recession was complete. The magnitude of the task achieved by the authorities can be gauged from the fall in real government spending on goods and services by 8 percent during 1982 84, and by 5 percentage points as a proportion of GDP.

A postscript needs to be added to this success story. Just as the fiscal adjustment program reached its conclusion in 1984, the external environment, both in terms of prospects for export earnings and foreign assistance, became more clouded. Despite this, the authorities adopted an expansionary fiscal stance for 1985, with real spending likely to rise significantly and reverse much of the economy achieved during the last three difficult years. The government also abandoned its earlier plan to eliminate such borrowing to finance its deficit by 1987. In many respects, there are parallels between the current situation and that in 1980–81 when budgetary policy was slow to adjust to a worsening outlook. It underlines the difficulty in effectively implementing a fiscal strategy, even one that is so clearly enunciated as in Papua New Guinea, both because of imperfect foresight and the political difficulty of subordinating other objectives of government policy, such as the desire for growth and development, to the need for fiscal austerity at a time when revenues are buoyant as a result of a boom that may well have passed.

Monetary Policy

Monetary policy generally plays a subsidiary role to fiscal policy in adjustment programs in the island economies. This reflects the relatively small size of private bank credit in relation to public borrowing requirements and the large swings in liquidity associated with an unstable external position. Nevertheless, monetary policy can still play a useful role in economic management in these countries.

What should be the main objective of monetary policy in island economies, and how can this be achieved? The answer to the first part of the question is that the objective is the same as that for fiscal policy—i.e., to contain the level of domestic demand within bounds consistent with external viability. The only main difference is that, whereas fiscal policy, of necessity, tends to have a longer-term focus, monetary policy can be fast acting and can, in addition, be directed to the short term.

In considering how to achieve this objective, policymakers in the island economies have considered the role of monetary targeting but, generally speaking, have found it to be of limited usefulness. Put in the simplest of terms, in economies subject to such large external shocks, the authorities have found they are relatively powerless to manipulate monetary aggregates to achieve the targets. In some cases, also, monetary officials have taken the view that because of the openness of these economies and the safety valve provided by changes in import demand that mitigates the impact with which external shocks are transmitted to the domestic economy, there is less need to limit monetary growth, especially when it arises from foreign transactions.

In Solomon Islands, few attempts have been made to control the money supply so as to mitigate the influence of external shocks. The deterioration in the terms of trade in 1980 and 1981 was reflected in a 25 percent decline in the stock of broad money in these two years. In the subsequent three years, broad money rose on average by some 20 percent per annum, reflecting mainly persistent external surpluses. Significantly, during most of this period the autonomous growth in total domestic credit was broadly in line with the combined growth in real incomes and foreign-induced inflation. This would seem broadly appropriate if domestic money creation is not to spill over into additional imports. However, in 1984 and the early part of 1985, domestic credit growth accelerated to over 40 percent as buoyant business conditions at the top of the cycle fed through into loan demand. This development forced the authorities, albeit reluctantly, considering the possible effect on growth and with some difficulty in view of the bluntness of the instruments at their disposal, to begin to constrain domestic credit expansion in 1985. This step became unavoidable if domestic monetary policy was to be prevented from adding to incipient external pressures.

In contrast, Papua New Guinea traditionally published targets for monetary growth, but developments in 1983 encouraged the authorities to abandon targeting. Against a background of weak private sector activity and a continuing deterioration in the international reserves position, the authorities, at the beginning of the year, established a target for broad money growth of 7–10 percent in 1983. Consistent with this target (and the weak external outturn they expected), the authorities also set a ceiling growth in private sector credit of 15 percent. However, events diverged markedly from this scenario. The external position strengthened sharply in the second half of the year. Although private credit grew by somewhat less than the ceiling established for 1983 and public sector recourse to the banking system was also less than expected, monetary growth jumped to 15 percent, well above the 7–10 percent target range. The authorities found that the magnitude of the external surplus was such as to leave them largely unable to contain monetary growth.

Although the arguments against monetary targeting in these circumstances appear convincing, this should in no way be taken to mean that monetary growth does not matter. Monetary developments are, after all, a key indicator of future domestic demand and trends in imports. Thus, although it may not be possible to project monetary growth rates accurately in view of the unpredictability of export developments (and equally the lags with which changes in domestic incomes are reflected in import demand), policymakers must aim to influence monetary developments in a medium-term context, consistent with their balance of payments objective. In this way, the operational element of monetary policy—influencing the rate of change in domestic credit expansion—remains just as important in the absence of monetary targeting as it is when targets are employed.

Interestingly, monetary authorities often do not have to act firmly to contain credit growth during the downswing of the cycle. Typically, by the time the authorities are forced to enact adjustment measures in the fiscal field, domestic income, activity levels, and confidence have fallen to a low ebb. In these circumstances, credit demand is likely to be low. Sometimes, the needs of the domestic economy lead the authorities to encourage banks to lend to private businesses at the same time that they are vigorously pursuing fiscal consolidation. Because of the lags between economic upturn and spending decisions, the period when greatest caution in monetary policy is required is often at, or just past, the cyclical peak in the terms of trade. Regardless of possible strong monetary growth in preceding periods, domestic demand conditions, and particularly import demand, may appear subdued. In these circumstances, the authorities may be inclined to disregard a surge in private credit demand—or even encourage it—to foster growth. However, a tight rein on domestic credit is vital at this point of the cycle to mitigate the impact of domestic demand on external pressures in the succeeding downswing.

While the objective of such a policy is to manage demand so as to avoid external crisis, more explicit forms of countercyclical policy have been developed, most notably in Papua New Guinea and Western Samoa. As an example, stabilization funds have been established in Papua New Guinea for coffee, cocoa, copra, and oil palm exports. These funds impose a levy on exporters when prices exceed a historical "normal" level and pay a bounty to growers when prices fall below this level. Thus, disposable incomes in the export sector are reduced at the peak of the cycle and are supported at the trough.[7] The smoothing out of incomes should also mitigate balance of payments variability arising from domestic demand instability. Experience with these mechanisms has been generally satisfactory in Papua New Guinea, although it would also be a mistake to ascribe to them too important a contribution in economic stabilization. Even so, this experience should seem to be favorable, almost uniquely so, among countries that have experimented with such schemes. Elsewhere, particularly in some African countries, governments have been unwilling to leave fund balances in the hands of growers, and the stabilization schemes have become, effectively, a means of export taxation and the funds have not been available to support exporter incomes when prices fall.

Difficulties in implementation can also arise in setting the appropriate threshold price below which levies turn to bounty payments. In Papua New Guinea the threshold price for cocoa is set at a high level, so that, even at the recent cyclical peak in prices, bounty payments were continuing to be made to growers. Rather than being countercyclical, the scheme was acting in these circumstances to reinforce cyclical

---

[7] A broadly similar arrangement, the Mineral Resources Stabilization Fund, operates to smooth fluctuations in government income deriving from the variability in mineral profits.

demand forces. Similar difficulties can emerge in the operation of commodity marketing boards where delays in reducing procurement prices when world prices decline can artificially support domestic demand and accentuate external problems. This has been a problem at times in both Western Samoa and Solomon Islands, being reflected financially in operating losses of the boards concerned.

A word needs to be said about the instruments of monetary policy. Financial markets in the island economies are small and the range of liquid instruments that would integrate markets is also small. Generally, Treasury bills and other short-term securities are not available, and in cases where they are, such as in Papua New Guinea and Fiji, they are usually held by the initial purchasers until maturity; secondary and interbank markets have not yet developed. Also, secondary markets in longer-term government and public sector instruments remain undeveloped. In these circumstances, the monetary authorities are unable to rely on intervention through open market operations in securities to influence banking activity. The monetary control instruments that are available are effective, but are generally less flexible and fast acting than such open market operations may be. In a monetary environment subject to large swings in bank liquidity associated with external cycles, this can create some difficulty for effective policy implementation.

The most commonly used instrument of monetary control in the Pacific islands is variable reserve requirements. Normally, there is a single requirement fixing a minimum ratio for bank holdings of government securities and related other assets to deposits, although in Fiji there is, in addition to this requirement, a minimum cash ratio requirement. The effects of variability in the liquidity position among banks can be neutralized through interbank deposit transactions and various refinancing and lender-of-last-resort facilities provided by the authorities. Experience shows that this works fairly well, and changes in requirements that initially bear more heavily on some sections of the banking community are evened out quickly. The greatest problem with this system derives from wide fluctuations in bank liquidity. This requires that the authorities adjust the required ratios rather frequently to ensure that they are effective in exerting the desired degree of constraint on bank lending. At times, this procedure can be a difficult undertaking. In Western Samoa the authorities have relied on direct credit ceilings applied to each bank to limit credit growth during their recent adjustment program. In this small system, and in association with the accepted need for discipline in view of an arrangement with the Fund, this mechanism has proved most effective.

Interest rate policy is generally viewed more as an instrument to mobilize domestic savings than to ration credit in most island economies. Freedom to pursue an independent interest rate policy is also seen to be circumscribed as a result of the close ties of the business community in the island economies with Australia and New Zealand. Shifting or large interest rate differentials with these centers can promote deposit and borrowing shifts through movements in intercompany accounts—even where direct capital movements are controlled. For these reasons, interest rate policy has not often been used actively to promote adjustment, its main role being to provide an appropriate financial environment for development. A noteworthy departure from this passive role was the major interest rate adjustment included in the Western Samoan program.[8] In February 1983 bank deposit rates were raised by 5–6 percentage points, and bank lending rates, by an average of 4 percentage points to become mostly positive in real terms. The effects of the reform were slow to be seen, although deposits did quickly shift into longer-term maturities. However, in time, the interest rate reform proved effective, not only in mobilizing savings, but in encouraging an increased flow of remittances from Samoans working abroad. Also, higher interest rates dampened import demand in conjunction with exchange rate depreciation, and also led to a rationalization of aggregate credit demand. This experience suggests that some of the other island states may benefit from a more active use of interest rate policy.

Wage Policy and International Competitiveness

While fluctuations in demand are the primary cause of recurring periods of external imbalance in the island economies, many also suffer from a lack of international competitiveness, which makes persistent external pressures likely if even moderate growth is pursued. This is a problem particularly common in Melanesia. Western Samoa has also experienced periods when international competitiveness was inadequate and contributed to external problems. But the origins of Western Samoa's difficulties were of the more standard kind—inflation compounded by inadequate monetary control and an inflexible exchange rate policy. In this case, orthodox corrective policies were applied and were successful. As part of the 1983 adjustment program, the tala was devalued by a total of 17 percent in nominal effective terms during February–May 1983 and by a further 12 percent during May–July 1984. Although much of the initial devaluation was offset by subsequent inflation, the cumulative adjustment has reduced the real effective exchange rate to its lowest level since early 1980. There is no doubt that, with the

---

[8] As an example of the wide scope of Fund technical assistance in the region, the author, in conjunction with Klaus-Walter Riechel of the Fund staff, visited Western Samoa in 1978 at the invitation of the authorities to offer advice on interest rate policy. The report prepared for the authorities following that visit contains a full description of the financial system and the issues of interest rate policy in Western Samoa.

support of appropriate demand restraint, exchange rate depreciation has been effective in restoring international competitiveness to Western Samoa's economy.

Part of the reason why a flexible exchange rate policy has been successful in Western Samoa is that real wages are relatively flexible. The labor market in that country is not strongly regulated, and increases in the cost of living do not flow through to wage rates automatically. The same has not generally been the case in Papua New Guinea and Fiji, and to some extent in Solomon Islands. In these countries, regulated labor markets (especially wage indexation) have inhibited the downward adjustment in real wage levels even when this has been necessary. On the other hand, real wages have increased in periodic bursts during affluent times. The result has been that high labor costs have tended to become endemic, bringing with them problems of retarded growth, distorted production patterns, and substantial unemployment.

The effectiveness of exchange rate policy as an instrument to restore international competitiveness is limited in these circumstances. A depreciation of the exchange rate aimed at restoring competitiveness is passed through quickly into import costs and, because of the openness of the economy, is largely reflected in an increase in the general price level. Higher prices are transmitted to higher wages through wage indexation, so that much of the adjustment in relative price and cost levels stemming from the depreciation is offset. Exchange rate depreciation can improve competitiveness in this situation, but only if the depreciation is much larger than the gain desired, and at the cost of a considerable increase in prices. This relative weakness of the exchange rate as an instrument of external adjustment has traditionally discouraged its active use for this purpose in the Melanesian island countries. Most explicitly in Papua New Guinea, exchange rate policy has in the past been directed principally at containing domestic price increases under the so-called hard kina policy. The task of maintaining external balance was assigned overwhelmingly to fiscal policy.[9]

During much of the period since independence in 1975, Papua New Guinea's economic policy was conducted around the cornerstones of the hard kina policy aimed at keeping import costs and wages growth low, and a tight budgetary policy aimed at keeping domestically induced inflation low and limiting domestic demand growth within bounds consistent with external viability. This policy was successful in maintaining broad external balance during the favorable years of the late 1970s, but was not successful in providing an environment conducive to invest-

---

[9] A lucid exposition of this strategy can be found in Garnaut (1980), and Garnaut, Baxter, and Krueger (1983).

ment, especially in traded goods industries, or the creation of employment. This was not so much because competitiveness weakened during this period—in fact, it probably improved somewhat—or that real wages increased in this period. The problem was created because of a doubling of real wages that occurred during 1972–75 on recommendations of the Isaac Report, which set real wages at a level beyond the economy's ability to absorb at full employment, and which, because of the inflexibility imposed by wage indexation, remained fixed at an excessive level thereafter.

The severity of the 1980–82 recession imposed intolerable strains on the external position, which could be sustained only through heavy recourse to external borrowing on commercial terms. As noted above, after a belated start, fiscal policy was by 1982 playing its maximum role in supporting adjustment, but more needed to be done. Thus, in March 1983, in a break with their past policy of revaluing in the face of a weak Australian dollar, the authorities devalued in line with the 10 percent depreciation of the Australian dollar at that time. This change in policy was encouraged by a potentially far-reaching decision, adopted by the Minimum Wages Board, that during 1983–86 wage levels would be adjusted for only the first 5 percent of consumer price inflation in each year.

The breaking of the nexus between import prices and domestic wages and costs opened up greater opportunities for exchange rate flexibility in support of improving competitiveness. The authorities certainly recognize this and have had some success in this direction, although not as much, perhaps, as they would wish. In 1983 the nominal exchange rate was gradually moved downward, with care being taken not to move too fast in order to avoid raising domestic inflation to double-digit levels, which would prove politically troublesome. Real wages declined by about 3 percent, and the real exchange rate depreciated somewhat. However, subsequent progress with this strategy was upset by disruptions caused by shortages in the domestic supply of a sensitive item of consumption—betel nut. A surge in betel nut prices pushed consumer price inflation to over 10 percent in the first half of 1984, forcing the authorities to adopt a more cautious approach to exchange rate policy in order to bring inflation down. This was essential to ensure that public acceptance of partial indexation could be sustained. Subsequently, with increased betel nut supplies, inflation receded quickly before a more flexible exchange rate policy could be implemented. Although little progress was achieved during 1984 in reducing real wages and strengthening competitiveness, developments served to reinforce public acceptance of partial wage indexation. Discussions on new wage arrangements to cover 1987–90 are now under way, and there appears to be a growing acceptance in the society of the need for a continuation of real wage flexibility. Indeed, this would seem to be essential if economic growth performance is to improve and be compatible with external viability over the longer run.

Fiji has experienced broadly similar problems. During the first half of the 1970s, collective bargaining arrangements were associated with considerable labor unrest and large wage increases. The present centralized arrangements were established in 1977 to overcome these difficulties. A Tripartite Forum was set up with representation from the trade unions, employers, and the government to set annual wage guidelines. Although adherence to the guidelines is voluntary, in fact they apply throughout the unionized labor force and are followed closely by wage councils which influence wages for nonunion employees, although some divergence has arisen in recent years. Importantly, sugar growers and cane cutters, who comprise the bulk of the export sector labor force, are not covered by the guidelines.

The main factor influencing the annual wage guidelines has been the rate of increase in consumer prices, which, as in the other Pacific island economies, are heavily influenced by import prices. Moreover, in recent years government employees have been granted merit and seniority increases in addition to the increases provided in the guidelines, while, at the same time, the terms of trade weakened considerably. Real incomes for the country as a whole declined, and those in the export sector fell substantially. In contrast, wage earners (especially in the unionized sector) were protected from any reduction in real incomes. As in Papua New Guinea, these developments tended to inhibit external adjustment and discourage investment and employment.

Although Fiji did not experience acute external difficulties on the scale of some other of the island economies, the authorities recognized the potential seriousness of the wage problem. By 1984 wages were estimated to be much higher than would have been the case had they moved in line with changes in real national income adjusted for the terms of trade since 1980. The implied redistribution of income obviously had major political and social ramifications. Beyond this, the pressure of increasing wage costs on public finances strained the authorities' ability to manage aggregate demand while promoting development, and the hike in wage costs inhibited private investment in tradable goods and service industries. The potential damage to the economy, were these practices to continue, would be severe. Thus, as noted above, at the end of 1984 the government introduced a freeze on public and private sector remuneration. The freeze was effectively implemented in 1985, and during that year average real wages are estimated to have declined by about 5 percent.

Obviously, a wage freeze can be no more than a temporary measure. Its success also cannot be measured only by developments during the period when it applies; indeed, developments after it lapses are probably a more significant measure of success. It is still too early to judge the success of the Fiji wage freeze, although indications so far seem generally favorable. The government has used the period of the freeze to engage the employers and unions in consultations regarding future national wage guidelines. For its part, the government has stressed that wage developments should be related to the overall strength of the economy's performance rather than an automatic result of price developments. If this approach can be accepted and implemented, it would alleviate one of the most troublesome rigidities in the economy, allow greater scope for flexible exchange rate policy, and promise increased potential for growth with external viability over the long run.

A final note on competitiveness problems and exchange rate management in the Pacific islands. The combination of two common structural elements—a high degree of openness, and high concentration of trade flows on both the import and export sides to a few, but different, countries—can serve to reduce the scope for independent exchange rate policy. Typically, the Pacific island economies obtain a large share of their import needs from Australia and New Zealand but export little to these countries, relying instead on markets in Japan, the United States, and the European Communities (EC). In these circumstances, changes in the strength of the Australian and New Zealand currencies that are not directly related to differential inflation rates can have significant effects on the Pacific island economies. First, their terms of trade will be affected: weakness (strength) in the Australian and New Zealand currencies will result in lower (higher) import prices and an improvement (deterioration) in the terms of trade. Second, the terms of trade change will translate through the effects on costs and prices into a change in the real exchange rates: weakness (strength) in the Australian and New Zealand currencies, through its effects on import prices will reduce (raise) domestic price inflation and subsequently wage changes, and result in a depreciation (appreciation) in the real effective exchange rate.

It should be noted that the effect on the real exchange rate is independent of the type of exchange rate system that the country follows. For example, in the case where the currency is pegged to a depreciating Australian/New Zealand dollar, the terms of trade change occurs through an increase in export prices, while domestic inflation and wage increases are not affected. Alternatively, if the currency is pegged to, say, the U.S. dollar against which the Australian/New Zealand dollar depreciates, the terms of trade improvement comes about through lower import prices, and domestic inflation and wage increases are affected. Although the impact on the real exchange rate is likely to be similar in either case, the incidence of the impact on the domestic economy would be different. In the first case, the benefit of the improvement in the terms of trade goes directly to the export sector alone. In the alternative, the export sector benefits to a smaller extent, but import-competing industries also receive some gain.

In practice, the indirect effects of exchange rate developments in Australia and New Zealand have been important in some cases. To cite Papua New Guinea's example, where some 40 percent of imports come from Australia, movements in competitiveness since independence in 1975 correspond broadly to developments in the value of the Australian dollar during this period. During the period 1975–79, the Australian dollar was weak relative to the currencies of Japan and the Federal Republic of Germany (Papua New Guinea's main export markets), and as a result the kina also depreciated significantly in real effective terms. Although under the hard kina policy the kina was appreciated in nominal terms when the Australian dollar was depreciated and depreciated modestly against an average for its trading partners, prices in Papua New Guinea rose by significantly less than the average abroad. Likewise, between mid-1979 and 1982, when the kina was more stable in terms of the Australian dollar, it appreciated significantly against its trading partners as a group, as the yen and the deutsche mark were weak relative to the Australian dollar, while inflation in Papua New Guinea evolved in line with that abroad. During both these periods, movements in the real value of the kina followed those of the Australian dollar, regardless of the exchange rate policy followed by the Papua New Guinea authorities. One can confidently expect that the weakening of the Australian dollar over the past year, to the extent that it is not eroded in real terms by price increases, will result in a parallel depreciation in the real effective exchange rate of the kina.

This experience serves to illustrate, by way of a rather unexpected example, the reliance of the South Pacific island countries on the economic policies and developments in the two larger countries in the region—New Zealand and Australia. This reliance has many dimensions, including development assistance, training and technical assistance, trade and market access, and the provision of employment opportunities. Trade and market access are also important aspects of relationships within the region, and trade and cooperation arrangements, such as those provided under the South Pacific Regional Trade and Cooperation Agreement (SPARTECA), can be of great potential benefit to the island countries. By and large, the Pacific island countries have dealt with the severe economic disruptions of the 1980s better than developing countries in most other regions of the world. But they remain vulnerable to external disruption, and their freedom of independent action is narrow in some areas. The final thought I would like to leave you with is that it behooves New Zealand and Australia, in taking economic policy decisions, to bear in mind the interests of the Pacific island economies and to help where they can to reduce their economic vulnerability.

V. Conclusion

The Pacific island countries are not a unique group that face different problems requiring special analysis and a separate approach to adjustment. Indeed, they share many of the problems common to developing countries anywhere. The general approach to their economic adjustment problems fits well within the broad framework that has evolved under the IMF's umbrella and has gained wide international acceptance. Nevertheless, there are elements of similarity in the circumstances facing the island economies that are strong enough, and different enough from countries outside this group, to enable us to identify certain common features in the approach to adjustment followed in these countries.

This paper has dealt mainly with two particular problems that confront policymakers in small island economies in the region—wide fluctuations in income and activity induced by external cycles, and inflexible wage determination arrangements. Shifts in the balance between aggregate demand and supply associated with external cycles are the principal underlying cause of periodic balance of payments difficulties experienced by these countries. Since the supply side of these economies tends to be relatively invulnerable to influence by policy except in the very long run, the main burden of economic adjustment inevitably falls on demand-management policies.

Fiscal policy, defined broadly to include public enterprises, marketing boards, and publicly administered stabilization schemes, where relevant, has the principal role in demand management. Because of the large size of the public sector and its typically close ties to the export sector, public finances are a major potential source of instability. The aim of public finance policy must be to eliminate this instability, operating to counter cyclical fluctuations when external viability is assured, while promoting adjustment when external difficulties so require. Thus, fiscal policy must be framed in a medium-term context and adjusted as external prospects change. A prompt response to changes in circumstances is essential to ensure that fiscal adjustment, when needed, imposes as little disruption on the economy as possible. The experience of the first half of the 1980s suggests that, even when these general objectives have been accepted by the island economies, it has not been at all easy to implement such a policy smoothly. Several of the Pacific island economies have, indeed, successfully implemented major fiscal adjustment programs over recent years, although both because of delays in introducing such measures and the depth of the last world recession, adjustment could not be achieved smoothly or without disruption.

In contrast, monetary policy plays a generally subsidiary role to fiscal policy in adjustment programs in the region. The magnitude of externally induced fluctuations is such as to virtually swamp monetary policy in many cases. The inability of the authorities to control fluctuations in money supply within reasonable margins and the safety valve provided by wide swings in import demand, which tend to insulate the domestic economy from the effects of such fluctuations in monetary growth, have discouraged reliance on monetary targeting. Nevertheless, over the medium term, monetary policy has to be in harmony with the objectives of fiscal policy, and in this, discipline in credit policy (especially around the cyclical peak in the terms of trade) is indispensable.

Inflexibility in real wages creates special problems for a number of countries in the South Pacific. Over time, wage costs have risen to levels that are clearly excessive in several cases, which has inhibited the effectiveness of exchange rate flexibility as a means of promoting international competitiveness. Excessive wage costs have exacerbated periodic balance of payments difficulties and, more important, have retarded growth, development, and the creation of employment opportunities. Several countries in the region are now actively endeavoring to address the issue of high wages and introduce greater flexibility into the labor market. Understandably, these steps have so far been cautious and need to be carried further if the social problem associated with high unemployment is to be effectively addressed and improved growth performance made possible.

The record of the first half of the 1980s reveals that the island economies of the South Pacific have, for the most part, effectively adapted their policies to meet the adjustment needs that the severe world economic recession forced upon them. Their adjustment programs were largely indigenously conceived and implemented, and in contrast to some other regions of the world, the Fund was not called upon to provide widespread active support. Nevertheless, we in the Fund are pleased to have been involved in this successful enterprise, and will continue our efforts to assist these countries in shaping their economic policies in the years to come.

References

Benedict, Burton, ed., *Problems of Smaller Territories* (London: Published for the Institute of Commonwealth Studies by Athlone Press, 1967).

Colclough, Christopher, and Philip Daniel, "Wage Incomes and Wage Costs in Papua New Guinea: Challenges for Adjustment, Distribution and Growth" (mimeographed, Sussex: University of Sussex, 1982).

Committee to Review the Australian Overseas Aid Program, and Sir Gordon Jackson, Report of the Committee to Review the Australian Overseas Aid Program (Canberra: Australian Government Publishing Service, 1984).

Demas, William G., *The Economies of Development in Small Countries, with Special Reference to the Caribbean* (Montreal: Published for the Center for Developing-Area Studies by McGill University Press, 1965).

Dommen, Edward, "External Trade Problems of Small Island States in the Pacific and Indian Oceans," in *The Island States of the Pacific and Indian Oceans: Anatomy of Development*, Development Studies Center, Monograph No. 23, ed. by R.T. Shand (Canberra: Australian National University, 1980), pp. 179–200.

Garnaut, Ross, "Economic Instability in Small Countries: Macroeconomic Responses," in *The Island States of the Pacific and Indian Oceans: Anatomy of Development*, Development Studies Center, Monograph No. 23, ed. by R.T. Shand (Canberra: Australian National University, 1980), pp. 313–31.

——, Paul Baxter, and Anne O. Krueger, *Exchange Rate and Macro-Economic Policy in Independent Papua New Guinea* (Port Moresby: Papua New Guinea Government Printer, 1983).

Jewkes, J., "Are the Economies of Scale Unlimited?" Chap. 6 in *Economic Consequences of the Size of Nations: Proceedings of a Conference Held by the International Economic Association*, ed. by E.A.G. Robinson (London: MacMillan, 1960).

Kuznets, S., "Economic Growth of Small Nations," Chap. 2 in *Economic Consequences of the Size of Nations: Proceedings of a Conference Held by the International Economic Association*, ed. by E.A.G. Robinson (London: MacMillan, 1960).

Legarda, Benito, "Small Tropical Island Countries: An Overview" (unpublished, International Monetary Fund, Washington, 1983).

Lloyd, Peter J., *International Trade Problems of Small Nations* (Durham, North Carolina: Duke University Press, 1968).

Selwyn, P., and Institute of Development Studies, *Development Policy in Small Countries* (London: Croom Helm, 1975).

Robinson, E.A.G., *Economic Consequences of the Size of Nations: Proceedings of a Conference Held by the International Economic Association* (London: MacMillan, 1960).

Smith, Bruce J., and Klaus-Walter Riechel, "The Financial System and Interest Rates in Western Samoa" (unpublished, International Monetary Fund, 1978).

Comment

Peter Nicholl

I. Introduction

I found Bruce Smith's paper very useful for my work as a policy advisor in a small island economy. Because he highlighted the general points and used the experiences of particular countries to illustrate them, his paper was easy to follow and the points it made were very clear. I intend to adopt the same approach in my comments, discussing Smith's general conclusions and using the experience of Seychelles to illustrate my points.

Seychelles cannot, even given the broadest interpretation of Smith's definition, be regarded as an independent South Pacific island state, and therefore based on geographic criteria, falls outside the group of countries Smith analyzes. But it is a small island state. Indeed, it is somewhat smaller than any of the four states Smith considers,[1] but its economy is sufficiently developed and sufficiently open to find relevance in Smith's analysis. There are, however, two differences between Seychelles and the South Pacific island states that struck me as significant. First, at $2,400, its per capita gross national product (GNP) is higher than most of the South Pacific island states. Second, its historical development has been quite different and, as a consequence, the problems associated with the dual nature of the economies common in Melanesia are much less significant in Seychelles.

It is interesting that when Seychelles joined the International Monetary Fund (IMF) in 1977, it chose to join the constituency headed by Australia that included three of the four island states considered in Smith's paper (Papua New Guinea, Solomon Islands, and Western Samoa), rather than a geographically closer African or Asian constituency. Seychelles perceived itself to have more economic commonality with these Pacific island states than with land-based states in Africa and Asia. It is therefore not illogical today for someone from Seychelles to act as discussant on this paper about South Pacific island states.

---

[1] Papua New Guinea, Fiji, Solomon Islands, and Western Samoa.

II. Characteristics of Pacific Island Countries

In his concluding remarks, Smith says that the "Pacific island countries are not a unique group that face different problems requiring special analysis and a separate approach to adjustment" (p. 260). I initially disagreed with this statement, as reports prepared under the aegis of the Commonwealth Secretariat make a strong case for the uniqueness of the problems of small island states. However, I find I can agree with his conclusion given the paper's concentration on economic adjustment. Nevertheless, small island states do exhibit many unique features, including:

1. An unusually high degree of specialization, and hence greater vulnerability to fluctuations in commodity markets or other crises in the world economy.

2. A lower capacity to borrow on the international capital markets. They may, however, have a greater capacity for getting funds from multinational agencies on a per capita basis or on a government-to-government basis than other developing countries. While that is a major advantage, it does introduce another element of vulnerability.

3. An asymmetry in their relations with other countries and with multinational companies.

4. Emigration of labor (frequently skilled labor) and a consequent inability to secure a balanced supply of manpower.

5. Diseconomies of scale in administration, defense, and infrastructural investment. A prime example is the international airport in Seychelles. In New Zealand there are periodic debates about whether three international airports are a luxury for a country with only three million people. The implication is that one such airport per million people may be excessive. Seychelles has only about 70,000 people and an international airport. The airport is crucial to the country's major industry and foreign exchange earner—tourism. In the year before the airport opened (1970), Seychelles had a grand total of 1,622 visitors; this number has since risen to over 70,000 visitors per annum. The costs of the investment in the airport have to be spread across a limited population. I realize that small states must temper their enthusiasm for the trappings of statehood and the infrastructure and industries of large societies. But there are limitations to the divisibility of certain necessary economic and social investments.

6. Multi-island configuration. Fiji, for example, has literally hundreds of islands and Seychelles has about one hundred. Often, one large island is the site for concentrated development, attracting crucial human resources away from the other islands. Some multi-island states, and Seychelles is a case in point, develop deliberate policies, akin to regional development policies in other countries, to try to prevent or even reverse this flow; such policies are costly to operate.

7. Problems of transport. Transport is a problem in two respects. Cost is the obvious one; but availability and reliability of transport links can also be a serious source of externally generated instability. The withdrawal of an established link may be a relatively minor operating decision for a major international airline or shipping company, but it can have a significant impact on an island economy. For example, Seychelles has been carefully marketing itself in the Far East as a tourist destination in order to increase tourist numbers and reduce reliance on European tourists. Between 1980 and 1985, the number of tourists from Japan and the territory of Hong Kong had doubled and Japan had become Seychelle's sixth most important source of tourists. In January 1986 the only direct link between the Far East and Seychelles was cut at a fortnight's notice, not because of problems in Seychelles but because of reduced traffic to and from the end point of that flight, Johannesburg. Seychelles' aviation authorities are trying to arrange a replacement connection. In the meantime, in the week ended January 26, 1986, only 1 hardy tourist arrived in Seychelles from Japan compared with a normal weekly figure of 70–80.

All of the features on this list relate to economic structure, development processes, and economic and political vulnerability to external pressures. Some of what I have called "unique" features exist in other developing countries, and in developed countries as well, but are more pronounced in small island states.

When it comes to considering adjustment processes and policies, the differences between small island states and other developing countries seem to be differences of degree.

III. Role of Supply Side

The second conclusion Smith draws is that since "the supply side of these economies tends to be relatively invulnerable to influence by policy except in the very long run, the main burden of economic adjustment inevitably falls on demand-management policies" (p. 260). While I do not disagree with Smith's point, I think it is overstated. There is no evidence in the paper to support the statement. The supply side of a small economy has a limited number of sectors and resources that could be influenced by policy. However, within that limitation, smallness may be an advantage. I can think of several instances where supply-side policies may actually operate more quickly in such countries as compared to larger, more diverse economies. Examples can be found in these states of supply responses that were quite rapid. For example, in Solomon Islands, the smallholder production (of copra) rose by almost two thirds in 1984 in response to sharply rising producer prices.

The tourism industry in Seychelles provides another example of a quick response from the supply side. A recovery in tourism of only a few months' duration was jeopardized in early 1983 when one major foreign carrier curtailed air services and another terminated service altogether. The loss in potential arrivals was more than 40 percent. In response, the Seychelles authorities converted their inter-island airline into an international carrier by leasing a plane. Although this action required considerable budgetary support, it apparently salvaged the winter season and also instilled confidence among tour operators for the coming year.

From the perspective of a third world country, Smith's assertion about supply-side response confirms the third world's view that the IMF is not really interested in supply-side adjustment, but markets a standard package of demand restraint. It is not an exaggeration to say that this stereotypical view of the Fund appears frequently throughout the African and Asian literature.

IV. Role of Fiscal Policy

Smith's third conclusion, with which I agree entirely, is that fiscal policy "has the principal role in demand management" (p. 260). Earlier in his paper he says that the "aim of fiscal policy in adjustment programs in broad terms must be to set limits to demand through government spending and financial deficits that are consistent with external viability" (p. 245). That is a sensible and appropriate aim, but the process of translating it into specific policy behavior is less straightforward.

The first requirement Smith lists is "a realistic assessment of future economic prospects," and, in particular, the "future flow of external receipts" (p. 245). Smith's paper makes it clear that this is easier said than done. That does not mean, however, that the exercise should not be carried out. I agree with Smith that the role of IMF missions is significant in policy areas like this, even when the country does not have an adjustment program with the Fund. The forecasting exercises for foreign exchange flows recommended by Smith are carried out in Seychelles. But we differ from the case studies Smith describes in his paper in two crucial respects: (1) our focus is still fairly short term, typically 12–18 months ahead; and (2) the foreign exchange forecasts do not yet have a central role in the formulation of fiscal policy.

In both of these areas, Seychelles can learn, I believe, from Smith's description of the fiscal policy framework in Papua New Guinea: "In Papua New Guinea, it is understood that fiscal policy is the principal instrument for ensuring external viability, and budgetary policy is directed toward this objective" (p. 248). Smith says that this is a "realistic approach to fiscal management in an island economy, combining elements of countercyclical and adjustment policies in a logical balance" (p. 248).

Fiscal policy is not so clearly assigned in Seychelles. In adjusting to the recession in the tourism industry from 1980 to 1983, fiscal policy seemed to play a smaller role than monetary policy and prices and incomes policies. The countercyclical element of fiscal policy was initially stronger than its adjustment element. When the overall deficit was reduced in 1983 and maintained at the lower level in 1984, the expenditure cuts fell on capital expenditure, an outcome Smith says is not unusual in these economies.

Through a fortunate coincidence of economic influences, Seychelles has, up until now, avoided the need to assign fiscal policy more explicitly to adjustment. The opening of the international airport in 1971 transformed the economy and ushered in a period of rapid growth without foreign exchange problems. Between 1970 and 1979, tourist arrivals grew at a cumulative annual rate of 54 percent. At the same time, as a newly independent country with links to two former colonial masters, strategically situated between Africa and Asia and adopting a nonaligned role in the East/West debate, Seychelles was the recipient of a significant amount of financial support from diverse sources.

As a consequence, gross domestic product (GDP) grew at around 10 percent per annum for a number of years over the latter part of the 1970s. Although investment and consumption expenditure both increased rapidly, Seychelles was still able to build up its external reserves from SR 75 million in 1975 to SR 165 million in 1980.

At that time the need to look to the future with "a wary eye" would not have been apparent. The events of the years since 1979 have, however, moved Seychelles much closer to the pattern described by Smith for the South Pacific states. Tourist numbers fell sharply for three years, and in 1982 were only 60 percent of the 1979 level. Numbers have recovered again in each of the last three years, but in 1985 they were still below the 1979 peak. Over the same period, aid and concessional loans have not been as readily available as before. The broad economic picture over the years 1980 to 1985 is therefore quite different from the remarkable progress of the 1970s. Average real GDP growth, which was negative in each of the years 1980 to 1983 before recovering lost ground in 1984 and 1985, was probably zero over that period. At the same time, external reserves have fallen from SR 165 million in 1980 to SR 67 million at the end of 1985.

Despite these setbacks, policymakers in Seychelles, and I suspect in other small island states as well, when framing economic policy, tend to cast an optimistic eye to the future, rather than the "wary eye" recommended by Smith. They believe, with justification, that they have come through a severe recession in their major industry tolerably well and that they can do the same again in the event, unlikely it is hoped, that they have to.

Two major changes in the situation of Seychelles do not yet seem to have been fully taken into account in the authorities' policymaking framework. These changes are certainly not being ignored but are, in my opinion, not being given sufficient weight. The first is that the cushion provided by a high level of overseas reserves no longer exists. The second is that more recent external borrowing has been on commercial terms, and this trend will probably continue. The Papua New Guinea model for formulating fiscal strategy, combining elements of countercyclical and adjustment policies in a logical balance, may well be one that Seychelles should now consider adopting.

V. Role of Monetary Policy

Smith's fourth conclusion is that "monetary policy plays a generally subsidiary role to fiscal policy in adjustment programs in the region" (p. 261). He says that, for valid reasons, policymakers in the island economies have found the value of monetary targeting to be limited. I think they are right to eschew targeting. The monetary authorities in these countries often have to take a large fiscal injection as given. They have at their disposal two means of implementing monetary policy, but these means have opposite effects on the measured money supply.

The first approach is to restrain private sector credit growth in order to limit a secondary expansion of the money supply fueled by the increase in the banking system's liquidity. The tools are quantitative regulation and/or high interest rates. This policy approach is often quite successful in these economies.

The second approach is what I would call a "savings policy" aimed at limiting the operation of what Smith calls the import "safety valve" by persuading people to hold financial balances rather than to spend. In Seychelles, the authorities use high nominal interest rates and the exemption of interest income from tax to bring about high real interest rates. The results of this policy in terms of its effects on the retail price index are shown in Table 1. Measured by the leakage of the monetary expansion of the last two years into imports, this policy has been successful, but cause and effect are not clear cut. Growth of M2 fell in 1981 and 1982, increased by only 2 percent in 1983, but then accelerated to 12 percent in 1984 and 21 percent in 1985. Imports grew by about 4 percent in 1984 but were fairly flat in 1985.

There are also quantitative and other administrative restrictions on imports. It could be argued that slow growth of imports is due entirely to these measures and has nothing to do with monetary policy. But Seychelles is unusual among small or developing countries in that it has another safety valve in the form of a liberal, open-door policy toward capital flows. This has always been the case, and the 1986 budget has

Table 1. Seychelles: Effect of Nominal Interest Rate Changes on Retail Price Index, 1982–85

	Nominal Interest Rate on Bank Deposits	Change in Retail Price Index
1982	9.75	– 0.9
1983	10.75	6.6
1984	11.00	1.2
1985	11.00	0.5

just reiterated the government's commitment to a liberal exchange and payments system. The statistics do not indicate that net private remittances or outward capital movements have increased over the last year in response to the strong domestic monetary growth. There may be other explanations for this development, but it appears likely that the high interest rates available domestically, helped by considerable uncertainty about trends in the major exchange rates, have prevented capital flight from Seychelles.

So, whether the safety valve operates through the current account, the capital account, or both, there may be a role for monetary policy to play via interest rates even in a small, open, island economy. Seychelles' experience is similar to Western Samoa's and reinforces Smith's conclusion that the Western Samoa "experience suggests that some of the other island states may benefit from a more active use of interest rate policy" (p. 254).

What is of concern in Seychelles' current policy mix of offsetting high fiscal injections by increasing the public's desire to hold financial assets through a high interest rate policy is that it may not be sustainable for long. Seychelles' experience of the last two years certainly confirms Smith's point that "the lag in the impact on real economic activity [of a surge in monetary growth] is variable and difficult to predict" (p. 242). Smith says that "the magnitude of the expansionary impetus is typically so large that, sooner or later, real spending increases. Most often, private consumption spending is the first component to pick up momentum . . ." (p. 242). We should find out over the next year whether this conclusion also holds for Seychelles.

Smith says that "the period when greatest caution in monetary policy is required is often at, or just past, the cyclical peak in the terms of trade" (p. 252). The problem is how to recognize when you are at this point in the cycle.

Again, the tourism industry in Seychelles illustrates the problem clearly. Forecasting tourist arrivals is a key element in projecting foreign exchange revenue in Seychelles. After the recession of 1980–82, tourist arrivals rose by 26 percent in 1983, 14 percent in 1984, and 14 percent again in 1985. The growth rate over 1984 and 1985 had been steady and spread across most markets, with the not surprising exception of South Africa. When we did our 1986 forecasts, we confidently forecast another year of 15 percent growth. Growth slowed in November and early December when, over a seven-week period, arrivals were only 3 percent higher than the preceding year; it bounced back strongly in the last half of December, but weakened again in January. Fewer tourists arrived in January 1986 than in January 1985, though this latter drop was due in part to the sudden termination of one air connection. The smooth trend that had persisted for almost two years became very unstable, making it difficult to know what to forecast for 1987.

Being able to pinpoint the moment at which the terms of trade have peaked seems to be a case of keeping what Smith calls a "wary eye." When the terms of trade are favorable (or in Seychelles' case, when the flow of tourists is increasing steadily), that is the time for monetary policy to be cautious. It seems to be one of the burdens that central bankers must bear that they should always be professional pessimists and never assume that good times will last. It is a role that is unlikely to endear the central bank to politicians in the small economies (or large ones for that matter), but one that they must assume if they are to do their job appropriately.

VI. Role of Wage Policy

Smith's fifth point in his concluding remarks is that "inflexibility in real wages creates special problems for a number of countries in the South Pacific" (p. 261). Wage inflexibility creates problems wherever it is evident. It lay at the center of many of New Zealand's structural problems and, as in the island states, it limited the ability to use other policy tools, such as the exchange rate. In small island economies, the special problem tends to be the size of the public sector where wage inflexibility is often most pronounced. Perhaps more important, automatic increment and promotion systems actually increase wages irrespective of the state of the economy. Though real wages are more of a problem for small states than large states, small states are also sometimes better at confronting it than large states, as exemplified by the experience of Papua New Guinea cited in Smith's paper.

In Seychelles one of the policy responses to the sharp downturn in tourism was to hold down increases in earnings. Over 1983 and 1984 average earnings rose by only 2.9 percent per annum. In the government sector, the rise was only 1.5 percent per annum. Though 1985 figures are not yet available, the policy of restraint has been continued and any increase in average earnings will be only modest. A policy of fairly firm incomes control has been sustained with apparent success for four years, with the only significant increases in that time being for those at the low end of the wage scale. Few, if any, large countries could maintain such a policy for that length of time. So this structural characteristic identified by Smith, though a source of vulnerability and instability, can also be a source of policy strength and stability for a small island economy if it has the right policy.

The dilemma for policymakers is that in containing the real wage problem, an inflexible wage structure is established that may, in time, worsen the skill shortage problem that all these small island economies face.

VII. Role of Exchange Rate Policy

In his brief remarks about use of exchange rate policy as an adjustment tool, Smith says there "is no doubt that, with the support of appropriate demand restraint, exchange rate depreciation has been effective in restoring international competitiveness to Western Samoa's economy" (pp. 254–55). In Seychelles, as a means of dampening the inflationary pressures that emerged in 1981, the rupee was appreciated by 15 percent. The strong exchange rate, along with other incomes and price control policies, reduced inflation dramatically. However, the use of the exchange rate as a tool to combat inflation may have exacerbated the downturn in tourism receipts, although how significant its effect was is difficult to determine, as a number of other strong influences were also at work at the same time.

Even if one agrees with Smith (p. 258) that "two common structural elements [of small island economies] . . . reduce the scope for independent exchange rate policy," some important policy decisions can still be taken with regard to the type of exchange rate arrangement to be used. The countries in Smith's study all use a basket arrangement. A choice is involved in determining which basket to use—does the country want to stabilize its export prices, its import prices, or its international competitiveness in a particular industry. As Smith's example shows, if a country's export trade and import trade are with different groups of countries, no exchange rate system will permit both export and import prices to be stabilized. A country can, of course, take the middle ground by choosing a trade-weighted rather than an export- or an import-weighted basket. Seychelles chose to peg to the SDR,[2] and this choice has had some significant consequences for its real exchange rate, which,

---

[2] See p. 239, footnote.[4]

until recently, had appreciated steadily because of the larger weight given to the U.S. dollar in the SDR than in Seychelles' trade pattern. There is probably no "correct" policy, but the authorities in these countries need to be aware that their choice of basket does have policy consequences.

VIII. Summary and Conclusions

In his concluding remarks Smith says that the adjustment programs followed in the island states he analyzed "were largely indigenously conceived and implemented, and in contrast to some other regions of the world, the Fund was not called upon to provide widespread active support" (p. 261). This description also fits Seychelles, which has made no use to date of Fund resources. There are probably three main reasons for the negligible use of Fund resources by the small island economies: (1) a conservative approach to policymaking, as Smith points out; (2) the heavy flows of aid and concessional finance from sources other than the IMF; and (3) the small size of their Fund quota, which has discouraged them from having recourse to the Fund. The Fund did consider the special case of small member states in the last quota review, and a marginal concession was made to them, but it was of little significance. Conditionality, as well as the scarce human resources that would be tied up in negotiating an arrangement with the Fund, is seen as a high price to pay for the funds that would be made available.

According to Smith, generally "the Pacific island countries have dealt with the severe economic disruptions of the 1980s better than developing countries in most other regions of the world" (p. 259). I believe the same conclusion can be drawn about Seychelles. Being small is not an entirely negative feature. Although smallness does impose major limitations on resources, including human resources, and makes the country very vulnerable to external shocks, the case studies Smith has used show the enviable ability of these countries to take comprehensive and firm policy measures when they are necessary. Smallness may actually give them a comparative advantage in policy flexibility over larger countries, which may explain in part their better relative performance.

Appendix

Participants

Moderator

Sir Frank Holmes
  Institute of Policy Studies, Victoria University of Wellington

Authors

Bijan B. Aghevli
  International Monetary Fund
Robin T. Clements
  Reserve Bank of New Zealand
Helen Hughes
  National Center for Development Studies, Australian National University
Ralph Lattimore
  Lincoln College, Canterbury, New Zealand
P.J. Lloyd
  University of Melbourne, Australia
Jorge Márquez-Ruarte
  International Monetary Fund
Stanley Please
  St. Anthony's College, Oxford University
Bruce J. Smith
  International Monetary Fund
Robin T. Spencer
  Reserve Bank of New Zealand
Peter Wickham
  International Monetary Fund

Discussants

Te'o I.J. Fairbairn
  Pacific Islands Development Program
Christopher Findlay
  University of Adelaide, Australia
Christopher Higgins
  Department of the Treasury, Australia
Colin James
  The National Business Review

David G. Mayes
　New Zealand Institute of Economic Research
Sang Woo Nam
　Korean Development Institute
Peter Nicholl
　Central Bank of Seychelles
Cho Soon
　Seoul National University, Korea

Observers

Geoffrey Bertram
　Victoria University, Wellington, New Zealand
Robert Buckle
　Victoria University, Wellington, New Zealand
Roderick Deane
　Reserve Bank of New Zealand
Peter Dixon
　University of Melbourne, Australia
Brian Easton
　New Zealand Institute of Economic Research
Ian Fitzgerald
　Westpac Banking Corporation, Wellington, New Zealand
Peter Jonson
　Reserve Bank of Australia
Roger Kerr
　The Treasury of New Zealand
J.Y. Kubuabola
　Ministry of Finance, Fiji
John MacFarlane
　Department of Finance, Papua New Guinea
Richard Manning
　University of Canterbury, New Zealand
Malcolm McPhee
　New Zealand Herald
Rupa Molina
　Department of Finance, Papua New Guinea
Tony Raynor
　Lincoln College, Canterbury, New Zealand
Graham Scott
　The Treasury of New Zealand
Feleti Sevele
　Copra Board, Tonga
Kerrin Vautier
　New Zealand Commerce Commission
Harilaos Vittas
　International Monetary Fund

PARTICIPANTS

Bryce Wilkinson
   Jarden and Company, Wellington, New Zealand
Richard Williams
   International Monetary Fund

Seminar Coordinator

Graham Newman
   International Monetary Fund

Biographical Sketches of Participants

Bijan B. Aghevli
Assistant Director in the Asian Department of the International Monetary Fund, and Chief of the Division for Japan, Korea, and Tonga. He has been a Research Fellow at the London School of Economics and has published various papers on international and monetary economics. He holds a Ph.D. in economics from Brown University.

Robin T. Clements
Manager of the Research Section in the Economic Department of the Reserve Bank of New Zealand. He is a graduate of the University of Canterbury, New Zealand.

Te'o I.J. Fairbairn
Research Associate with the Pacific Islands Development Program (PIDP) in Hawaii. He holds a Ph.D. in Pacific History (Economics) from the Australian National University, Canberra, and has been Senior Economist with the South Pacific Commission and Senior Economic Planning Adviser for the United Nations Development Program.

Christopher Findlay
Visiting Senior Lecturer in the Department of Economics at the University of Adelaide, Australia. Previously, he was associated with the Research School of Pacific Studies at the Australian National University, Canberra.

Christopher Higgins
Deputy Secretary (Economic) in the Australian Treasury. Previously, he served as Director of the General Economics Branch of the Economic Statistics Department of the Organization for Economic Cooperation and Development. He was educated at the Australian National University, Canberra, and the University of Pennsylvania.

Sir Frank Holmes
Visiting Fellow at the Institute of Policy Studies at Victoria University of Wellington. An economic and planning consultant and director of several companies, he served previously as a government adviser and as Chairman of the New Zealand Planning Council.

Helen Hughes
Professor of Economics, Research School of Pacific Studies, and Executive Director of the National Center for Development Studies, Australian National University, Canberra. Previously, she was Director of the Economic Analyses and Projections Department at the World Bank.

Colin James
Political journalist and analyst. A frequent commentator on radio and television, he has been political editor and editor of *The National Business Review*, and has contributed to several books.

Ralph Lattimore
Reader in Agricultural Economics at Lincoln College in Canterbury, New Zealand. Formerly, he was at the University of British Columbia. He has done research and consulting work in New Zealand, the United States, Brazil, and Canada in the areas of trade and policy.

P.J. Lloyd
Visiting Professor in the Department of Economics at the University of Illinois at Urbana-Champaign. Also a Professor in the Department of Economics of the University of Melbourne, Australia, his area of specialization is international economics.

Jorge Márquez-Ruarte
Assistant Division Chief in the Asian Department of the International Monetary Fund. Previously, he was with the Fund's Western Hemisphere and Exchange and Trade Relations Departments. He holds a Ph.D. in economics from the University of Chicago.

David G. Mayes
Director of the New Zealand Institute of Economic Research, Wellington, and Head of Statistics and Computing, National Economic Development Office (NEDO) in London. Previously, he was Senior Lecturer in Economics and Social Statistics at the University of Exeter, and Editor at the National Institute of Economics and Social Research, London.

Stanley Please
Senior Associate Member of St. Antony's College, Oxford, and a member of the Governing Councils of the Overseas Development Institute and of the Institute of Development Studies. Previously on the staff of the World Bank, he continues to act as consultant to the World Bank on policy-based analytical work on sub-Saharan Africa.

Bruce J. Smith
Assistant Director in the Asian Department of the International Monetary Fund. His Fund service has involved extensive work on Asia and the South Pacific. Previously, he worked with the Australian Government. He was educated at Sydney University.

BIOGRAPHICAL SKETCHES

Robin T. Spencer
Chief Manager of the Economic Department at the Reserve Bank of New Zealand. A graduate of Victoria University of Wellington and the London School of Economics and Political Science, he spent three years on secondment to the International Monetary Fund, where he worked in the Research and European Departments.

Peter Wickham
Assistant to the Director of the International Monetary Fund's Research Department. He received his undergraduate degree from the University of Essex and subsequently studied at the University of British Columbia and the Johns Hopkins University.

DATE DUE